ROPE
BURNS

Robert Scott

Beth's

Phone (780) 882-7996
Fax (780) 882-7266
12419 - 99 Street
Grande Prairie, AB T8V 6Y5
Email:
bethbook@telusplanet.net

Books

NEW & USED

– BUY –
– SELL –
– TRADE –

Photocopy & Fax Service

PINNACLE BOOKS
Kensington Publishing Corp.

http://www.pinnaclebooks.com

PINNACLE BOOKS are published by

Kensington Publishing Corp.
850 Third Avenue
New York, NY 10022

All Kensington Titles, Imprints, and Distributed Lines are available at special quantity discounts for bulk purchases for sales promotions, premiums, fund-raising, and educational or institutional use. Special book excerpts or customized printings can also be created to fit specific needs. For details, write or phone the office of the Kensington special sales manager: Kensington Publishing Corp., 850 Third Avenue, New York, NY 10022, attn: Special Sales Department, Phone: 1-800-221-2647.

Pinnacle and the P logo Reg. U.S. Pat. & TM Off.

First Printing: September 2001
10 9 8 7 6 5 4 3 2 1

Printed in the United States of America

TORTURE VAN

September 29, 1997, 10:15 P.M.: Michelle Michaud was at the wheel of the dark green minivan. James Daveggio waited in the back, ready to pounce at a moment's notice, while looking for a new victim.

Spotting pretty twenty-year-old Juanita Rodriguez walking home from a night class, Michaud halted the van beside the startled young woman. Jumping out in a heartbeat, Daveggio grabbed Rodriguez. She screamed hysterically, "What have I done? What have I done?" before she was dragged into the van.

As the van pulled away from the curb, Daveggio growled at Rodriguez, "Shut up, or I'll kill you." After ordering her to strip, he forced her to orally copulate him. When Michaud turned her head to see what was happening, Daveggio yelled, "Keep your eyes on the damn road!" His own clothing off, Daveggio brutally raped and tortured Rodriguez for hours.

The van finally stopped on a dark, deserted road deep in the woods. As Rodriguez hastily dressed, Michaud said, "If you turn around for one second, he'll shoot you." Then she opened the door and shoved Rodriguez out. "Next time you won't be so lucky."

BOOK YOUR PLACE ON OUR WEBSITE AND MAKE THE READING CONNECTION!

We've created a customized website just for our very special readers, where you can get the inside scoop on everything that's going on with Zebra, Pinnacle and Kensington books.

When you come online, you'll have the exciting opportunity to:

- View covers of upcoming books
- Read sample chapters
- Learn about our future publishing schedule (listed by publication month *and author*)
- Find out when your favorite authors will be visiting a city near you
- Search for and order backlist books from our online catalog
- Check out author bios and background information
- Send e-mail to your favorite authors
- Meet the Kensington staff online
- Join us in weekly chats with authors, readers and other guests
- Get writing guidelines
- AND MUCH MORE!

**Visit our website at
http://www.pinnaclebooks.com**

ACKNOWLEDGMENTS

If I had to thank everyone who helped me on this book, the list would be several pages long. But I wanted to be sure to thank the following people for all their help and support: First is my wonderful editor at Pinnacle Books, Karen Haas, and my terrific literary agent, Damaris Rowland. I'd also like to thank Paul Dinas for giving me a chance to do this book. I couldn't have gathered all the facts without the help of newspaper reporters Christina Proctor, Cory Fisher, and David Holbrook, or without law enforcement agents David Trimble, Patrick St. John, and Michelle Quattrin. Lastly, thanks to Cameron Wallace, Mark Lee Chapman, Shelley Stafford, Sandi Thomas, and Jan Olson.

"The van had been prepared as what I would describe as a murder and abduction chamber."

—Bill Eastman, Pleasanton Police Chief
Press Conference, December 10, 1997

PART I
SEASON OF FEAR

Prologue

Sacramento, California, September 1997

At 8:00 P.M. on a mid-September evening, a dark-haired, thin woman in her late thirties drove her green minivan to the house of thirteen-year-old Nancy Baker. Nancy was best friends with the woman's teenage daughter and knew the woman well. The girl's parents weren't home at the time and the woman asked Nancy if she wanted to accompany her as she ran a few errands. Since Nancy had done this in the past, she thought nothing of it and said, "Sure." But it seemed strange to the teenager as they took off and the woman began to drive around in circles, up one street and down another, until the girl was completely lost. Twenty minutes elapsed before they pulled in front of a suburban home, one that was much like the house the woman lived in. Nancy was sure she had never been there before.

Since the teenager had been holding the woman's drink on the long crosstown drive, the woman said, "Bring it into the house with you."

"OK," Nancy responded, and followed her up the steps without hesitation. But once inside she immediately spotted the woman's burly boyfriend and grew nervous. Nancy knew he was a biker who belonged to a local motorcycle gang called The

Devil's Horsemen. The man, also in his late thirties, was beefy, his arms covered with tattoos, and he had a pronounced raspy voice. Nancy saw that he was sitting at a dining room table doing crank (methamphetamines). The owners of the house were nowhere in sight.

"Come on and have some crank," the woman said to Nancy.

"I don't want to," she replied.

Nancy had done crank with the man and woman before and hadn't liked it. It had made her heart race and she had felt sick.

"Oh, come on!" the woman implored. "This will be the last time you have to."

Finally coaxed into taking a snort of the meth, Nancy and the adults all got high. When the drug had taken effect, the woman said to Nancy, "I want to tell you something in private."

The teenager followed the woman down the hall, into the bathroom. The woman locked the door behind them.

"I've been thinking about you a lot lately," the woman said. "Take off your shirt. We're going to party."

Baker knew that to the woman "party" meant sex.

"I don't want to!" she cried.

"Well, you have to," the woman replied, pulling a .22-caliber automatic from the back of her pants.

Faced with the shiny black weapon, the frightened girl had no choice but to comply. She peeled off her shirt, but balked at taking off any more clothes. Only when the woman threatened her once again did the teenager reluctantly remove the rest of her clothing.

Excited now, the woman stripped off her own garments and demanded, "Rub my breasts."

Nancy refused.

Irritated by the refusal, the woman pushed the naked girl into the dining room in front of her biker boyfriend. Nancy Baker tried to cover herself with her arms, but the burly man pushed them aside and studied her. Then, without a word, he grabbed her and dragged her toward the bedroom as the woman began to loosen his clothing. Once in the bedroom the man held the girl's arms aside while he stood in front of her, his eyes roaming over her naked body. The woman knelt down and licked his anus while he forced his fingers into Nancy's vagina, even though she told him to stop. He became so aroused that he pushed the teenager onto the bed and nuzzled between her legs while the woman sat on the edge of the bed and masturbated. In a fit of passion the woman began to moan, "Daddy. Oh, Daddy."

Suddenly, the man heard a strange noise in the backyard and got up to retrieve something from his clothing. Nancy saw with sudden terror that it was a .38-caliber pistol. She knew its size and caliber because he had shown it to her before and told her what it was.

The man checked the window that faced the backyard and saw that it was just a false alarm. Satisfied that there were no intruders in the yard, he refocused his attention on Nancy and the woman.

He sat down on the edge of the bed and had the woman orally copulate him. When he was thoroughly aroused, the woman stopped and said to Nancy, "It's your turn."

The woman tried forcing the girl's head down upon his penis, but Nancy fought back with all her might and refused to do it. Even though the woman pushed hard, Nancy resisted with even more force and managed to keep from doing what they wanted.

Tiring of the impasse, the burly biker grabbed Nancy, flung her back onto the bed, and spread her legs. Without any hesitation he held the thirteen-year-old virgin down and penetrated her. He had sex with her for nearly fifteen minutes while the woman once again licked his anus and pleasured herself. The man tried kissing Nancy on the mouth, but she twisted away and at least denied him this one small satisfaction.

Finally, it was over. The man and woman allowed the girl to return to the bathroom and clean herself up. As Nancy was running the water, the woman entered the bathroom with the pistol in her hand.

"Do you know what will happen if you ever tell about this?" the woman asked the teenager.

"Yeah, I'll be in trouble," Nancy Baker replied.

"Yeah," the woman responded. "I'll personally kill you if you tell."

Chapter 1

The Cul-de-sac

It was a cool evening on September 29, 1997, in Reno, Nevada, presaging the winter to come. This city, with its 4,000-foot elevation, was known for its casinos and fast life, but these attributes were the furthest things from Juanita Rodriguez's mind as she walked home from her night class at Morrison Business College. The pretty and petite twenty-year-old from El Salvador was trying to better her life with a business education while working a full-time job. She tugged at the collar of her coat and hurried her steps as leaves whirled by on the sidewalk.

It was 10:15 P.M. when she arrived at the corner of Washington and Sixth Streets and waited for a ride from her boyfriend. The outlines of the high-rise casinos glowed dimly in the background, especially the Circus Circus only a few blocks away. She checked her watch as the minutes ticked along, but her boyfriend was nowhere in sight. As she marked time at the curb, she was dimly aware of a dark green minivan that slowly cruised by and made a U-turn at the corner. The man and woman inside seemed to be studying her.

The van quietly returned in Rodriguez's direction

and came even with her. For a moment everything was still except for the cold breeze that rustled the leaves of the cottonwood trees. Then the side door of the van suddenly swooped open and a large burly man hurtled from its interior and grabbed her. In the next instant everything was a whirlwind of terror, shouts and cursing. The man slipped on the curb, banged his knee and swore, but still managed to hold on to her hair and backpack. Startled and confused, all Rodriguez could think to say was, "What have I done? What have I done?"

Even the dark-haired woman driver seemed to be momentarily in a state of shock. Instead of pulling to a halt, she slowly drove past as the man and Juanita struggled on the sidewalk in the deserted neighborhood. In sheer anger the man yelled at the driver, "Stop, you fucking bitch! Stop the van!"

The van slowly came to a halt as the heavyset man muscled Juanita Rodriguez into the van and slammed her to the floor between the rear captain's chairs. Then the driver took off into the night, Rodriguez still babbling hysterically, "What have I done?"

The man growled back at her, "Shut the fuck up or I'll kill you!"

Rodriguez saw instantly that he wasn't kidding, and ceased talking.

Then her worst fears came true. He ordered, "Take off your shirt." Meekly, she complied.

But his lust was temporarily cooled by the woman's erratic driving. She seemed to be going around in circles. The man directed the driver through several streets until they were on Interstate 80. Once they were past the lights of Boomtown, a gambling complex on the western side of town, the man's attention fully returned to Juanita Rodriguez. He rapidly took off his own clothes and forced her to do the same. He said, "You're going to enjoy this!"

To her disgust, he inserted his finger into her anus and had her do the same to him. He moaned slightly as she did. Then he made her kneel down and orally copulate him, withdrawing in time to ejaculate on her face.

The thin woman driver turned around only once to see what was going on. But the man snapped at her, "Turn the fuck back around and watch the road! And keep the speed down."

The nightmare ride was far from over for Rodriguez, however. As the van drove through the night, into the wall of the high Sierras, along the twisting canyon of the Truckee River, the man kept sexually abusing her. When they approached the California agricultural station at the town of Truckee, there was suddenly a new and terrible tension in the van. The man climbed into the captain's chair just to the rear and side of the woman driver, and he cradled Juanita Rodriguez's head in his lap with a pillow over her head. He said, "If you make a sound, I'll kill you."

For one agonizing moment they were in the full glare of the border guard station. The woman made some innocuous comment to the guard and then the van was rolling again. Only after they were past the bright lights did the man pull the pillow away and Rodriguez gasped for air, at least thankful that he hadn't smothered her to death then and there.

As the van cruised up and over Donner Pass, where the Donner Party had been reduced to cannibalizing itself, the man resorted to sexual torture and various forms of intercourse. This unending nightmare was visited upon her as the darkened, tree-covered mountains rolled by outside the windows. Rodriguez's head was placed in such a position that she could see the van's dashboard and a rosary hanging from the rearview mirror. She tried engaging the woman in a conversation, hoping that she might help her, but the woman ignored her. Finally, out of desperation, Juanita reached forward and gently tugged on the back of the woman's hair and asked, "Have you ever been in love?"

"You ask too many questions!" the woman snapped.

As the van sped down the mountain road, the woman put a country-and-western tape into the tape player. She and the man began to sing along. Juanita Rodriguez noticed that the man called the driver "Micki." Her attacker was particularly keen on one tune sung by Johnny Cash and asked for it to be played over and over while he repeated a phrase to himself. Juanita asked what the song was about. The man's reply made her blood run cold. He explained that the song was about a man in Reno who shot another man, "Just to watch him die."

Frantic now, Rodriguez devised a desperate plan in an attempt to keep herself alive after this ordeal was over. Turning once more to the silent woman driver, she pleaded, "Please help me. I have a mother who will miss me if I am killed." And then she lied, "I also have a baby."

For the first time the woman seemed to take interest in her.

"How old is your baby?" the woman asked.

"Nine months old," Juanita lied.

A few more questions by the woman and at last Juanita Rodriguez knew she at least had gained some sympathy with her.

Even as she started to connect with the woman, the man's hands kept roaming all over her body. It wasn't until the high mountains receded into gentler hills that the man seemed to tire of his abuse on her. She begged him to be returned to Reno unharmed and she wouldn't tell anyone. Seemingly almost remorseful now, he answered, "I know I did bad. I kidnapped you. I abused you. And I raped you. I don't want you to do something stupid. I can't take you back."

He then turned to the woman driver and asked, "What do you think?"

The clear implication: What were they going to do with her?

For a long, terrible moment the woman was silent. Then quite unexpectedly she pulled off the freeway and drove to a dark, deserted cul-de-sac deep in the woods. She took one long look at Juanita and uttered, "Let her go."

Juanita Rodriguez was allowed to put her clothes back on and told to get out and count to twenty before turning around. On her way out the door, the woman whispered to her, "If you turn around for one second, he'll shoot you. Please believe me. You will die. So don't turn around."

Then in a louder voice the woman gave her one more bit of advice. "Don't walk by yourself again. Next time you won't be so lucky."

As Rodriguez stood shivering in the cold and dark, her back turned toward the van, she suddenly heard the vehicle drive away, leaving her alone on the deserted cul-de-sac. Everything was silent now, except for the distant freeway traffic and the chilly wind sighing through the pines. But in her mind she distinctly heard over and over her assailant singing, "I shot a man in Reno, just to watch him die!"

Chapter 2

Wheels in Motion

In the darkness of the now deserted cul-de-sac, Juanita Rodriguez heard the sounds of the freeway in the distance. She stumbled toward the noise, still afraid that the pair might return. Shaken and disheveled, she made her way to the margin of Interstate 80 and waved frantically for the vehicles to stop and help her. Even though it was after midnight, a car full of young people finally pulled over on this forested, desolate part of the road. In halting English she made them understand that she needed to get to a phone. They drove her to a phone booth close to the county seat of Auburn, and Rodriguez contacted the Placer County Sheriff's Department.

Two deputy sheriff officers, Don Murchison and Jeff Adams, responded to her phone call and picked up the distraught young woman at the phone booth. Even though she was clearly shaken and her English was not the best, she made them understand that she was from Reno and that she had been kidnapped, raped and abandoned in the forest. Wanting to get as many details correct as possible and look for evidence, the Placer County officers immediately took Rodriguez back to the cul-de-sac where she had been dropped off. They asked her to recount as best she could everything that had happened and searched for clues at the isolated spot. But there was scant evidence left at the scene of what had transpired there—only a comb that may or may not have been dropped by the perpetrators and nothing else of value.

Juanita Rodriguez was transported to the hospital at Auburn where Nurse Vickie Sewell examined her and used a sexual assault kit, standard procedure in these kinds of situations, to obtain evidence. Nurse Sewell knew that every step she now took would be important later if the suspects were ever caught and the case did come to trial. With great care and precise methodology, she obtained an array of swabs and other material for her sexual assault kit. From Juanita Rodriguez she gathered a saliva reference sample, fingernail scrapings and head hair samples. She also obtained control swabs from Rodriguez's thighs, forehead, neck, cheek and mouth. Then she did a pubic hair brushing.

The whole process of gathering sexual assault evidence was very time consuming and exacting, but Nurse Vickie Sewell was lucky in one regard—Juanita Rodriguez had been brought to the hospital soon after her rape. The longer the span of time between a rape and the medical exam, the more time the seminal fluid of the attacker had a chance to break down under enzyme activity and pH factors.

After taking the vaginal swab, Nurse Sewell air-dried it under a fan to keep microorganisms from growing and degrading the evidence. She then collected Rodriguez's clothes, especially panties, which were a good potential source of seminal fluid and a possible retainer of the attacker's pubic hairs. The head and pubic hairs from Juanita Rodriguez were extremely important just in case the assailant was soon caught and her hairs might be discovered on him or his clothing.

Vickie Sewell understood that any minute bit of evidence she garnered might be extremely useful later on at a criminal justice DNA lab. Even more than fingerprints, DNA testing in this case might be the difference between a conviction and an acquittal if things ever got that far.

Juanita Rodriguez's night of dredging up the horror of her ordeal was far from over. She was next met by Placer County Sheriff's detective Desiree Carrington, who had her recount the details of the attack once again while the details were still fresh in her mind. Even though it was the early hours of the morning, Juanita struggled through the litany of her terror-filled ride. She made it quite clear that she had escaped with her life by the narrowest of margins. Detective Carrington was considerate of Rodriguez's situation, knowing how traumatic a rape experience can be, but she was also very thorough. A restrained sense of modesty would be no help in catching this violent man and woman pair.

Detective Desiree Carrington was one of a growing number of females working in a field dominated by male detectives. She knew at the outset it would not be easy, especially in a rural area where the Western macho myth died hard. But she began earning her badge and the respect of fellow officers when she was the spark plug behind the cracking of a major theft ring, in July 1996.

It started out innocently enough. An eighty-seven-year-old Placer County woman complained of having some checks from her checking account turn up missing. Not much was thought of it until the woman's checking and savings accounts began to be drained of money. Detective Carrington followed a long and twisting path to a thirty-six-year-old man with the improbably larcenous name of Jeffrey Gordon DuFault. He was being held in a Yuba City jail, about fifty miles away in a different county, for passing bad checks. But by the time she got there to question DuFault, he had already been released on his own recognizance and simply disappeared.

Not one to give up so easily, Carrington kept following a new and ever-widening trail of bogus checks and stolen identifications that spanned four counties. There was nothing to link them directly to DuFault, but by now she was pretty sure she knew her man and his mode of operation. As the summer of 1996 progressed, it became apparent that over eighty individuals and thirty businesses were being defrauded mainly by thefts of checks and credit cards from mailboxes and PO boxes. The very sophistication of the larceny became evident when it was learned that DuFault was obtaining blank interim driver's license cards and documents from the Department of Motor Vehicles, then creating fraudulent identification cards and documents using the personal information of real people whose checks had been stolen. By this means he could open accounts and obtain credit cards. He had a scam going that was starting to run into the hundreds of thousands of dollars.

But DuFault overstepped his bounds when he used a counterfeit Sacramento Municipal Utility District identification card. Tracing him to a house in Roseville, near Sacramento, Detective Carrington and a team of officers raided Jeffrey DuFault's home on October 15, 1996, and arrested him and four others in the fraud and stolen property ring. The house was literally stacked to the ceiling with stolen goods: furniture, television sets, VCRs, kitchen appliances, stereo equipment, computers, bicycles, car parts and art objects. It took three large moving vans to haul all the stuff away for evidence.

Detective Desiree Carrington realized she was going to need all the same patience and persistence that she had used on the DuFault case to unravel who the perpetrators were in the abduction and rape of Juanita Rodriguez. But she also realized that time might be a luxury in this case. If the man and woman in the minivan had tried it once, they were apt to try it again. The chilling thought entered her mind and every one else's in the Placer County Sheriff's Department: "Uh-oh, here we go again. We have another Gallego-type case on our hands."

Back in 1978, Sacramento resident Gerald Armand Gallego and his wife, Charlene, used a van for the abduction, rape and ultimately murder of teenage girls. Their first depredation began on September 11, 1978, when Charlene cruised Country Club Plaza mall in Sacramento; she was looking for likely "love slaves" for her husband, Gerald. She hit upon sixteen-year-old Kippi Vaught and seventeen-year-old Rhonda Scheffler. With promises of marijuana she coaxed the girls back to the van parked strategically in a nearby deserted parking lot. As soon as the sliding side door slid open, the girls found themselves looking down the barrel of Gerald Gallego's .25-caliber automatic pistol that he held firmly in his hand. He sternly told them to keep quiet and they wouldn't get hurt. Without a struggle they complied. Within minutes the van was motoring out of town, Charlene at the wheel, and Gerald ordering the girls to remain silent. Charlene drove through Auburn on I-80 to a secluded area in the mountains near Clipper Gap—the very area where Juanita Rodriguez had been let go. Gallego pulled the girls out of the van at gunpoint and marched them into the dense forest. For hours he raped them. Later that night he dispatched Kippi and Rhonda with gunshots to the back of the head.

No one knew more about the man and woman kidnap and murder team of Gerald and Charlene Gallego than Desiree Carrington's partner, Placer County detective Bill Summers. He had found the body of their last victim, Sacramento college student Mary Beth Sowers, dumped in rural Placer County, in 1980.

Mary Beth and her date, Craig Miller, had been attending the Founder's Day Dance at their college when they were suddenly confronted by a gun-wielding Gerald Gallego and his wife, Charlene. Forced into Gallego's vehicle, the couple was driven into the rural hills of El Dorado County, onto Bass Lake Road. Once they were beyond all the houses and farms, Gerald made Craig Miller exit the car, minus his shoes, and they walked only a short distance up the road. Then in the glare of the headlights, Gerald Gallego summarily shot Craig Miller three times right in front of his girlfriend, until he was dead.

Hysterical Mary Beth Sowers couldn't have had too many illusions of what was going to become of her at this point. She was driven back to the Gallegos' apartment, where Charlene immediately flopped down on the couch, while Gerald dragged the unfortunate young woman into the bedroom. Through the thin bedroom door Charlene could hear the unmistakable sounds of forced sex for the next few hours.

It wasn't until the early-morning hours of the next day when Mary Beth Sowers was forced back into their vehicle and driven up into Placer County, near Roseville, where Detective Desiree Carrington would one day bust the DuFault fraud ring. She was marched down into a small gully out of sight of the road, and just as the sun was coming up, Charlene Gallego heard the sounds, *pop pop pop*, emanate from the gully. Gerald Gallego had just dispatched his last victim.

A week later two teenage boys, who were out target shooting, discovered the body of Mary Beth Sowers. Placer County Sheriff's detective Bill Summers was summoned to the scene and he never forgot the sight. The dew-soaked body of the college coed was still wrapped in the blue silk evening gown she had been wearing to the dance. She had been shot in the head three times.

Detective Summers, along with other local agents, soon began putting the pieces together about all the rapes and murders that the Gallego couple had committed. On the run, Gerald and Charlene Gallego were caught in Utah, after leaving a trail of nine dead victims scattered around the Sacramento area. Charlene would get life imprisonment. Gerald would end up on death row.

About the Juanita Rodriguez kidnapping and rape, Detective Summers said to *Contra Costa Times* reporter David Holbrook, "This new crime made us all remember the day we found Mary Beth. It was the same description, a male-female team using a van to lure in their victims."

Juanita Rodriguez was returned to Reno on October 1, 1997, after an intensive interview with Detectives Desiree Carrington and Bill Summers, but her relationship with law enforcement authorities was far from over. The FBI now became involved in her kidnapping, or as they put it, in federal legalese, "The Conspiracy to Commit Kidnapping in Interstate Transportation." The case came into the hands of Special Agent Lynn J. Ferrin, a Reno agent who had seen more than his share of these types of crimes. In his early fifties, with a trim dark mustache and sandy-colored hair, he definitely looked younger than his years. Robust, but not portly, he stayed in shape by a regimen of exercise. Only the glasses he wore while reading papers attested to his more studious side.

He got right on the Rodriguez case by conducting a long interview with her and sending out an FBI team to canvass the area around Washington and Sixth Streets in Reno where the abduction had occurred. Among the agents were Bruce Wick and Mike West. They talked to people throughout the neighborhood who might have noticed anything peculiar on the day and night of September twenty-ninth. A few interesting tips came from the Midtown Motel and the St. Vincent de Paul kitchen nearby, and they duly noted them down.

Special Agent Lynn Ferrin was very well trained in how to handle these types of investigations. He had spent his entire adult life in law enforcement, starting as a deputy in the Davis County Sheriff's Office in Utah and then the North Salt Lake City Police Department. Transferring to the FBI, he'd spent the last twenty-four years moving around the West with the Agency. By 1997 he'd settled down in the Reno Residential office under the command of Agent Jerry Hill, on Kietzke Lane on the south side of town. With its spectacular views of the eastern rampart of the Sierra Nevadas, the new office complex surely beat some of the offices he had been stationed at in the past.

Agent Ferrin realized that solving the Rodriguez

case wasn't going to be easy. He'd learned from Juanita that the man and woman had a lot of personal items in the van, including sleeping bags, as if they had been staying in it. If the pair had no fixed address, they could be anywhere by now. But his specialized training in the investigation of violent crimes, especially Title 18 criminal offenses, which covered kidnapping and sexual assault, had taught him that apprehension often turned on small factors that could be overlooked if not thoroughly investigated. Agent Ferrin was determined to leave no stone unturned in this case. He, too, had heard of the Gerald and Charlene Gallego depredations, and he wanted no repeat in his jurisdiction.

Across town other wheels of justice were in motion as well. From Juanita Rodriguez's verbal description, Officer Wong of the Washoe County Sheriff's Department was able to put together a composite drawing of the male assailant using computer imaging. This new high-tech technique was light years ahead of the old artist renderings. Able to program in over a thousand different shades of coloring and texture, it was a terrific boon to the justice system. It could detail eye shapes and colors, bone structuring and facial peculiarities, all with a high degree of sophistication.

Using Rodriguez's description, Officer Wong produced the mock-up of a heavyset man with close-cropped salt-and-pepper brown hair that was receding in front. He possessed a round face with a large mustache and puffy eyelids. Juanita hadn't seen the woman driver well enough to give a good description of her, other than she had dark hair and wore glasses some of the time.

Within the Washoe County Sheriff's Office crime lab complex, another individual began working on the Juanita Rodriguez abduction and rape as well. Criminalist Renee Romero obtained the rape kit that Nurse Vickie Sewell had used on Juanita. With her blond shoulder-length hair and striking features, Romero could easily have passed for a model in a glamour magazine rather than a criminalist in the Sheriff's Department. But along with her good looks she also possessed a keen intellect attuned to small important details. She had studied forensic sciences at the University of Nevada, Reno, and published a thesis on DNA typing.

As Renee Romero took the swabs that Nurse Sewell had procured, she used only a minute sample from each to analyze the semen contained therein by a method known as PCR testing. PCR testing was faster than the more exact RFLP method and it could use smaller initial samples. It could also be amplified and copied better than RFLP, much like xeroxing a copy of an original document. Not only could Romero use what she found, she could send the samples to other labs for verification as well as to double-check her findings.

When Renee Romero ran her DNA tests, she came up with one very interesting observation: the semen sample contained no sperm. It was a significant fact. It meant that the attacker had produced no sperm either because of natural causes or he had had a vasectomy.

The Placer County Sheriff's Department, Washoe County Sheriff's Department and FBI were beginning to put together a sketchy outline of a man and woman who had used a van for abduction and rape. But before they had progressed very far, the couple struck again.

Chapter 3

"Act Like You Enjoy It."

While Renee Romero was checking for DNA evidence in late October, police investigators later learned the dark-haired woman who owned the green minivan was back in Sacramento, California. She and the tattooed man planned a trip to Oregon. Somehow her twelve-year-old daughter learned of their plans and cajoled her way into coming along. Once they were rolling along the freeway, the girl fell asleep on the long drive up the Sacramento Valley. Somewhere south of the Oregon line, she was suddenly awakened when she felt a strange sensation on her leg. She realized with a start that the tattooed man was rubbing her legs.

"Make him stop, Mommy!" the girl cried to her mother, who was driving.

The dark-haired woman turned around and glared at her daughter.

"No," she responded. "I want him to."

Then the woman drove off the freeway into a secluded area and stopped the van. While the man held her daughter down, the woman unzipped the frightened girl's jeans. The man bent over and began to perform oral sex on the girl—with no objections from the woman.

Even when they reached Klamath Falls, Oregon, the girl's torment wasn't over. They forced her to take drugs and both took turns molesting her.

The couple enjoyed the torment so much, in fact, that the next week they drove the woman's daughter and her friend Nancy Baker down to Santa Cruz on the northern California coast, and again the man's hands freely roamed over the young girls' bodies. He was filled with such bravado over his exploits that he stopped the van somewhere in the Santa Cruz Mountains just to fire his .38-caliber pistol next to the head of the young teenager. He even told her what caliber it was and what would happen to her if she ever told anyone what they had done. The girls were under no illusions that he meant business. They knew he was a rough member of a motorcycle gang and would resort to violence if he felt he had to. Nor did they have any illusions about the woman as well. The woman had bragged about killing someone in the past and then hanging the body in a tree.

On November 3, 1997, seventeen-year-old Patty Wilson, who was a friend of the tattooed biker's daughter by his first marriage, was working at Q-Zar, a game arcade for teenagers near Pleasanton, California. She stepped outside for a cigarette break that evening and saw the familiar green minivan approach. The dark-haired woman gestured for her to come over and she complied.

"Want to do a line of meth?" the woman asked.

"Sure," Wilson answered.

It wasn't a big deal for her. She had done meth

with the woman and her boyfriend several times before.

As Patty Wilson stood by the driver's window, they all talked for a while about the man's daughter being pregnant. Then Wilson asked if they wanted to do the meth in the arcade's bathroom.

"No, we'll do it in the van," the woman answered.

"I've got to tell my boss I'll be gone for a little while," Wilson said, excusing herself. When she returned and climbed into the minivan, she noticed that all of the backseats had been removed except for the long benchlike seat in the far back. There were pillows on the floor and a mirror above it.

The man began driving east, away from the city lights. As Patty Wilson gazed up at the mirror, thinking they were just out for a drive, the woman suddenly came up behind her and pushed her down, attempting to place handcuffs over her wrists. Wilson struggled wildly and elbowed the woman in the ribs. But the heavyset man stopped the van and tore out of the driver's seat. He jumped into the back of the van and punched Wilson hard in the face.

As Wilson remembered later, "I didn't know you could actually see stars when you get hit. I passed out for about five minutes."

The next thing Wilson knew when she revived was that there were handcuffs on her wrists, and her hands were behind her back.

Now the woman was driving and the man was yelling at her that every place she attempted to stop was either too open or too conspicuous. Patty Wilson knew the general lay of the land in the area and realized that they were headed for the hills south of Livermore, a nearby town. While they were still moving, the man could no longer restrain himself. He undid his pants and ordered Wilson to go down on him. Fearing for her life, she did as he demanded.

The man wasn't satisfied with her performance. "Act like you enjoy it!" he growled.

But Patty Wilson wasn't enjoying it. After a minute she stopped and told him, "I can't do this! It reminds me of my stepdad. He used to force me to do this."

This seemed to spoil the effect for the man. Sullenly, he said, "OK, you don't have to do it anymore. But you know who is going to want her turn," and he pointed at the woman.

Indeed, the woman did want her turn. She found a place to pull over in the darkened hills near Livermore, parked, and came in through the sliding door. She pulled Wilson's pants and panties off and went down on her as the man sat nearby and masturbated. When they were finally through, they forced Wilson to take off all her clothes and they snapped a couple of photos of her nude.

It was only after this that they said, "We can't take you back to work. We're not going to jail."

Patty Wilson was scared out of her mind. She knew how dangerous this pair could be. She also knew they had a gun because she'd seen it the day before behind the passenger seat. And she realized that the man could kill her with his fists at any time if he wanted to.

Wilson begged, "If you let me go back to work and don't hurt me or kill me, I won't tell. I'll make up some dumb lie to the police. I know my manager will call the police because I'm not like that. I wouldn't take off from my job like that. As long as you let me live, I won't tell."

The man and woman drove on and thought it over. The minutes seemed like hours to Wilson. Everything was dark and deserted outside with no houses in sight. A perfect place for a murder.

Finally, after an excruciating amount of time had elapsed, the couple agreed to let her go. They concocted a story she was to tell the police.

"Listen," the woman said. "You're to tell the police that you were kidnapped by three teenage boys from the parking lot of Q-Zar. The boys took you out in the hills and raped you."

To make it more convincing, the woman reached over and ripped Patty's shirt. They drove her to a gas station on Dublin Boulevard and dropped her off. Then they simply vanished.

Patty Wilson called her manager from a phone booth and repeated the story about the teenage boys and he believed her. But when she told the Dublin police the same story when they arrived, they were more skeptical. Too much of her tale did not ring true.

Nonetheless, Wilson stuck to her story, even though her assailants were no longer around. It didn't matter. She recalled how the savage man's punch had knocked her out for a full five minutes. And she remembered the large pistol behind the passenger seat. But more than anything else, Patty Wilson remembered that these two knew where she lived.

Two weeks later, on the night of November 18, 1997, a curious event took place on the streets of Sacramento, California. A Sacramento police officer received information that two young girls had been molested and went to investigate. When he arrived at Nancy Baker's house, he found her and the dark-haired woman's daughter there. His mere presence must have given them courage. First Nancy, and then her friend, blurted out stories of sexual molestation and rape at the hands of a man and woman who owned a green minivan.

Detective Willover of the Sacramento Police Department got the particulars of their statements on November 20 and began to fill out a report. Under the crime description he wrote, "Rape of drugged victim," concerning the rape of the girl who was a daughter of the woman who had been driven to Klamath Falls and Santa Cruz. For a date of the crime he penciled in "Sept '97?" He wrote down the vehicle used in the crime as a '95 Dodge Caravan, dark green.

Nancy Baker, who had been raped in the strange house, also told about her ordeal. She not only gave vivid testimony, she gave one more very important fact—the names of the couple. James Daveggio and Michelle Michaud.

Nancy Baker also gave one more bit of electrifying information. On an evening back in October, a news item had come on the local television station about the Reno abduction and rape of Juanita Rodriguez. Michelle Michaud's daughter and Nancy had been sitting on the couch when Michelle suddenly pointed at the screen and said proudly, "We did that!"

By "we" she had meant herself and James Daveggio. And by "that" she had meant the abduction and rape of Juanita Rodriguez.

Daveggio and Michaud had not only done "that"—they had also done a lot of other things that hadn't come to light. When Detective Willover checked the computer data bank, he found that both Michelle Michaud and James Daveggio had indeed had their problems with the law in the past. Michaud had been arrested for prostitution and

Daveggio's transgressions included kidnapping and forcible rape.

When asked where the couple might be at the present time, Nancy Baker didn't know. She said they now lived out of their van and could be anywhere.

One thing Detective Willover knew for sure, they were on the loose, they were armed and dangerous, and they meant business.

PART II
BLOOD BROTHERS

PART II

BLOOD BROTHERS

Chapter 4

"Froggie"

James Anthony Daveggio had been born in San Francisco at Mary's Help Hospital on July 27, 1960, the son of a delivery driver for a liquor supply company. He already had one brother and a sister was soon on the way. But before James was five years old, his father divorced his mother, Darlene, and moved out of the area.

Even though his mom remarried in 1964, Daveggio sorely missed his dad. At some point he found out that his father not only got remarried, but he always seemed to have several girlfriends on the side. According to Donetta Rhodes, a woman Daveggio would later marry, "James always wanted to be like his dad. He idolized him. He even insisted at one point that we go live with him in Pacifica. He wanted the nice things his dad had: the nice house, the good cars, all the kids. But the thing James wanted most was more wives and more girlfriends. I thought that was a real odd thing to tell me. But where it seemed to work for his father, it never quite worked for him. James had a way of bullshitting people for a while. He had this real open manner. But once you got to see what he was really like up close,

it was a different story. Everything had to be for
him. He really at heart didn't care about anyone
else. And it always tripped him up. It's like he
couldn't control himself. James always managed to
get into trouble at some point."

When James Daveggio got into minor scrapes as
a boy, the one person to always back him up was
his mother, Darlene. To her, he was special, even
though he did have a speech impediment that
made his voice very low and rough. And he was not
the quickest learner. If James got into a scuffle with
a neighborhood boy, it was always Darlene who
found a ready excuse why her son was the innocent
party. If he was found to have stolen something, she
surmised it must have been a mistake. And when
even darker rumors started to circulate about him
later, she drove them out of her mind. It couldn't
be her son who was at fault, not the James she knew,
who was a loving son.

One woman who had been a classmate of James's
in high school, and still works in the area, remembered him at Union City's Logan High School as
quiet and kind of shy. "He really didn't stand out.
He wasn't bad-looking or anything. I remember he
had long blond hair and blue eyes. I guess I remember the eyes more than anything. They were
very bright blue. But other than that he wasn't
someone you really noticed all that much."

James Daveggio's photo in the 1976 Logan High
School yearbook, *The Epitaph,* revealed a stocky boy
with longish blond hair that reached to his collar.
He had one characteristic, though, that could not
be captured by just a photo—his voice. Even by the
time he was sixteen, it was already deep with just a
bit of a rasp to it. It earned him the nickname
"Froggie." He was intimidating because of his size
and deep voice, but also approachable because he

tended to smile a lot and was fairly quiet. His eyes, girls agreed, were the best thing about him. They were a very deep blue and tended to light up when he smiled. And he didn't use foul language around girls like some teenage guys did, just to act tough.

But if the girls had looked a bit more carefully at his smile, they might have noticed it contained a strange quality. Both his 1976 and 1977 yearbook photos reveal a secretive nature to his smile, as if he had hidden thoughts. Perhaps it was a smile that masked the bizarre sexual fantasies that were beginning to bubble to the surface of his mind. For by 1976 Daveggio was already showing tendencies of antisocial behavior and deep-seated sexual problems.

The move to Pleasanton from Union City did not help. He didn't make many friends at his new school, Foothill High, and always seemed to be getting into fights. The more he was punished, the more he rebelled. And his penchant for stealing only increased. He became involved in a robbery of a local gas station and was caught. For his part as the driver of the getaway car, he spent some time in the Alameda County Boys detention camp.

He was also becoming more outgoing and aggressive with girls. According to one source, "He couldn't keep his eyes or his hands off them. He had roaming hands, if you know what I mean. If he wanted something, he just went after it. That went for people as well as things."

The move to Pleasanton also brought him into contact with a boy a year older than himself—a boy with sexual fantasies just as wild and violent as his own. The boy's name was Michael Ihde.

The two bumped into each other on Pleasanton's old Main Street. Before long they were both skipping school and hanging out. It was here, not at school, that Daveggio got into his true element and made friends. Never a model student, he began to disregard his homework even more. He was never much into books anyway. It was more fun just to hang out with "tough" guys like Mike around Main Street. Not that either Mike or James were all that tough at this point. They didn't do hard drugs then, but they weren't above caging a few beers from older boys and smoking marijuana. Then they would go down to an area known as "the Creek," behind Main Street, and drink their beer or smoke their dope.

One of the places they hung out at was the Pastime Pool Hall on Main Street. A bartender who currently works there grew up with Daveggio. Like everyone else who knew James from that era, he referred to him as "Frog" or "Froggie."

"Frog used to hang out at the creek [Arroyo del Valle] behind Main Street a lot," he said. "You could look over there and there would be Frog. Not really causing any trouble. Just back there goofing off. He'd rather do that than go to school. I don't remember the other guy, Mike what's his name. I'm not even sure how much of friends he and Frog were. I think they just kind of were in the same crowd, you know what I mean. Birds of a feather. That kind of thing. But I heard about him [Mike] later."

In fact, nearly half the patrons sitting at the bar on a summer's day in 1999 remembered Frog. They, like him, were somehow on the fringes of the new upscale Pleasanton—and not particularly pleased at what had become of "their town." What had once been a working-class city was now becoming snobbish and elitist, according to them.

Pleasanton, as the name implies, is a peaceful upscale community thirty-five miles southeast of San

Francisco. It is a place where families move to escape the urban blight and crime of the city. By 1997 this city of 60,000 hadn't had a murder for over two years. In fact, the eighty-one officers of the Pleasanton Police Department didn't even have a homicide unit. Murders and violent crime were something that happened in Oakland and over the hill in San Jose.

But San Jose's close proximity did bring one good thing to Pleasanton. Prosperity. What had once been a quiet backwater town devoted to agriculture and ranching was transformed almost overnight by the computer revolution in Silicon Valley. Suddenly by the late 1970s, thousands of people were moving to Pleasanton for the cheaper prices of homes. Not long thereafter, the high-tech jobs followed. Software and hardware companies took advantage of the space around Pleasanton with its cheaper land prices and flooded the area.

But these were jobs for people with college degrees and advanced technical skills—not the kind of people James Daveggio hung out with. With their minimal education and low-paying jobs, Daveggio and his friends were more likely to be merely service people to these new "techies," who now inhabited their town in such abundance. Daveggio and his buddies were more aligned with Old Pleasanton, whose roots went back to Spanish California land-grant days, when Don Augustine Bernal had owned all the land in the vicinity as far as the eye could see. A land of rolling, oak-dotted hills and lush green valleys along winding streams, it was suited for cattle raising and an agrarian way of life. But by the late 1970s the agricultural land was quickly going under the bulldozer's blade to make room for the high-tech firms and the expensive new homes of the workers in those establishments.

Needless to say, Daveggio and his Pastime friends looked on the newcomers with ill-disguised envy and hatred. These were the people who were destroying the way of life they knew.

With its old-fashioned saloon appearance and its cool, dark, funky interior, the Pastime Pool Hall is the last throw-back to the old era. There is no Brie and Chablis being served there, just beer and pretzels. Anyone wandering in wearing a three-piece suit would be immediately eyed with suspicion if not outright contempt.

None of the patrons wished to give their real names when the news about Daveggio broke, perhaps worried about the ramifications in a town that knew all too well about James Daveggio by 1997. But they were more than willing to talk about their old friend Frog. "Stan," a patron wearing a T-shirt and beat-up baseball cap, said, "Frog was actually a nice guy back when he used to come in here in the late 1970s and early '80s. He didn't cuss and he didn't have tattoos and all that stuff. He liked smoking some dope, but just about everybody did then. He wasn't into any of the harder drugs, like crank or cocaine. At least not when I knew him. To tell you the truth, I think a lot of girls kind of liked him, despite what his voice sounded like. Mainly because of his long blond hair and blue eyes. But he was pretty shy around them. I don't know how much he hung around with that guy Michael Ihde. They knew each other, that much I know. But I wasn't really a friend of Mike's. He was real strange. More of a loner."

"Jeff," another pool hall patron, agreed for the most part. "Froggie was all right. Except when he had too much to drink. He couldn't drink here at the Pastime 'cause he was underage, but he had ways of getting it elsewhere and drinking down by the creek. Then he turned into a loudmouth. It was pretty evident he couldn't handle booze very well."

One thing none of them mentioned was Frog's views and fantasies about sex. Whereas in most cases teenage boys will brag to one another about their exploits, Frog never did. He clammed up on the subject when asked about it. Whatever his sexual inclinations and tendencies, he kept them to himself.

One acquaintance, who was not part of the Pastime crowd and who still lives in the area, remembered Daveggio and Ihde in less favorable terms. "They were always getting into some sort of trouble. Stealing cigarettes and crap like that. I don't know. Frog wasn't too bright. He kinda went along with things. He was easily led around by others. They were just trying to be a couple of hard-asses."

There were also other recollections of Frog—not by his friends, but by the police.

"I particularly remember Daveggio at that time," Captain Gary Tollefson of the Pleasanton Police Department said years later. "I knew exactly who he was. I knew his nickname was 'Froggie.' He wasn't into hard-core criminal activity then. Just penny-ante stuff. He was always on the periphery of trouble. Like he couldn't stay away from it. I guess it had some kind of fascination for him. When I think of him back then, he wasn't really what you'd call a bad guy. A hard case. He actually was pretty friendly and gregarious and I had several conversations with him when I was a patrolman. But like I said, he was always on the fringes."

The combination of James Daveggio and Michael Ihde and the company they hung out with was a bad mixture. Separately they had their various problems to deal with—together they exacerbated the problems, bringing out the worst in both of them. The fact that they didn't do hard drugs in 1977 was not going to help them in the long run. They had an affinity for alcohol, and neither of them could handle the stuff. Daveggio's interest in school deteriorated even more, and by mid-1977 he was transferred to Valley High Continuation School in Dublin, California, a town adjacent to Pleasanton, after cursing out one of the administrators at Foothill High. This put him into even closer contact with Michael Ihde, who was already attending that institution.

Dublin, if anything, was even more an upper-middle class town than Pleasanton. It made both Ihde and Daveggio feel like absolute outsiders, coming from working-class backgrounds. Ihde, in particular, felt uncomfortable and isolated there. "Dublin was a stuck-up place," he proclaimed years later. "A bunch of hypocrites who thought they were better than everybody else. The teachers really had it in for me."

Even Daveggio admitted to a friend in Sacramento almost twenty years later, "I didn't like Dublin. I didn't fit in."

By 1978 both James Daveggio and Michael Ihde were staking out their turf as the perpetual outsiders. Someone or someplace was always out to get them or put them down. The prosperity and pretensions of Dublin were like corrosives on their low self-esteems and the only real place they found relief was on Pleasanton's Main Street with boys just like themselves. Drinking and smoking, talking tough with the other guys, they saw Main Street as a haven from the mores and upscale society that they were learning to despise.

* * *

Michael Ihde was even less imposing than James Daveggio. Standing at five feet nine inches, with an angular face and reddish brown hair, he had a thin pinched sort of look about him. His hair was long, with pencil-thin sideburns, and his green eyes had a disturbing yellowish tinge to them. He was the youngest of the three children of Charles and Colleen Ihde of Pleasanton. His parents had divorced when he was eight years old, remarried, and divorced again for good when he was eleven. All of this did not bring any stability to the Ihde household.

Mike's life became even more unusual when his mother took a job as a civilian employee at Santa Rita Prison, just one mile outside of Pleasanton. He spent his teenage years in employee housing virtually "behind the wire."

The prison itself sat in a basin surrounded by hills just north of Pleasanton. In the distance, Mount Diablo, or the Devil's Mountain, made a suitable backdrop to the enclosure. With its bleak gray walls and strands of barbed wire atop its fences, Santa Rita was in stark contrast to upscale Pleasanton, just a mile away.

With more than 800 employees and nearly 5,000 prisoners, Santa Rita was a small city unto itself. In fact, Santa Rita was really a conglomeration of internment facilities; the Santa Rita County Jail, Federal Institution, and Federal Prison Camp, dubbed "Club Fed." The Federal Prison Camp had been started as a minimum security facility to house bootleggers in the 1930s. Over time the enclosure accepted more hardened cases. Through its gates passed Patty Hearst, newspaper heiress turned brainwashed terrorist, and Sara Jane Moore, would-be assassin of President Gerald Ford. Also serving time there were the likes of junk bond king Michael Milken, Unabomber Ted Kaczynski, and Los Angeles police officers Stacey Koon and Laurence Powell, who had beaten motorist Rodney King nearly to death.

More daring than these was inmate Ronald McIntosh. In 1986 he hijacked a helicopter, flew it to the prison yard of the women's facility, and airlifted his inmate girlfriend, Samantha Lopez, from the grounds. They enjoyed ten days of freedom until caught buying wedding rings in Sacramento.

Michael Ihde certainly had interesting company in his youth. And if it wasn't enough that his mother was an employee of the facility, one of his uncles was a full-time Alameda Sheriff's deputy as well. All of this should have had a beneficial impact on young Mike's upbringing. But ironically, it seemed to have had just the opposite effect. He began to harbor respect for the cons while turning his back on the cops and prison guards. He had enjoyed school until his freshman year in high school, and then he said, "The teachers were prejudiced against me because I had long hair and was a slow learner." In Mike Ihde's world it was always someone else's fault for the problems he faced. His "slow learning" and truancy got him thrown into Valley High Continuation School—and into the orbit of James Daveggio.

The two boys started spending more time around each other once they were both in the continuation school, feeding off each other's neurosis and disdain for the law. More often than not, Friday and Saturday nights would find them inebriated with the other boys down on Main Street, even though they were underage. The most compelling evidence of their friendship came from a source in the Alameda

Sheriff's Department who knew them both as teenagers. He told *San Francisco Chronicle* reporter Patricia Jacobus, "In a bizarre coincidence, Daveggio was friends with Michael Ihde, who was sentenced to death in 1996. . . . Daveggio has had run-ins with the law since his teenage years."

Whether James Daveggio and Michael Ihde discussed their sexual fantasies of dominance and control at this time, nobody knows except them. There's even some debate as to how well they knew each other. But in a strange parallel course they were already setting the patterns for their future lives in crime.

It was odd that after 1978 neither one kept in touch with the other. But in an ironic twist, their crimes would be so similar in scope and violence, covering the same locales near Pleasanton, that half a dozen police agencies would eventually ask about a number of victims: "Who did it? James Daveggio or his old friend Michael Ihde?"

Not until the dawn of a new century would they know for sure.

For a time both boys attempted to keep their demons down by marrying young women in the area and joining the armed services. But nothing was destined to work out for these two. They would give in to their most bizarre and violent desires and leave a bloodstained trail from the San Francisco Bay Area to Nevada and Washington State.

James Daveggio was able to keep his demons in check a little longer than his friend. By 1978 Michael Ihde was already on the path to hell.

Chapter 5

Blood Brother

Michael Ihde dropped out of school in 1978, married his already pregnant girlfriend, Becky, and joined the marines. Perhaps he hoped they would make a man out of him, just like the television ads promised. But nothing ever worked out quite right for Mike. He injured his foot in the first few weeks of basic training and was released from the marines with an honorable discharge.

Suddenly at a loss of what to do and unemployed, Ihde moved with his new wife up to the small town of Ione in California's Gold Rush Country. With its false-front buildings and Gold Rush architecture, it looked more like a Hollywood movie set than a real town. Strangely enough, Ihde had chosen a town with a large penal institution dominating the skyline. The Preston School for Boys belied its innocent-sounding name. It was a large, dark, glowering nineteenth-century building made out of sturdy cut stones. Sitting high on the hill on the west side of town, it seemed like a fantasy right out of Charles Dickens' imagination. There were some pretty hard cases inside, despite their ages—criminals who somehow mirrored Michael Ihde's own troubled mind. Consciously or not, Ihde kept finding himself living in the shadow of prison walls.

He obtained a job as a laborer in a nearby locale with the American Forest Products Company, but right from the start he missed a lot of work because of his injured foot. Never one to believe very strongly in the American work ethic, he found it more enjoyable to stay at home and dwell on his fantasies of sexual dominance. Not with his wife, but with a stranger.

By March 24, 1978, Michael Ihde was no longer willing to dream those fantasies. He was ready to act. He walked to the Safeway parking lot in the nearby city of Jackson, and directly into the path of Gloria Hazelwood, who was getting into her car.

Thirty-two-year-old Hazelwood had just finished work at Garibaldi's Studio in Jackson's old downtown and had climbed into her '73 Dodge Dart at about 5:00 P.M. As she put the car in reverse and backed up, she nearly ran into Ihde. He dashed to her driver's-side window and begged, "Please, lady, I need to get to the top of the hill," indicating a direction just outside of town. "It's urgent."

Hazelwood didn't know him and was about to refuse, but he persisted.

"Please take me," he said. "I'll give you five dollars if you do."

The money seemed to do the trick. Not that she wanted it, but if he was willing to give her five dollars just to drive him out of town, she decided it must really be an emergency. Despite some misgivings, she opened the door for Ihde and he climbed in.

He directed her onto State Route 49, then to

Electra Road, and had her drive halfway down its narrow blacktop to an isolated spot near the Mokelumne River. When they reached an uninhabited area, he suddenly said, "That's enough."

Gloria Hazelwood stopped the car and without any warning Ihde balled his hand into a fist and punched her in the face and stomach. Scared witless, she started screaming. This only made him punch her harder as he yelled, "Shut up!" Taking a red rag out of his pocket, he tied her hands together behind her back and jerked her panty hose and panties down. He shouted at her to spread her legs. When she was slow about it, he forced them apart. With her head up against the car door, he brutally raped her.

When he was done, he allowed her to pull her panties and panty hose back up. He took her car keys and forced her out of the car and up an embankment by the side of the road. Ihde told her to face the Mokelumne River. She dutifully complied, still scared out of her mind, while he searched on the ground for something.

In the next instant Gloria Hazelwood found out exactly what he was looking for. Ihde came up with a large rock in his hand and slammed it into her head. She tumbled down the embankment and he followed, pounding her with the rock.

"Please stop it!" she cried. "I won't tell anybody!"

"Do you expect me to believe that?" he scoffed. He kept right on pummeling her head with the large stone.

It was only when Hazelwood pretended to be dead that he stopped. She put on a good act, pretending to have stopped breathing, as he looked her over to make sure. Ihde threw the rock away, convinced she was indeed dead. He scrambled up the embankment and disappeared into the forested countryside.

Hazelwood never passed out, but she had been beaten into a daze. She said, "After he was gone, I struggled to get to the top of the hill. I just thought if I don't get up there no one will see me. No one will help me. I was trying to climb up the hill and I was sick and so dizzy and I fell a couple of times when I tried to stand up. So I crawled to the top of the hill and I got in the car and locked the doors. Then I blew the horn until someone stopped."

Hazelwood was first taken to nearby Amador Hospital and then to Sacramento Medical Center. She required numerous stitches to her head, but luckily for her there was no brain damage. Unluckily for Michael Ihde she was still alive.

Gloria Hazelwood had no doubt as to his intentions. She told the investigating officer, Amador County Detective Sergeant Norman Pettingill, "He wanted to kill me."

Detective Pettingill took a description of the assailant. Hazelwood described him as "a white male, twenty years of age, about five feet nine inches tall, with a slender build. His hair is medium brown with a reddish tint. It is collar length and combed straight back without a part, curling up at the bottom near the collar. It is closely cut, and possibly a layer cut. The sideburns are very narrow, coming straight down to approximately the jaw line, with no flare."

From this description the police were able to create a sketch, which they published in the *Amador Press News*. But even with this, after a month-long search of the area, they had to admit, "We've run into a brick wall."

But Michael Ihde never was lucky for very long. In June 1978 an unknown informant called the sheriff's office and turned him in. Perhaps as usual, he had not been able to keep his mouth shut and had bragged about his exploits with Gloria Hazelwood. At 8:00 A.M. on June 14, the authorities converged on his home in Ione. They stormed into the house and arrested Ihde, handcuffing him, before placing him in the patrol car. Then his luck turned even more sour. The woman he had picked at random to kidnap and rape turned out to be the wife of his own foreman at American Forest Products.

There were soon dark rumors of vigilante justice by Ihde's coworkers at American Forest Products—something not so far-fetched in this Gold Rush Country town. A few miles down the road in Sonora, Ellie Nesler would stride into a courtroom one day and shoot the alleged molester of her boy, dead.

It was only the efforts of Gloria's husband that finally cooled down the hotheads before they did something rash. He told a reporter for the *Amador Press News*, "I don't want any retribution on his [Michael Ihde's] family. I think the law should take its course. I'm not going to do anything about this but let the courts do their work and I don't think anybody else should do anything either."

At his trial Michael Ihde was all outraged innocence. "I know I am innocent," he declared. "My wife and a lot of other people believe in my innocence. I feel I should have been granted a change of venue because of the prejudice here and the newspaper articles. I feel very sorry it happened to Mrs. Hazelwood. If I was Mr. Hazelwood, I would want to get the guy too. I have always put women on a pedestal because I love my mother so much."

Despite his protests, the only ones to buy his "innocent routine" were his mother and wife, Becky. She stated that her sexual relationship with him was completely normal and he had never tried anything "weird." She went on to say that he never beat her or abused her.

But his wife would find out soon enough just how "weird" he was.

The jury had no problem finding Michael Ihde guilty on November 30, 1978, of Count 261 (2), Forcible rape, and Count 217, Assault with intent to murder.

Ihde, who had spent his childhood in a prison compound, now got a one-way trip back to a prison, except this time he was going behind the walls instead of just looking at them from a distance. From his early years around cons and a few hard cases who hung around Pleasanton, he already knew some of the ropes about life behind bars. He was well on his way to becoming an "institution man," one who finds it almost easier to live in prison than on the outside. The world outside had too many options, too many chances to get into trouble. On the inside, everything was regulated. A man knew just where he stood with the guards and the other prisoners.

The authorities tried to mend his ways and give him a different outlook on life. He got the prerequisite counseling about finding a regular job once he was released and how to conduct himself back in society. But the authorities had little success with Michael Ihde.

Lessons that should have been impressed upon him in prison didn't stick. The only real lesson he took to heart was "Don't leave the next victim alive." By 1982 he was on the outside again, minus a wife. Becky had gained a new insight into his real nature and had promptly divorced him when she discovered he was not an innocent who had been framed. The terrible things people had been saying about Mike were now obviously all too true.

He was paroled to his old stomping grounds in the East Bay, not too far from where James Daveggio lived. Ihde was just as violent as ever, covered only by a thin layer of civility. Hanging out in the less than palatial environs of Ashland Avenue in San Lorenzo, Ihde began to have a fling with the bottle. He made halfhearted attempts to find a job, but more often than not he found himself sitting around the sparse apartment with a six-pack or a bottle of booze. He did manage to gain a new girlfriend, Rachel Piazza, but she was just as slovenly and prone to drinking as he was. Too often their drinking bouts turned into arguments and then into fights. Neither one of them could hold down a job for very long. Ihde felt stifled in the shoddy surroundings. He took to wandering down the Southern Pacific tracks to a spot beneath a large freeway overpass. The area had been turned into a hobo jungle, with discarded beat-up furniture stashed away in the bushes and screen of small trees. It was a place where he could drink in peace, away from the hectoring of Rachel and her demands that he get a job. Basically, he had been a loner all his life and this spot's isolation gave him a chance to think about what he really liked—sex with someone fresh and exciting. Sex with someone who didn't expect it. Sex with someone he could abuse and dominate. Someone like Gloria Hazelwood. Within a year he was ready to strike again.

Chapter 6

In the Shadow of Charlie Chaplin

If James Daveggio had paid more attention to his old friend Michael Ihde's fate of imprisonment, he might have avoided its consequences. But Daveggio had problems that were remarkably similar to Ihde's. He married a young woman in Pleasanton named Annette and had a daughter, born in 1980. But Daveggio had a roving eye when it came to other women. He also had a hard time keeping a steady job. Generally soft-spoken, despite his raspy voice, he became a different person when drinking—and he turned to alcohol more and more often. He constantly promised to get his act together, but one excuse followed another. He would rather be out drinking with his buddies than at home helping raise a family. And like his father, he really had a thing for the ladies. He met a pretty young woman named Donetta Rhodes at Niles Canyon, a place where teenagers hung out and went swimming in the creek. Many people told Rhodes to stay away from Daveggio. They knew the real man behind the charming facade. But she was only seventeen at the time and in love. All she could see was the handsome young blond with blue eyes.

As she laughed ruefully later, "I thought I knew better than them. I was going to change his ways. Some things you just have to learn the hard way, I guess. And I learned some pretty hard lessons with James."

In July 1980 Daveggio left his wife, Annette, for Donetta. Rhodes didn't realize he was still sleeping with his ex-wife, who became pregnant by him again. A daughter, April, was born on July 13, 1981. Just like his father, he was accumulating wives, girlfriends and children at an increasing rate.

Donetta Rhodes was furious at him when she learned of Annette's pregnancy. She threatened to leave him, but he was a smooth talker. He convinced her to marry him, even though his divorce with Annette wasn't final. Daveggio and Rhodes drove up to Reno on May 7, 1982, and were married at the Chapel of the Bells on West Fourth Street by Reverend Frank Murtha. Inside the small chapel, which resembled more of an office space than a church, were Denice Bickford and Lisa Bradshaw as witnesses. One thing Donetta quickly learned in Reno was that James loved to gamble. It wasn't just a passing love affair with the slots and cards, it was an addiction.

Returning to Pleasanton, James and Donetta moved into a stylish new home on Clovewood Avenue that his mom, Darlene, and his stepdad owned. For a while it looked as if they might settle down to be a typical part of the suburban good life.

But living under the same roof with Daveggio's mother was not easy for Donetta. According to Donetta, "She thought James was God's gift to the world and that I should do everything for him. Make his bed, cook his meals, worship the ground he walked on. And this was when I was holding down two jobs and he wasn't working at all! I had a job at Denny's in Pleasanton and one at a 7-Eleven. James finally did land a good job at a sheet metal company and I heaved a sigh of relief. But in a couple of weeks he quit it for no reason. He was allergic to work."

Daveggio was also a dreamer and a schemer with 101 get-rich-quick schemes that never quite worked out. Of course it usually took the money that Donetta made from her jobs to get him started on these schemes. "The grass was always greener on the other side of the hill for him," she said. In pursuit of these schemes they moved to Oklahoma for six months and then back to California near Pacifica, where Daveggio's dad lived.

Donetta related, "James always wanted to be like his father. He really didn't even know him until he was sixteen. Then it was his dad this, and his dad that, all the time. He told me once that he wanted to have more wives, more women and more kids than his dad did. I thought it was an awfully strange goal. His dad had been married four or five times and he had eight kids. James's admission made me feel real uneasy. What kind of person would want those kinds of things?"

In fact, this admission did not bode well for their marriage. Neither did their prospects when they moved back to Pleasanton and started living in motel rooms and even in their car. It wasn't long before they found themselves right back underneath his mom's roof on Clovewood Avenue.

"It was tough," Donetta said. "He hit the bars again and started doing cocaine. And he had a terrible gambling habit. More than once, I just barely got my paycheck and he was running off with it up to Reno or Tahoe to lose it all at the card tables.

He also began to play a lot of poker at the Pastime Poolhall with his buddies. This didn't make things any better, because I didn't like to drink or gamble. So I got left home a lot with his mom. Life with him was becoming hell!"

Donetta admitted that Daveggio never physically abused her, but the verbal and mental abuse was becoming almost constant. And he was also becoming "weirder" as time went by. He shocked her one day by saying, "We can make some money if we let a guy I know come over and watch while we have sex."

Donetta put her foot down and said, "No! Absolutely not!"

Equally strange was an incident that occurred while they were driving through Niles Canyon toward Union City, his old stomping grounds where Michael Ihde now lived. As they rode in the car, he turned toward Donetta and said, "I once knew a girl who was killed and her body dumped by the side of the road. It was by a creek."

She didn't know which creek he was talking about or whom he was referring to, and she let the comment pass. But in time she would wonder.

About the only job James Daveggio cared to do was bartending, and he found one just over the hill in the hamlet of Sunol, alongside Niles Creek. It was at a dive that catered to bikers. By this time, just like them, he sported numerous tattoos. They included an eagle, a skull and a lion's head.

A few doors down, at the only other bar in town, was a man named Hans Kuendig. He, too, was about to see something lying beside the road near a creek. It was something he would never forget.

* * *

Don't blink if you're passing through Sunol in Alameda County, only ten miles from Pleasanton, or you'll miss it. With an antique shop, flower boutique, general store, tavern and a population of 900, Sunol hardly seems a part of the Greater Bay Area. The old Victorian homes and ranch houses of this quaint village are tucked into sheltering hills dotted with black oaks and pines.

It wasn't always so quiet and serene, though. In the first years of the twentieth century, Sunol's neighboring town, Niles, was the home of Essanay Studios and America's first movie cowboy hero, Broncho Billy Anderson. In 1910 he brought movies out of the studio and into the real world, filming on location around Niles and Sunol. Broncho Billy strutted along its dirt streets, filming shoot-'em-ups and horse operas. In all, Essanay Studios made 450 pictures in the area with other silent film stars such as Ben Turpin, Wallace Beery, Zasu Pitts and Marie Dressler. But one of its actors in particular was destined for greatness—a thin English chap who had a gift for comedy and mime, Charlie Chaplin. In the hills and canyons around Niles and Sunol, he shuffled into the sunset with his signature cane and into the hearts of millions of people and cinematic history in the movie *The Tramp*.

For a while it seemed that the area would become the movie capital of California. But then Chaplin and the film industry moved south to Hollywood, taking advantage of the better weather and unparalleled sunshine. Niles and Sunol once again slipped back into a quiet lethargy.

Not that the present-day residents minded. It was the very peacefulness and beauty of the area that drew them there in the first place. But on December 2, 1983, local resident Hans Kuendig, an acquaintance of James Daveggio's, spotted something from his car, alongside narrow Kilkare Road just a half mile north of Sunol, that was neither peaceful nor beautiful. It appeared to be the body of a young woman.

Fourteen-year-old Kellie Poppleton of Fremont was a very pretty girl. Standing five feet five inches and weighing 123 pounds, she looked much older than her tender years. People often thought she was eighteen or nineteen years old. She had blue eyes and reddish brown hair, which she wore in a stylish cut. When she smiled, her eyes had a particular sparkle to them that people noticed.

She was a member of the Christian Group called Young Life, and acquaintance Kathy Wilson knew her as "a really nice kid." Other neighbors agreed. "She was just your normal teenager. She was interested in clothes and all that stuff. And boys too. But she didn't seem to have a serious boyfriend."

Some of the classmates at her old junior high, Wells Middle School in Dublin, remembered her as trying to act more worldly than she really was. But they agreed she wasn't a troublemaker. "She liked to make up stuff about herself," one of them said. "Act like she was older than she really was. She was kind of lonely."

For whatever reason she started skipping a lot of school, even though she lived only a few blocks away. She was bright and intelligent, but she didn't quite fit into junior high.

It was ironic, if anyone had taken the time to notice, that her middle school was directly adjacent to where James Daveggio and Michael Ihde had spent their days at Valley High Continuation School.

When her family moved to Fremont, Kellie Poppleton attended teacher Dave Dillon's Junior High Opportunity Class in that city. This class was filled with nineteen other students who weren't bad kids either, but just needed a little help in motivation, the way that Kellie did.

Dillon spoke of her as being a "good kid. Very, very bright." But she had been missing a lot of regular school since her family had moved from Dublin to Fremont. She seemed confused, sad and out of place. She didn't even know the numbers of her new address at The Mission Peak Lodge on Mission Boulevard in Fremont when Dillon asked her. Her real father lived about 150 miles away in the Sierra foothill town of Grass Valley, and the divorce of her parents had hit Kellie hard. Dillon was determined to help her get back on track. "After all, she was just a kid," he said. "She had a lot of potential if she would just remain focused."

He remembered Kellie Poppleton leaving his class about 1:15 P.M. on Friday, December 2, 1983. Already clouds were forming and the winds picking up from a Pacific storm that was moving in. As she left his class, Kellie was wearing a dark blue Adidas jogging jacket with red striped sleeves, blue jeans and brown, white and black slip-on tennis shoes. She walked down the street and met a boy from school at the shopping center on the corner of Fremont Boulevard and Darwin Avenue. The boy talked with her for about fifteen minutes and then Poppleton went to a pay phone nearby. One thing a coworker of her mom's, Kathy Wilson, said, "Kellie would never step willingly into a stranger's car." Others weren't so sure. Since a storm was brewing and she was quite a ways from her home at the shopping center, a nice dry car might have looked appealing at the moment raindrops started to pelt down.

The boy at the shopping center was the last one to see her before motorist Hans Kuendig found her lying motionless alongside Kilkare Road in Sunol at 5:25 P.M. that same evening.

Kuendig got out of his car to investigate and was shocked to find that it was indeed the partially clad body of a young woman with her jeans pulled down and shirt pulled up, exposing her breasts. But the most shocking sight of all was the rose-colored necktie wound tightly around her neck and plastic bag wired around her head. It was later determined the hyoid bone on the right side of her neck had been badly damaged.

He later told a *Tri-Valley Herald* reporter, "I was sure it was a body and my first reaction was to think that someone had been hit by a car. I backed up for a closer look and was shocked to see it was a woman. Her head was in a plastic bag."

Kuendig didn't touch her. Instead, he raced home and called the sheriff's office. Within minutes they relayed a call to Ken Hale, the nearest government authority, at the Department of Forestry Office. Hale hurried up Kilkare Road and against all expectations found the victim still breathing, though unconscious. He loosened the necktie, but the plastic bag was more of a hindrance.

"It took probably a minute to take the wire off her neck," he said. He then proceeded to give her cardiopulmonary resuscitation (CPR) as best he could. But her entire face was a battered mess, as if it had been smashed in by a rock. He could see that she was small, white, with short reddish brown hair. Being a resident of Sunol who knew all the local girls, he realized she wasn't one of them. But beyond that he couldn't tell much. "She didn't really look human," he said. "She was pretty hard to identify."

At least she was still alive, if just barely. With any luck she would pull through and be able to identify her brutal attacker.

About ten miles down the road to the southwest in Fremont, Trese Rusk, working at Fremont Ambulance Company, dispatched an ambulance to pick up the victim and transport her to Washington Hospital in Fremont. Rusk had no way of knowing at the time that the victim at Sunol was her own daughter from a previous marriage.

The ambulance crew picked up the battered young woman and placed her in the vehicle as night fell in the silent canyon. But the silence was soon shattered by a wailing siren and flashing lights reflecting off the darkened walls. They sped down the winding roads toward the large city of Fremont and delivered Kellie Poppleton into the ER at 6:11 P.M. But here all efforts at reviving her proved futile. At 6:18 P.M. she was pronounced dead by Dr. Harry Andrews. Along with her went all hope of easily identifying her attacker.

As Poppleton was moved to a holding area in the hospital, she was now the only one beyond the disturbing fracas that soon broke out. It was caused partially by the entanglement of jurisdictional lines that had been crossed by just removing her from the scene of the crime. Poppleton was a Fremont girl—still a Jane Doe—who had been found in the sheriff's territory, by a state official, and transported to Fremont City. All of this combined to create chaos among the converging authorities as she lay upon the gurney, immune to their mounting frustration that soon erupted into a shoving match.

Coroner's Investigator J.L. Shaw tersely registered it all in his official report: "On the P.M. of 12-2-83, this C.I. [Coroner's Investigator] received a call from Sgt. Neal [Everett], ACSD [Alameda County Sheriff's Department], requesting this office to give authorities to view the remains at Washington Hospital. I was informed the remains had been removed from the scene by the fire department [ambulance], and he wanted to see what they had! This C.I. advised Sgt. Neal [Everett], and the R.N. Supervisor she could allow Sgt. Neal [Everett] to look at the remains only! They were both advised nothing was to be removed, nor was the remains to be disturbed any further than what was done in the emergency room. I was advised some clothing had been removed prior to arrival of the ACSD and Sgt. Neal [Everett] had them."

As if there weren't enough authorities on hand getting in each other's way, a Fremont police officer now arrived at the hospital, sent there by Lieutenant Reed of the Fremont Police Department, and in the words of Coroner's Investigator J.L. Williams, "It was learned that Fremont P.D. had become involved in this case and it was reported that a hassle occurred between the FPD [Fremont Police Department] officer and nursing staff at Washington Hospital."

Lieutenant Reed's report stated, "When the remains were removed to the holding area, the Fremont Police officer became concerned that a bag of clothing was being left behind. The clothing reportedly had been removed by the hospital staff and placed in a sealed bag. The Fremont Police officer took possession of this sealed bag. Reportedly the hospital nursing staff became concerned with Fremont Police taking charge because of the orders from this office were that only Alameda County Sheriff's Department was involved. A physical exchange between the nursing staff and the Fremont Police Officer apparently occurred."

Poppleton's mother Trese had been worried ever since Kellie didn't show up on Friday afternoon at the usual time. Kellie was a dependable girl and it wasn't like her to be so late without calling. Trese, and Kellie's stepfather, Tracy Rusk, conducted a four-hour search on Friday night as the weather worsened. At 11:00 P.M. they filed a missing person's report with the Fremont Police Department. Because Kellie looked so much older than her years and had no identification on her when her body was discovered, the Fremont Police did not connect the Jane Doe in Washington Hospital with the Rusks.

The parents spent most of Saturday retracing the steps of their daughter and talking to acquaintances of hers. It was a horrible day. A vicious storm hit the Bay Area with hurricane-force winds, knocking down trees and snapping power lines. The Rusks staggered through the pelting rain with a deepening sense of fear and foreboding.

Saturday evening Mrs. Rusk watched a report on the television news describing the clothing worn by a victim whose body was in Washington Hospital. She later remembered, "Even though I heard about the clothing, still I denied it to myself."

At 3:30 A.M. on Sunday morning she panicked and called the Alameda Sheriff's Department. They escorted the Rusks to Washington Hospital and there lying on the gurney was the battered remains of her daughter. The Jane Doe found in Sunol finally had a name.

The sight was not a pretty one. The CI listed more than thirty blunt injury wounds to the neck alone. Nine more were found on the face—one so bad, the skull bone showed through. Her sixth rib had been fractured as if someone had kicked it.

George Comte, Alameda County Coroner, pronounced on his report that the death was caused by "asphyxiation due to strangulation associated with multiple blunt injuries." But that hardly said it all. Sergeant Neal Everett related, "We think she may have suffered a lot before dying."

The Rusks were distraught. Trese cried out in anger, "Anybody who would do that to another human being has to be an animal."

Tracy Rusk went even further. "He's a mad animal and should die the same way she did!"

On December 7, a memorial service was held for Kellie Poppleton at Alder Avenue Baptist Church in Fremont. The parishoners really didn't know the girl that well, but they wanted to honor her memory. An elderly lady said, "She seemed like a nice young girl. Kind of quiet. It's terrible what happened to her."

The Rusks arranged for their daughter's body to be shipped to Sacramento for cremation so she could be interred next to her maternal grandmother. The fact that she was cremated instead of buried would have unforeseen ramifications. Law enforcement criminal labs would not have a body on which to use new scientific techniques not even dreamed of in 1983.

If the Rusks thought they were interring the commotion surrounding Kellie's violent death, they were sadly mistaken. There was an incident about to be revealed that would make the fracas at Washington Hospital seem like child's play in comparison.

Chapter 7

The Morass

On December 9, 1983, the Alameda Sheriff's Department conducted a very interesting interview. It concerned a thirteen-year-old girl named Trina Bence, who had known Kellie Poppleton at Fremont's Centerville Junior High School. Bence's story about her whereabouts on the day of Poppleton's disappearance was so inconsistent that the police brought her in again for questioning on December 10. Under intense scrutiny, Bence's story began to unravel. By midafternoon she admitted that she and another thirteen-year-old girl, Cynthia Reppond, had lured Poppleton to a liquor store where a seventeen-year-old boy and a twenty-seven-year-old drug dealer, Julian Ramirez, were waiting. Bence and Reppond were sure that Poppleton had been snitching on their drug operations with Ramirez at Centerville Junior High. They vowed to teach her a lesson.

But according to Trina Bence, the "lesson" soon got out of hand after they hustled Kellie into Ramirez's 1973 Grand Prix. Driving up Niles Canyon Road, Reppond and Bence held Kellie's arms while the seventeen-year-old boy hit her repeatedly in the face and chest with brass knuckles. When Ramirez stopped the car in a rural location, he began working Kellie over with a wooden billy club. Then things really got out of hand. According to Bence, Ramirez and the boy sprawled Poppleton on the ground and pulled her pants down. In a frenzy they sexually mutilated her with a nine-inch butcher knife. The boy took off his red necktie and tightened it around Poppleton's throat while Ramirez stuck a plastic bag over her head and fastened it with a wire. They drove to Kilkare Road in Sunol and dumped Poppleton's barely alive body alongside the pavement into the wet grass.

At 6:00 A.M. on Sunday morning, December 11, Alameda County Sheriff's deputies swooped down on three separate addresses and arrested Cynthia Reppond, Julian Ramirez and the seventeen-year-old boy. The news hit the papers and airwaves like a thunderbolt.

It certainly seemed like the twenty-seven-year-old Ramirez was the right man for the crime. He was a known drug dealer with arrests for heroin possession, assault with a deadly weapon, burglary and possession of stolen property. It seemed logical that he had decided to get even with a "snitch" who threatened his operations by killing her in the most brutal fashion possible, thereby scaring off any other future snitches. For all intents and purposes it seemed like the Kellie Poppleton murder had been solved.

Then things began to fall apart.

Teacher Dave Dillon said, "I can't believe about those drugs. It just doesn't seem possible."

Rob Taylor, an ex-boyfriend of Cynthia Reppond's, echoed Dillon's comments regarding Reppond. He told a reporter for the *Fremont Argus*, "It's a shock. I can't believe it. I know she wouldn't kill anyone."

It was true that a different portrait of Kellie Poppleton was now being painted by students at Wells Middle School in Dublin, where she had attended classes before moving to Fremont. Several said she had been a depressed girl who often cut classes, talked about using marijuana, and sometimes wept for no apparent reason. But all of them doubted she had been part of any drug ring or a snitch.

"Kellie was not a discipline problem," Assistant Principal Ken Kohler at the middle school stated. "Her aptitude tests showed above average intelligence. She was just a nice little girl who didn't have any direction."

At some gut level these people sensed something the Alameda Sheriff's Department did not: Trina Bence was a liar.

It soon became apparent to even the Alameda Sheriff's Department that something was amiss. Bence kept contradicting the statements she had given earlier. Her story always seemed to change in small details. Under further questioning her original story of the murder began to unravel until it was in shreds. In their rush to make an arrest, the Alameda Sheriff's Department had fallen into Bence's deranged fantasies. She had made up details wholesale as she went along, taking what she needed from the news reports she had read and heard on television, and what the police were feeding her. She knew just enough about the case to let them hear what they wanted to hear. It was a case of self-fulfilling expectations.

Sheriff Glen Dyer of Alameda admitted on December 12, "Miss Bence recanted some of her testimony and is vacillating on some statements about the murder."

But it was much worse than just a recantation and vacillation. Her story had more holes in it than a colander.

Tom Orloff, the Alameda assistant district attorney, was furious. It was making his office and the sheriff's department look like a bunch of fools. He told reporters for the *Argus* that the Alameda Sheriff's Department "had acted prematurely in arresting suspects and that the case was drug related." Deputy District Attorney John Burke went even further to state that no physical evidence even linked the suspects to the Poppleton case. Cynthia Reppond and the seventeen-year-old boy were released from juvenile hall on December 13. Julian Ramirez was kept in Santa Rita jail on an unrelated charge.

The fallout from the rush to arrest the killer of Kellie Poppleton was just starting. The seventeen-year-old told a Fremont *Argus* reporter, "I don't like having a label as a murderer. I guess Trina was trying to cover up someone's name or something. I got a bum rap. I'm a known hoodlum in the neighborhood. I even burglarized a police officer's house four years ago. But I didn't kill Kellie. I didn't even hardly know her. I was home with a friend when she was killed."

Julian Ramirez was even more outraged. "I'm not a sex-perverted killer," he told a reporter of the *Argus.* "Whoever beat and strangled Kellie should be sentenced to death. That's a terrible crime. That's as low as a person can get. I might have had drug problems, but I'm not violent."

Ramirez went on to say that he didn't know Kellie Poppleton, Cynthia Reppond, Trina Bence or the seventeen-year-old boy. "She [Trina] must have known about my background and made it all up," he said.

In fact, he didn't know at the time that Trina Bence lived in the same apartment complex that he did. She had watched his drug operations in the neighborhood and fingered him as a likely suspect in the Poppleton murder.

Ramirez went on to tell the reporter that inmates at Santa Rita's maximum security unit, Big Greystone, had made life for him "difficult" after they had seen a report on the television news about him and the murder. It made him very nervous.

It should have done a lot more than that. At 8:25 A.M. on December 15 someone in the day room of Big Greystone stabbed Julian Ramirez in the neck with a sharp object, attempting to sever his jugular vein. He was attended to by Lieutenant Dale Berry, who said, "There's no doubt in my mind, this was done with the intent to kill." Ramirez had to be rushed to Oakland's Highland Hospital for surgery—all because of a crime he didn't even commit.

Phillip Schnuycrson, Ramirez's lawyer, was beside himself. "The Alameda Sheriff's Department released a kind of feeding frenzy, a blood lust [when they made their arrests]. It seems we turned the clock back to the 1940s when people said, "We don't care about who it is, just arrest someone."

All the police had left now was scared, confused, lying Trina Bence.

But not for long. Her hearing was scheduled for March 14, 1984, but on Friday, February 17, Richard Iglehart, Alameda County assistant district attorney, brought the whole sordid matter before Judge Richard Hodge. He told the judge that Trina Bence had concocted the entire story. After reviewing 600 pages of transcripts and other evidence, he pronounced, "I'm convinced she wasn't even there [at the death scene] and never even knew Kellie!"

Robert Shuken, Trina Bence's attorney, was furious. He blasted the Alameda Sheriff's Office, saying they should have known she was fabricating the story. "She [Trina] comes from a troubled, confused background, and fabricated the story to get attention. She garnered information from the police and the press, and then fed it back to them, making them believe she had firsthand knowledge of the slaying details." In effect, Bence was giving the police and press exactly what they wanted to hear. He went on to say that she barely knew Julian Ramirez, who lived across the street from her, and knew the seventeen-year-old boy and Cynthia Reppond only by sight.

Berry Simon, one of Shuken's private detectives who had been put on the case, concurred. "We were surprised with the lack of quality of the [sheriff's] investigation. We refuted every point in their investigation by proving it impossible."

Investigators had already searched Julian Ramirez's home on December 11 for brass knuckles and a billy club and came up empty. They had also impounded Ramirez's 1973 Grand Prix to test bloodstains in the backseat.

But as Assistant District Attorney Iglehart said on February 17, "You would have heard about it by now if the bloodstains linked Ramirez to the slaying."

Phillip Schnayerson, Ramirez's lawyer, chimed in. "The one ground they were holding him on is the complicity in a murder. He was never involved and he damn near was killed over it!"

ADA Iglehart did stick up for the Alameda deputies, saying, "Hindsight is 20-20. It's not every day that police officers are faced with a situation where someone is strongly implicating themselves and other people. The police are in the difficult situation of having to make a charging decision within forty-eight hours after an arrest."

All in all, the Alameda Sheriff's Department came off looking pretty bad. Only Trina Bence's mom, Pam Hansen, was ecstatic. She announced, "This terrible ordeal has brought our family together. It's made us learn a lot about ourselves. We've become closer."

But perhaps not close enough. Trina opted to live in a distant foster home for a while after she was released, to put some distance between herself and those she had implicated. The obvious reason was feared retribution.

Pam Hansen said, "Trina experienced some problems with other kids in juvenile hall, her first two days there. But on Friday, after her release, all the children clapped for her as she left."

But there were no happy endings to this whole miserable affair. Everyone in the case had been damaged as it sank further and further into a morass. Cynthia Reppond had been tarred by the false accusations and scorned by classmates. Trina Bence continued to have her own problems, finding it hard to get back to a normal life. Three years after the incident, Julian Ramirez was right back in Santa Rita Prison once again. He may not have been the one responsible for Kellie Poppleton's abduction, rape and murder, but Trina Bence must have known something about his character to have made him such a viable suspect. On the night of September 12, 1987, he lured a fourteen-year-old girl to his doorstep. She had been walking to a high school dance at American High School and was thirsty. Ramirez promised her a glass of water. When she reached out for the glass, he grabbed her arm and pulled her into his apartment. He tried to rape her, but she struggled free and called the police. Ramirez ran, but he didn't get far. The police caught and arrested him on a corner not far from where Kellie Poppleton had disappeared three years before. Julian Ramirez found himself heading right back to Santa Rita Prison, where he had been stabbed in the neck almost four years earlier.

Worst of all was the fact that Trina Bence's lies had kept the authorities from looking for the real killer for nearly three critical months while the clues were still fresh. When they went back to pick up the pieces, many of the key witnesses' memories had already begun to fade and evidence that might have remained in the area was either washed away by the winter rains or degraded by time.

For the parents of Kellie Poppleton, life became a living hell. Tormented by the memory of their slain daughter, they moved out of the area. Even with their absence, the case, like a festering wound, refused to heal.

By 1997 Kellie Poppleton's murder remained unsolved. By then the Alameda Sheriff's Department had gone through several "changeovers" at the top. All of those who had been implicated in the "screwups" surrounding the Poppleton case were now gone. The department looked at the case with a fresh viewpoint by officers not tainted by the original debacle.

With a clean slate and some new information not available in 1984, they drew up a fresh list of prime suspects in her violent murder. It was a very small list. On top of that list were two names: James Daveggio and Michael Ihde. Daveggio had been a bartender in Sunol at the time. He even knew Hans Kuendig, the man who had found Poppleton's body lying by the side of the road. Ihde lived fairly close to where Poppleton had been abducted. Just like Gloria Hazelwood of Jackson, California, Poppleton had been beaten in the face by some blunt object. Her hyoid bone had also been bruised on the right side. And just like in the case with Hazelton, a red rag or red tie had been attached to her body. A red rag had been used to tie Hazelwood's hands together while she was being raped. Poppleton had had her life choke out by one.

Chapter 8

The Overpass

A curious thing happened in Pleasanton before the furor over the Poppleton case had even died down. It occurred on April 5, 1984, only a quarter mile from James Daveggio's home on Clovewood Avenue. Fourteen-year-old Tina Faelz was walking home from Foothill High School, the same high school that Daveggio had attended, on a route used by students as a shortcut. It paralleled Clovewood Avenue below West Las Positas Road and crossed under freeway I-680 via a large culvert toward Faelz's home on Virgin Island Court. Students had been warned not to use the culvert and it had even been boarded up several times. But it was so much closer for students who lived on the eastern side of the freeway to crawl through it rather than walk a half mile north or south to use an overpass. Each time it was boarded up, students pulled down the barriers and kept on using it. James Daveggio may have even used the culvert himself as a teenager. Certainly, he would have known about it.

Tina Faelz began to use the culvert shortcut because she had stopped riding the school bus when other students began to pick on her. Faelz acted young for her age and one other girl on the bus in particular had tormented her constantly. Rather than face the abuse, she began to walk home alone.

Her best friend, Mary Lou Eisma, said, "She was more on the child side. She had a hard time fitting in [at high school]."

Tina Faelz stayed a bit late at Foothill High on the afternoon of April 5, 1984, before starting her walk home. Several students saw her leaving the school yard about 2:25 P.M., heading toward the freeway culvert. It was a typical spring day with sun and clouds and a few showers. Tina passed down the row of houses and out of sight toward the culvert.

At 3:27 P.M. truck driver Larry Lovall of San Jose happened to glance down from his big rig at the drainage ditch alongside I-680 as he drove along and spotted a strange object. Even from his height and the speed he was traveling, the object looked eerily like the body of a young woman. He was so shaken by the sight that he turned off at the next exit and doubled back, parking alongside the freeway. He got out of his truck and scrambled halfway down the embankment, where he did indeed see a girl's body lying in the ditch. She wasn't moving and she appeared to be bleeding from multiple wounds.

Lovall didn't touch her. Instead, he hurried back to his truck and drove to the Alameda County Fairgrounds on Bernal Avenue and called the Pleasanton Police.

Sixteen-year-old Eric Voellm of Foothill High and his friend Jay Dallimore reached the culvert just one minute after Lovall left for the fairgrounds. They, too, spotted a girl's body in the drainage ditch, her backpack and schoolbooks scattered all around.

Voellm was more brave than prudent. He crawled up to the body and later told the *Valley Times,* "I felt to see if she was breathing. But she wasn't. There was blood everywhere. Her body was still warm."

The two teenagers hightailed it out of there, not knowing if the killer was still around. They ran down the streets and phoned the police from a home on nearby Lemonwood Drive.

Within minutes of the two phone calls, Pleasanton's new police chief, Bill Eastman, had officers on the scene cordoning off the area. It was easy enough to identify the victim, Tina Faelz, because her name was scrawled in all her books and on her backpack. It was also easy to tell the way she had died. There were multiple stab wounds on her head, back and side.

Eastman soon told reporters, "Whoever attacked the girl wanted to make sure she was dead." He continued, "We believe she was probably surprised on her way home. There is no doubt in my mind that she was killed in that exact same spot where she was found."

Police Chief Eastman pulled out all the stops to apprehend the killer. There hadn't been a murder in Pleasanton in recent history, making the town fully live up to its pacific name. Eastman had been a cop ever since the Watts riots had erupted near his neighborhood back in the 1960s, and he decided to get involved. He'd earned a law degree at Pepperdine University and at the University of Southern California as well. He had been a patrolman for fifteen years in Culver City, California, rising to the rank of captain before taking over the police chief position in Pleasanton in 1981.

Eastman was honest and plainspoken with a large dose of common sense, and his officers admired him for it. Even Craig Eicher, president of the local Police Officers Association, not generally known for agreeing with police chiefs, said of Eastman, "He's done a good job." City Manager Deborah Acosta agreed by stating, "Bill came to Pleasanton to make the police force more professional and he's done that. He created a reputation that Pleasanton is tough on crime."

Eastman had half his entire force, twenty-four officers, working overtime on the Faelz case. They interviewed hundreds of students, friends and family of the dead girl and went over the entire area of her route from school with a metal detector searching for the murder weapon. One of the investigators on the case was Officer Gary Tollefson, the same officer who remembered James Daveggio so well as a troublemaker on Pleasanton's Main Street. He and another policeman took minute blood samples from the dirt and grass around the area where Faelz had been killed. They never found the murder weapon. They also did not link the murder at the time to James, a strange young man who lived nearby on Clovewood Drive.

Eastman, in frustration, told reporters on April 7, "I have some leads I hope will pan out. But at this time no leads should be labeled as substantial." In fact, the leads soon drifted off into nothing as the police force tracked down a hitchhiker who had been in the area on April 5 and a student wearing a blue backpack who had been seen there that afternoon as well. Both suspects were located, questioned and released, leaving the leads to all dry up. All that was left was a hunch in Police Chief Eastman's mind that the killer was not some random person merely passing through. Deep down he felt that the murderer lived in the area and had possibly used the culvert himself at one time.

As April progressed, the case began to disappear from the front pages of the local newspapers and then from even the inside pages as May approached. All that was left was an echo of the words that Foothill High senior Lisa Foster told a reporter, "This is Pleasanton. Things like that don't happen here!"

But things like that did happen around Pleasanton and in the summer of 1984, James Daveggio, who had lived for so long in the shadows of this community, was going to be suddenly caught in the bright spotlight of a policeman's patrol car.

The summer itself was hot, one of the hottest on record, with every week having some day up in the hundreds. Daveggio certainly felt the heat in more ways than one; married or not, he couldn't control the urges that plagued him. Unlike his old buddy Michael Ihde, he hadn't been apprehended for anything yet. But all that was about to change. He drove to a Black Angus restaurant on the edge of town one hot midsummer night, July 8, 1984, and soon was at the bar drinking with a young woman. Just like so many things in his life, there are two versions of what happened next.

According to one report, she found him fairly attractive, as many women did, but she also turned down his proposals to "get it on." One drink led to another, and as the clock passed midnight, the woman finally got up to leave. She didn't notice Daveggio was right behind her, walking quietly through the almost deserted parking lot.

He was half drunk and so was she, but he wasn't so drunk that he didn't know what he wanted. As soon as she reached her car, Daveggio was right beside her; a pistol slipped quietly from his pocket into his hand. As the terrified woman caught a glimpse of the pistol, she begged for mercy. What she got instead was an order from Daveggio as he unzipped his pants: "Suck it!"

Too frightened to even scream, and very aware of the pistol, she complied.

But if James Daveggio thought he was getting away scot-free on this one, he was wrong. A witness on the far side of the parking lot had seen the whole thing and called the police. Before Daveggio barely had his pants back up, a patrol car pulled into the lot and shone its lights on the pair. The woman went running toward the cops and told them what had just transpired.

The official police record differs from this version, citing that the woman was having a fight with her boyfriend at the Black Angus and Daveggio intervened. He escorted her out of the bar and they drove away in his car. About an hour later they returned to the Black Angus parking lot and the woman was in hysterics. She claimed to have been kidnapped and forced to copulate him orally. The Pleasanton Police took James Daveggio into custody and charged him with kidnapping and forced oral copulation.

But even then Daveggio's strange sort of luck still held out. The woman had been very drunk at the time and her story was garbled. On key elements of the incident she was completely blank and on others she had only a vague recollection. Even the assistant district attorney who was to try the case admitted, "She had a bad memory lapse. She started going sideways on us." He frankly told the court that he didn't believe the case could be tried to the satisfaction of the state.

The charges against James Daveggio were eventually dropped for lack of evidence and the unreliability of the woman's testimony. The incident gave him a temporary scare, but not enough to make him quit for good. The urges were just too powerful. Little did he know at the time that his old buddy Michael Ihde was also about to give rape another try right across the hill. Ihde was living in Daveggio's old backyard in the Bay Area, just up the road from Logan High School, where Daveggio had first begun to toy with the idea of sexual dominance.

At this point Michael Ihde had developed a strong love affair with the bottle. He still had his girlfriend, Rachel Piazza, with him, and they spent most of their time either crashing at friends' houses or living in his car. They hung out around Ashland Avenue in San Lorenzo for lack of any better place to go. By the fall of 1984 Piazza was pregnant and about to have Ihde's baby. On her birthday, November 27, she had to be rushed to Highland Hospital in Oakland by her mother for a possible premature delivery. Ihde was more interested in booze than in babies. Often seen at local liquor stores, he would find some out-of-the-way place to drink his liquor and watch the world go by. But on his girlfriend's birthday the world unexpectedly came to him. It appeared in the shape of Lisa Ann Monzo, an eighteen-year-old high school girl. She couldn't have fit into his fantasies any more alluringly than if he had dreamed her. She was pretty, with light brown hair, and as he would remember later, she had nice breasts. She was young and shapely, and best of all, alone.

On November 27, 1984, Monzo had been dropped off at her doctor's office in midafternoon in San Lorenzo to be treated for a sinus infection. She completed her appointment by 3:30 P.M., but her ride was already gone. Home was not very far away, so she decided to walk.

More than likely she was thinking of her upcoming role in the school play *The Lion in Winter.* Monzo had never acted before, but she garnered the lead role by applying herself with the same diligence and tenacity she had put into her job in school government and on the school newspaper. Her mom and stepfather had abandoned her when she was fourteen years old and she had grown up in various foster homes around the Bay Area. Instead of depleting her self-esteem, the experience seemed to make her stronger. She thrived on everything she came into contact with. By the time she reached the age of sixteen, she elected to stay in the home of a friend so that she could continue her education at San Lorenzo High School. Barbara Wong, the play's director and drama coach, had picked Monzo over the other candidates for the role because "of her strong vocal quality and strength in her face."

Brian Larsen, her leading man in the play, remembered, "She was friendly and outgoing and this was her first involvement in theater. She said she was just interested in seeing what the experience was like."

Lisa Ann Monzo was an independent girl, in good physical shape from jogging and working out. Her best friend, Laura Wells, said of her, "She had a lot of will. No one got in her way. She was nobody's fool." School principal Joanne Knowles knew Lisa Ann as a "bright young lady . . . a student body judge who was innovative in school leadership. A strong-willed young lady who was making such a defined mark on our student government."

Of all the students and teachers who knew Monzo at San Lorenzo High School, perhaps none knew her better than Mary Milton, the librarian. Because Monzo took only five classes per day, instead of six, she spent one hour each school day in the library. Ms. Milton remembered, "Lisa had an unquenchable thirst for knowledge. She was very eclectic. If she found something interesting, she would pursue it until she was satisfied that she had learned everything about it. For one so young she had a profound self-knowledge of who she was and what she wanted. Because she in essence raised herself since an early age, she set very high goals for herself.

"She had such an open mind for one so young. She once asked me if I thought palmistry was for real. I laughed because I knew she was aware of the palm-reading establishment near Hesperian Boulevard a few blocks away and was curious to its legitimacy.

" 'Why don't you go there and find out for yourself?' I asked. 'Then you can decide.'

" 'I will,' she answered, and promptly followed up on her promise. She was like that. Not willing to judge others until she looked into the matter herself. She had such confidence for someone who had endured a not-so-wonderful childhood.

"Lisa talked to me often about going into the military after high school for various reasons. One was that she needed the college grants they offered if she was to get a higher education after graduating. She had no parents who were saving for a college education. Another reason was that she thought the discipline would do her good, since she never knew any parental authority. But it was evident that Lisa was already very self-disciplined. She never used the excuse that she didn't have parents to mask any failures she might experience along the way. She was willing to accept responsibility for her own life and actions. The impression you got of Lisa was that she was very beautiful and very independent."

Lisa Ann Monzo also knew how to have fun in high school, perhaps making up for lost time when she was younger. One memorable school photo shows her on the pep squad leading cheers. Leaping in bare feet, a headband around her forehead, and wearing a tiger-print outfit, she was captured between heaven and earth by the photographer. She cups her hands to her mouth and shouts in exultant joy. She seems to almost float, suspended in space and time.

But there was another side to Lisa Ann besides the "strong-willed" go-getter and carefree cheerleader. She had a compassionate heart as well. In her column in the school newspaper, "Just for the Record," she wrote on November 19, 1984, about calming a sobbing youngster at nearby Lake Chabot park: "He didn't know me and I didn't know him. What could it hurt to be a friend for an hour or so?"

In fact, this strong-willed, resilient girl of eighteen had become friends to many people in the community. She had a new family who loved her, and her future looked bright as November reached its waning days of 1984.

As Lisa Ann Monzo walked home from the doctor's office on that windy November afternoon, her route took her through a small commercial area where local teenagers remembered her passing. She took a shortcut toward an overpass of Highway 238 that crossed the Southern Pacific railroad tracks. The area was deserted near the highway overpass except for one lone man, who appeared to be drinking from a bottle. Monzo hurried her steps to pass him by. The lone man was Michael Ihde.

Already half drunk from a day of imbibing, Ihde saw the girl coming in his direction. As she got closer, he could tell she was very pretty. No one else was around, and the urges were back hard and strong. Even the rough times he had endured behind bars were not enough to dissuade him from what he already knew he would do. He couldn't pass up an opportunity like this. God only knew when he would get another chance like it.

As the girl walked by, trying to ignore him, he suddenly pounced on her, grabbing her by the waist and punching her in the face. She let out a series of screams and struggled wildly, but she had been taken by surprise and was no match to his repeated blows to the head. Ihde dragged her toward the slanted concrete abutment of the overpass and slammed her against its cold surface. The girl kept screaming, so he pulled her jacket and shirt up over her head to muffle the noise. Then he pushed her to the ground and beat her nearly senseless. In a frenzy, he pulled her bra cups up over her breasts, then pulled her jeans and panties down around her ankles. In another moment he was inside her.

Whatever mercy Lisa Ann Monzo might have hoped for after he was done with her was futile. Ihde had learned his lesson well after leaving Gloria Hazelwood alive. As soon as he was through raping Monzo, his hands sprang to her neck and began choking the life out of the teenage girl. He did it with such violence that he fractured the hyoid bone of her throat on the right side, just as had happened to Kellie Poppleton a few months before.

Monzo struggled only momentarily and then lay dead.

Ihde left her that way, jacket and shirt pulled over her head, and jeans and panties pulled down around her ankles. His only pretense at burial was to cover her with some dirt and pine needles. Then he walked away, unseen.

Across town at the Alameda Sheriff's Department on 150th Avenue, it had been a routine day with the usual number of calls and incidents. Inspector William Smith, a twenty-year veteran of the force, was working homicide, but on this particular week he caught what was called "Night Detective Duty." He remembered, "On the night of November 28, 1984, I was in the watch commander's office reading reports that had been turned in that day, and one of the reports that I found was a report of a missing person, Lisa Monzo. In reading the report and making some phone calls and doin' a little follow-up, things didn't seem right to me as far as she didn't seem to be the kinda person that wouldn't come home after going to a doctor's office as reported in the missing persons [report].

"So I left a note for Detective Sergeant Tanna, because I had to go home 'cause I was working nights and he was working day shift, that this needed a little bit more attention during the daytime hours because the people need to be contacted . . . school, the doctor's office, and so on.

"When I returned back to work in the afternoon of the twenty-ninth for my night detective shift, I was told that they were having a meeting regarding Lisa Monzo's last movements, where she was last seen, and I was given at that time the assignment to organize the search on the railroad track area.

"[As I was on my way] I was notified by radio that they had found a purse by that overcrossing of Highway 238, and Detective Sergeant Little and myself arrived. We were walkin' into the crime scene and found her body. . . . My role then [became] to secure the crime scene, to allow personnel in that needed to come in, and observe what they did."

Securing a crime scene was like a well-scripted military operation with guidelines set forth by the California Commission on Peace Officer Standards Manual. The first thing Inspector William Smith, the team leader, had to do was to assume control over the area and designate assignments for team members as they came in. This was broken down further into some key components:

1. Secure and protect the scene.
2. Initiate a preliminary survey and determine scene boundaries.
3. Evaluate physical evidence possibilities.
4. Prepare a narrative description.
5. Depict the scene photographically.
6. Prepare a diagram/sketch of the scene.
7. Conduct a detailed search.
8. Record and collect physical evidence.

As Inspector Smith approached the crime scene, he determined to what extent it had already been protected and then made arrangements to keep out unauthorized personnel. He next made a cautious walk-through, watching where he stepped, while taking notes. He had to concentrate on the most transient evidence first, then focus on the easily accessible areas in open view and work toward the possible out-of-view locations while keeping an eye out for purposefully hidden items. He had to make a judgment call on whether evidence was moved inadvertently or whether some of the evidence looked "contrived."

The guidelines read: "Do not permit narrative effort to degenerate into a sporadic and unorganized attempt to recover physical evidence—it is recommended that evidence not be collected at this point."

Forensic scientist George Schiro even went further, recommending, "As the walk-through progresses, the investigator should make sure the hands are occupied by either carrying notebooks, flashlights, pens, etc., to prevent depositing unwanted fingerprints at the scene. As a final note on the walk-through, the investigators should examine whatever is over their heads (tree branches etc.). These areas may yield such valuable evidence as blood spatters."

As Inspector Smith made his walk-through, two official photographers came into the area and began snapping photos of the vicinity and Monzo's body. One was Deputy Lancher, who was on duty as a tech man, and the other was Ernie Erler, who was the crime lab photographer. None of this was new to them. They went through their own checklist by photographing with various lenses the overall, medium and close-up views of the scene. They set out recognizable scale devices to determine how large things were, and photographed from eye level to represent the scene as it would be observed by a normal view. Lastly, they took into account the admonishment from the Crime Scene Response Guidelines: "Film is relatively cheap compared to the rewards obtained—do not hesitate to photograph something which has no apparent significance at the time—it may later prove to be a key element in the investigation."

Lancher and Erler had seen plenty of bodies in all states of rigidity and decomposition over the years. But there was something particularly disturbing about this crime scene. The victim had obviously been so young and pretty until her life had been horribly snuffed out in this lonely spot beneath the bleak concrete supports of an overpass.

As the photographers snapped their shots of the scene, one more key player arrived on the scene. Sharon Binkley, a criminalist with the Alameda County Crime Lab, was an expert in criminalist serology and latent fingerprinting, as well as an evidence technician. In some ways her methods were the most exacting of all the law enforcement personnel present. She collected various evidence, constantly writing down what she found and checking her packaging notations for accuracy. She well knew that a cautious painstaking approach would avoid evidence loss and contamination. Each item was carefully placed into specially marked paper bags and plastic containers with the realization that no two items could be stored together and risk cross-contamination. She also checked Lisa Ann Monzo's clothes and body for tiny clothing fibers that might have come from the attacker.

All of this was a slow and laborious process amid the glare of spotlights. Binkley thoroughly went over the murder scene with a fine-tooth comb until nearly two o'clock in the morning, looking for minute clues and all the information she could assemble. She gathered an incredible number of miscellaneous items that ran the gamut from "probables connected to the crime" to "barely tangibles." But the most important thing she did that night was one small procedure that would have huge implications down the line. She took a couple of vaginal swabs from the body of Lisa Ann Monzo and kept them safely in storage.

The news that Lisa Ann Monzo had been murdered hit the teachers and students of San Lorenzo High School very hard. She had been a popular girl and had many friends there. There was a dance scheduled for the night after her body was found and news of the discovery caused a debate whether to let the dance go ahead as scheduled or cancel it. Finally, it was decided to let the dance go forward as an impromptu memorial to Lisa Ann.

The school librarian Mary Milton remembered the dance as a surreal event. "Even though the music was playing, most students just huddled in groups, talking about Lisa. Many were crying. Brian Larsen, her leading man in the play, was devastated. Another boy named Kenneth kept banging his head against one of the bleachers and moaning. Not one person there hadn't been affected by Lisa's life and death."

Across town Michael Ihde was not affected adversely or devastated. He was certain he had gotten away with it. So certain, in fact, that he soon committed an action so outrageous that it defies the logic of any reasonable person. He discovered through one of his cousins where Lisa Ann Monzo had been living. In an act of incredible audacity, Ihde went to her former home and passed himself off as a grieving friend. He cried and sobbed and wondered aloud who could have done such a terrible thing.

Whatever soul Ihde might have once possessed, he left behind in prison. He was as stone-cold a killer as ever walked the streets.

Meanwhile, just over the hill in Pleasanton, James Daveggio was on the way to losing his soul as well. Things were becoming increasingly rough for his second wife, Donetta, who didn't find James to be the same wonderful individual that his mom, Darlene, found him to be. If he wasn't chewing her out about something, he was down at the Pastime gambling their money away. Things reached a crisis point on July 25, 1985, when Donetta informed her husband that she was pregnant. She realized that he did not take the news well; but what he did next, not even she could have imagined.

Chapter 9

Country Roads

On July 25, 1985, thirty-five-year-old Janet Stokes of Tracy, California, was pulling a double shift at Tracy Beauty Supply and Gifts. She started work at 5:00 A.M. in the morning on what promised to be a hot summer day in this Central Valley town. As if her day wasn't already long enough, she drove over to her employer's house at 5:00 P.M. and began some housework for his wife, Anna Bucklin.

At least here Stokes was able to take a short break, drinking a couple of beers just to cool off and relax before returning to ironing the Bucklins' laundry. Mr. Bucklin unexpectedly returned to the house around 6:00 P.M. and sighed that he was going back to the store to do some more work. Surprisingly, Stokes announced she would accompany him and help out. It would be an incredibly long day, but she would appreciate the extra money on payday.

From about 6:00 P.M. until 11:00 P.M. Janet Stokes helped with clerical work, UPS shipping and unloading packages until even Mr. Bucklin grew tired of the drudgery and called it a day.

He drove her back to his house and said good

night. As she got into her car, she had a decision to make—drive home for some well-deserved rest or out to nearby Joey's Bar for some fun and relaxation.

Joey's Bar won out. Located on Grant Line Road and MacArthur Avenue in Tracy, it wasn't much to look at and the interior was still warm after a hot day, but at least the beers were cold. Stokes sauntered up to the bar and asked for a beer and some quarters for the cigarette machine. The bartender shrugged and said he didn't have any change. But a patron did. In her own words, "I met a nice man . . . and this nice gentleman offered me the quarters."

The nice gentleman in question was James Daveggio.

He was seated at the bar with a friend, John Huffstetler, who for the most part was very quiet and aloof. But not Daveggio. He was talkative and friendly. He soon had Stokes engaged in a cordial conversation and she found him quite charming. True, his voice was kind of rough, but he had a fairly handsome face, blue eyes and long blond hair. He also seemed to be quite taken with her, which after a long hard day of hot work was gratifying.

One beer led to another. After about thirty minutes Stokes asked Daveggio if he wanted to follow her to Bill's Club across town. It at least had airconditioning, something she truly desired at this point.

Daveggio said he'd be glad to.

Her offer was more or less for Daveggio alone, but as she looked back, Huffstetler was tagging along as well. Stokes walked out to the parking lot, saw both of them climb into a car, and as she drove the five miles to Bill's Club, she kept glancing in her rearview mirror. Daveggio's car was right behind her the whole way.

Tending the establishment that night at Bill's was David Bradshaw. He looked up to see three new customers sitting at his long bar, asking for drinks. He recognized Janet Stokes slightly, having seen her in the tavern a couple of times before, but the two men were complete strangers. He served up the mixed drinks they ordered, and before long the blond-haired young man had him engaged in a conversation about bartending. It turned out that the stranger also tended bar once in a while at Sunol, about forty miles away.

Everything seemed to be going smoothly. Huffstetler had loosened up enough to engage Stokes in a game of pool while Daveggio spun stories about bartending. Bradshaw remembered everyone having a good time: "It looked like they were having an evening on the town. A nice evening."

But lack of sleep, hard work and alcohol began to have an effect on Stokes. She'd already drunk two beers at the Bucklin residence, two beers at Joey's Bar, and now three Separators (brandy, kahlua and cream) at Bill's. Feeling a bit tipsy and light-headed, she began to worry about the lateness of the hour, and she harbored a knowledge of her limit for alcohol. She'd never passed out from drinking before, but sometimes if she drank too much, she did get sick and would vomit. This was not an appetizing prospect. It was time to call it a night.

She thanked the "nice gentleman" for a good time and started to exit the back door. She knew she was in no shape to drive, but at least she could make sure her car was locked before she walked the few blocks to her home. In her tired haze she almost didn't notice that Daveggio and Huffstetler were right alongside her as she departed.

Checking her parked car as planned, Stokes suddenly found Daveggio looming right in her face, insisting that he give her a ride home. She resisted at least twice, but the tiredness and alcohol were beginning to take their toll. And Daveggio was very insistent. In almost a complete daze now, Stokes somehow found herself sitting in their car, squeezed in between Daveggio and Huffstetler. Daveggio started the engine and quietly began to roll down the street.

Nothing was said as the car passed one street corner, then another, until it was motoring out of town past the city lights and into the dark country.

Janet Stokes began to get scared.

"Let me out. I want to go home," she implored, but the only response she received from Daveggio was, "Shut up!"

Her initial uneasiness now turned to sheer panic.

"Please, if you let me out right now, I won't say a thing," she pleaded.

Huffstetler told her to shut up and Daveggio kept right on driving down Tracy Boulevard into the darkened orchards and farmland.

Stokes was thoroughly scared and crying, but it brought no sympathy from the two men. They continually told her, "Shut up and you won't get hurt."

As if to emphasize the point, Huffstetler suddenly brandished a large handgun. With its appearance Janet Stokes knew that her "fun evening" had taken a terribly wrong turn. Tears streamed down her cheeks and she wondered how all this would end.

She didn't have long to find out. Daveggio pulled the car off the road into the orchards and parked by the side of the road in a deserted area. Only the reflection of the moon shone into the car's interior, highlighting the chrome pistol in Huffstetler's hand.

Daveggio stared over at Stokes without a trace of pity, even as she continued to cry. Then without any preamble he ordered, "Suck my dick."

Stokes rocked backward and summoned up her last reserves of dignity. She remembered later, "I was cocky and said no. But then I started to cry because he started to slap me and pull my hair."

She continued to beg, "No, no," but he simply replied, "Oh, yes, you are."

Everything was becoming a horrible blur for Stokes now. Huffstetler was lifting her blouse and removing her bra. In another moment she felt his cold hand on her breast. Daveggio unzipped his pants and pulled his penis out. She tried to move away, but he grabbed her hand and placed it on his genitals. She couldn't stop crying and he repeatedly beat her about the head, grabbing her hair and pulling her face down toward his crotch. Huffstetler was laughing at her all the time and constantly repeating, "Shut up and you won't get hurt."

She tried pulling her head back, but Daveggio's grip was too strong. Afraid now for her life, she finally decided to give in and did what he wanted.

When asked later in court by a prosecutor, "When you were sucking his penis, was it soft or hard?"

All these years later, one can still hear the outraged anguish in her reply, "Oh, God! I don't know. I can't remember!"

Afterward Stokes was sick. Huffstetler, for some reason, had departed the car and she begged him to let her out so she could urinate. He thought about it for a moment and then said OK. As she started to move toward the back of the car, his pistol suddenly erupted right behind her ear. Stokes dived to the ground, shivering like a wet puppy, while Daveggio ripped out from the driver's side and began yelling at Huffstetler for his stupid bravado. Daveggio was so mad he looked as if he could kill Huffstetler. Stokes prayed the next bullet wouldn't be in her head or in her back.

The argument seemed to go on forever—both Daveggio and Huffstetler wildly gesticulated. Finally, Daveggio won out and ordered Stokes and Huffstetler back into the car.

Daveggio was still angry and swore at Huffstetler as he started the engine, pulling back onto the roadway. He had hardly driven a mile toward Tracy when red lights flashed in the rear window. John Huffstetler had picked the worst possible moment to fire his pistol into the night. A San Joaquin patrol car had been cruising by at just that moment and heard the gunshot. Unlike the incident at the Black Angus restaurant in Pleasanton, Daveggio was not going to be able to get out of this accusation.

Chapter 10

Doing Time

James Daveggio and John Huffstetler were detained by a Tracy policeman while Janet Stokes was taken in for questioning and medical attention. In the course of a three-hour interview with the police, she revealed all the sordid details of what had happened earlier the previous evening. Soon thereafter, Detective Sergeant Chuck Crawford swore out a complaint against Daveggio and Huffstetler.

Count 1 alleged that Huffstetler violated Section 207 (a) of the California Penal Code: kidnapping, a felony, by "willfully, unlawfully, and forcibly stealing, taking, and arresting" Janet Stokes.

Count 2 dealt with Huffstetler in the count of oral copulation while acting in concert and abetting another individual. Count 3 was against Daveggio: 288(d) of the Penal Code, oral copulation, acting in concert with force. Counts 4 and 5 dealt with both defendants and the use of a firearm, in this case a Smith & Wesson .38-caliber Model #15.

James Daveggio was in deep trouble this time.

A preliminary examination was held on August 26, 1985, in Tracy, California, before the Honorable James E. Cadel. William Harrell, deputy district attorney, appeared as council for the state; David Harris, attorney-at-law, appeared as council for Daveggio; Janine Sheaffer represented Huffstetler.

In a somewhat plodding but thorough manner, ADA Harrell laid out a litany of damning facts before Judge Cadel. His main witness was Janet Stokes and he took her back through the ordeal of that terrible night. She was naturally embarrassed in recounting her plight, but Harrell was taking no chances with ambiguities. After all, Daveggio had already skated on the forced oral copulation charges in Pleasanton only the year before.

He asked Janet, "While your head was being pulled down, what were you doing at this point?"

A. "Pushing back, trying not to let my head go down."
Q. "Were you successful in resisting the push?"
A. "No."
Q. "Okay. So after it was pushed down, what happened next?"
A. "I just went ahead and did it. I couldn't fight it off no more."
Q. "Now when you say you did it, what did you do?"
A. "I did what he told me to do."
Q. "And what was that?"
A. "Suck his thing."
Q. "And when you say 'thing,' what are you referring to?"
A. "His penis."

In response to ADA Harrell's thorough questioning of Ms. Stokes, Daveggio's attorney, Harris, attempted to show that all throughout the evening at

Joey's Bar and then Bill's Club, there had been no trouble among the threesome.

He asked Stokes, "Everything was nice and easy and happy between you and the two defendants at that point, is that right?"

"Just the one defendant [Daveggio]," she answered. "The other guy was very quiet and unfriendly."

Harris went on to point out that Daveggio had not "forced" her into the car at the parking lot behind Bill's Club. He also related that even by her own admission she was "foggy" about this period of time. Further defending his client, he noted that Daveggio had not removed one article of her clothing while parked out in the orchard, nor had he ever held the pistol in his hand.

Huffstetler's attorney, Sheaffer, zeroed in on Janet Stokes's long day of work and drinking, which led to questioning about her memory. She was quizzed on many different points, especially the period in the parking lot. Quite a few times her response was the same: "I don't remember." In fact, Sheaffer kept pounding away at all the things that Janet didn't remember.

Q. "You indicated that his [Daveggio's] pants were down enough so that you could orally copulate him, correct?"
A. "That's right; well, it had to be, right?"
Q. "Do you remember whether he had no clothes from the hip to the knee?"
A. "No."
Q. "You don't know which hands he used to unfasten his pants?"
A. "No."
Q. "And you're not really sure whether his penis was erect or not, are you?"

A. "Not then, I don't, but once something is stuck in your mouth like that, you would remember."

Q. "So it was erect. I'm not asking you whether you remember it was stuck in your mouth or not, I'm asking whether it was hard or not."

A. "Once it was in my mouth, yes, but before that I don't remember."

Q. "You are sure it was erect once it was in your mouth, but before that you don't remember?"

A. "I'm not sure."

Q. "You are not sure whether he ejaculated or not?"

A. "That's right."

Q. "Your eyes were closed, so you don't know whether there were any distinctive marks around his penis?"

A. "That's right."

Q. "Now, you say he grabbed your hands and put them down in his crotch, down by his penis. He grabbed both your hands and did that?"

A. "Just one of my hands."

Q. "Just one of your hands?"

A. "I'm not real clear about that either."

Q. "So that's sort of a fuzzy recollection?"

A. "The whole thing is."

Only one other witness was called to the stand, David Bradshaw, the bartender who had served the threesome liquor that night at Bill's Club. He explained that everyone seemed to be having a good time while in his presence. There had been no trouble, and, in fact, Daveggio had been quite pleasant relating stories about the bartending business. But in the end, despite a good effort by both defense attorneys, there was no getting around the fact that there was a mountain of evidence against both Daveggio and Huffstetler.

Daveggio contacted his new attorney, Timothy Rien of Pleasanton, and on September 17, 1985, he stood before county judge Stephan Demetras with a new plea—guilty to Counts 1 and 2, not guilty on Counts 4 and 5 (the use of a firearm). Along with this went an understanding that he would be referred to Vacaville Medical Facility where they would assess his mental stability and capacity for rehabilitation. Vacaville's report would determine if he was to serve anywhere from five years in state prison down to three years or less in county jail.

Even the judge cautioned about Vacaville's decision: "It is often a term of art. Sometimes they disagree, but whatever the bottom line recommendation by the staff, even though it may be a split decision, that will be the factor that allows either a three- or five-year term."

Judge Demetras then asked Daveggio if he understood that he was forfeiting a chance for a jury trial where he could present evidence, call witnesses, and even take the stand in his own defense.

"Yes," Daveggio answered.

The judge went on, "Mr. Daveggio, if you plead guilty, since prison sentence is anticipated here, they can place you on parole once you leave prison. That could be up to four years. If you violate any parole terms, you can be returned to custody up to a year on each one of these. Do you understand that?"

Daveggio once again answered, "Yes."

Judge Demetras continued, "This kind of situation requires you to register pursuant to Section 290 of the Penal Code [as a sex offender] with law enforcement offices once you are back out, wherever you move and wherever you live. Do you understand that?"

"Yes" was all Daveggio said.

The judge's decision on sentencing was delayed by one day as Count 2 was amended (there being some late evidence that had been presented to Daveggio's attorney from the prosecution). Suddenly with this amendment, the most Daveggio now faced was two years in state prison. Already, things were turning in his favor.

Things even got better once he was whisked away to the Department of Corrections Reception-Guidance Center in Vacaville, a city fifty miles north of Tracy. Through its doors had passed Charles Manson and Sirhan Sirhan, the assassin of Robert Kennedy. Now as James Daveggio underwent his court-ordered "diagnosis and treatment for a period not to exceed ninety days," he spilled out his own story of the events that had taken place in Tracy, and about his life in general. According to him, he and Janet Stokes had been drinking and things just got out of hand. He thought she wanted to do it just as much as he did. Vacaville didn't need ninety days to evaluate James. By December 22 he was back before Judge Demetras, who, report in hand, admonished Daveggio's lawyer, "I have considered the Vacaville study which is back which recommends formal probation. They do find him marginally qualified. I did indicate to him one of the terms of his plea would be that I would go along with their recommendation; so I am prepared to do that. I am going to suspend the imposition of sentence for a period of five years, placing the defendant on formal probation under the following terms and conditions.

"1. He is to obey all laws that apply to his personal conduct.

"2. He is not to commit the same or similar offense.

"3. He is to serve 365 days in county jail. I have him having credit for three days before he went to Vacaville, and sixty-two days at Vacaville.

"4. He is to register pursuant to Section 290 of the Penal Code. [Sex offender]

"5. He is to obtain employment of a nature to be approved by the probation officer and remain continuously employed thereafter."

One other key point was mentioned. James was to refrain from the consumption of any alcohol and stay away from taverns.

So by Christmas 1985 James Daveggio could thank his lucky stars that he was only serving one year in county jail instead of five years of hard time in state prison.

By April 1986 his "jail life" had become even less restrictive. He was placed behind the wire at the San Joaquin Honor Farm and was given work furloughs during the day to be out and about beyond the "walls." His second wife, Donetta, later related, "He actually liked it there. He said he didn't have to do anything except watch TV and go to church once in a while. He said he really had them fooled. I believe him. He could bullshit just about anybody for a while. Until they really got to know him."

In an attempt to gain even more freedom, Daveggio put in an application for early release on April 17, and in his own words he wrote, "If I'm aloud [sic] modification, I still have my full time job. At present my family is on welfear [sic]. I feel I have learned that what I have done was very wrong and that I have a drinking problem. If modified I can get my family off welfear [*sic*]. I thank you for your consideration."

Even his probation officer seemed to be convinced of his mended ways. She wrote on the back of the report, "It is my opinion that James can stay sober, and become a very productive member of society if involved with AA [Alcoholics Anonymous] upon release."

But then James Daveggio could be very persuasive when he wanted to be. Even his rape victim, Janet Stokes, had referred to him as "this nice gentleman" before things had turned bad.

The judge reviewing his request, on the other hand, didn't buy his "nice gentleman" routine. Early release was denied.

But all in all, Daveggio's time behind bars was not that onerous for such a serious crime, and as spring turned to summer, he went about his daytime job and whiled away the hours "inside" with magazines and television. Not quite the "institutional man" that his old friend Michael Ihde had become, he nonetheless made the best of his jailhouse days. Because he couldn't drink alcohol in his present circumstances, he became the soft-spoken James of old. He was one of those guys who could turn on the charm just enough to meet any situation.

In July 1986 he was once again a free man. Almost immediately he began to recede from the consciousness of the courts and the police. But it was only a matter of time before he would be in trouble again.

Chapter 11

Adrift

James Daveggio really didn't have much to come home to in 1986 after being released from prison. His second wife, Donetta, had had enough of his chicanery and sexual infidelities and divorced him while he still was in jail. She said later, "I made a clean break from him. Moved out of his mother's house, changed my last name, changed my life. He was a big mistake in my life, but I learned a lesson the hard way. I became more wary of people. It was obvious that some could put on a pretty good act. And James was the master of that. They just can't keep up the act once you really know them and live with them. Then all their faults came out. The only good thing to come out of my time with him was our daughter, Deborah. She's a good sweet kid. I didn't want her to have anything to do with him. As it turned out that was the right thing to do. The farther anyone is away from James, the better."

In fact, daughter Deborah would do Donetta one better. Much later, when she learned about what her father had done, she would tear up all his photos, making him disappear from their lives.

Now instead of one set of kids to support and a single ex-wife, Daveggio had two. The prospect did not make him happy. A couple who were visiting Daveggio's mother in Pleasanton after he was out of jail remembered how moody he was. They didn't really know Daveggio and were struck by his unfriendly nature.

"The guy acted very strangely," the woman said. "I got the feeling there was something wrong here. But I didn't know what. He just sat there on the couch and watched as we looked the house over. He hardly said a word. It was nothing you could put your finger on. He was just very creepy."

Even longtime neighbor Emily Brighton, who lived across the street, felt there was something wrong with Daveggio. "It wasn't something that was real blatant," she said. "But there were warning signs that he had a troubled past. Maybe from his childhood."

Brighton was one to know. She had been the victim of incest as a child, and was now an advocate for other women who had gone through the same terrible circumstances. She'd read quite extensively on the subject, particularly citing *The Courage to Heal,* and she wondered if Daveggio might have been abused or had some problems as a child. Problems that would not allow him to become a normal adult.

From her own experience and intensive reading on the subject, she told how children growing into adults try to cope with the trauma. "You recover one piece at a time in a slow and painful process. All the puzzle pieces that make up who you are have been jammed together in a distorted and wrong configuration. You have to take them apart and try to put them back together in a proper manner. But sometimes, no matter how hard you try, you can't make the pieces fit correctly. The pieces have been too damaged.

"Children learn a sense of right and wrong by the age of eight or so. If they have suffered an intense trauma, like abuse, or maybe they lose the affection from a parent, they may never truly be able to distinguish what is right and what is wrong. And it is a progressive situation. Things don't get better with time, especially if the victim tries to cover up what has happened. The rage and sense of alienation only become worse."

She surmised that this may have been the case with James Daveggio. "The symptoms were certainly there," she said. "Especially when I found out what he did later. Often boys who have been abused or molested will take it out on others when they become men. It is a vicious cycle. Their self-esteem is so damaged at a young age that there is a rage inside that becomes harder and harder to control. It sometimes manifests itself in strange ways. One of these is by hurting others; another is alcoholism or drug abuse; another is self-mutilation."

James Daveggio as an adult would show signs of all four.

Emily Brighton's comments seemed to hit the nail right on the head as she cited passages from *The Courage to Heal,* a book about childhood abuse and molestation:

About Daveggio's sexuality she used as an example,

"Many survivors (of abuse) can feel sexual arousal or have orgasms only if sex incorporates some aspects of abuse. . . . The context in which we first experience sex affects us deeply. Often there is a kind of imprinting in which whatever is going on at the time becomes woven together. So if you experienced violation, humiliation, and fear at the same time as you experienced arousal and pleasurable genital feelings, these elements (become) twisted together leaving you with emotional and physical legacies that link pleasure with pain, love with humiliation, desire with an imbalance of power. Shame, secrecy, danger, and the forbidden feel thrilling."

Even though Brighton didn't know about Daveggio's self-inflicted three-inch burn mark on his back at the time, she intuitively suggested that he might be a candidate for self-mutilation, to try and expatiate his feelings of guilt. She read on,

"Many survivors have hurt themselves physically—carving into their bodies with knives, burning themselves with cigarettes, or repeatedly injuring themselves. It is natural that survivors struggle with self-abuse. As children they were indoctrinated to abuse, and now they continue the pattern themselves, never having known other choices. Self-mutilation provides an intense feeling of relief and release that many survivors crave. It also is an attempt to control, a type of punishment, a means of expressing anger, and a way to have feelings. Self-abuse is a way to re-create the abusive situation, producing a familiar result."

Just how right she might have been would surface years later when one of Daveggio's friends in Sacramento heard him admit that he often cut and burned himself. There was no explanation given by

James to his friend about why he did this, just a statement of the facts.

Without knowing it, Emily Brighton had a report backing her contentions, written by Amy Goldman in her presentation *The Life of a Child*. Ms. Goldman wrote, "For one reason or another, when a child is left alone for long periods of time and frequently, his mind begins to keep him company. Thus begins the fantasy/daydream world. During the fantasies, the masturbation begins."

Right on top of a list compiled about known serial killers and their childhoods, by Robert Ressler, Ann Burgess and John E. Douglas, is the common theme of daydreaming, compulsive masturbation, isolation and chronic lying.

Amy Goldman went on to write,

"Many people want to know if serial killers were abused as children. The answer is in most cases, yes. The levels and type of abuse range from sexual to physical beatings. However, the abuses can also be very subtle, not easily identified . . . such as neglect. Often though, when there was one type of abuse, there was another. For example, as the parent is hitting the child, the parent is also calling the child names. Although not understood why one child deals with this better than another, it is obvious that the abuse leaves an impression on the future killer which alters his life drastically. The history of abuse in the killer's background is extremely indicative of the effects of child abuse. This is not to say the abuse specifically caused the killer to be a killer, but I do think it is not unfair or untrue to say that the abuse was a key component."

James Daveggio's mother vowed she had never abused her son as a child, and ex-wife Donetta, who knew mother and son well, backs her up. Perhaps in some strange way it was the total opposite of abuse—the unrestrained adoration that had a telling and negative effect on young James. In the world he grew up in, he could do no wrong, which meant there were no limits to his excesses. Without the counterbalance and supervision of a father, and with the unyielding and sometimes misplaced devotion of his mother, he grew up with a skewed sense of self. Even Donetta Rhodes admitted, "You ended up doing whatever James wanted to do. The number one person in his life was himself. The only hole in that life was the worry that he couldn't be as good as his father—a father he never really even met until he was sixteen. And it was a real strange set of goals he set for himself as concerned his father. His father had nice houses and nice stuff, but he worked for those things. James never did. He didn't have to with his mom taking care of him, or some other woman doing it. That's what James really wanted, some woman to take care of him and go along with whatever he wanted. The only time self-doubts crept in were when he was drinking too much and he realized he couldn't scam everybody. Then he could be hard on himself. Not to be a better person, but to try harder at the scamming. He was the king of bullshitters. If things went wrong, it was always someone else's fault, never his own. When he got that same message from his mom, what was he supposed to believe? He just remained kind of a kid. A big, dangerous kid."

Reeling now with two wrecked marriages and indeed plagued by self-doubts, James Daveggio moved back in with his mom, Darlene, in Pleasanton for a while. His mom was the one person who never seemed to criticize him. Even more than Daveggio, she always saw the blame in others for his shortcomings. It was just the sort of reassurance he needed to try and get back on his feet. Donetta Rhodes even contended that James saw her (Donetta) as the reason why he had gotten into trouble in Tracy with Janet Stokes in the first place. If she hadn't told him she was pregnant, he would never have gone out drinking with John Huffstetler and ended up forcing Stokes to copulate him orally. To his mind it was all his second wife's fault. He was so off base that that "fact" became established in his mind, and it began to make him feel better.

Daveggio made a few halfhearted attempts at getting a steady job. He even took a course in diesel mechanics school and got a certificate in the program. It was here that he met his third wife-to-be, another trainee named Deta. But he could not stay focused on a regular work life for long. Once he got the certificate, he didn't do anything worthwhile with it. His life had already fallen into a pattern of never living up to expectations. Not the stint in the army, not his marriages, and now not the diesel school. Just like his old Main Street acquaintance Michael Ihde, he seemed to fail at everything he touched. He hadn't quite crawled into a bottle the same way Ihde had, but he was certainly adrift.

Daveggio began to go to the Pastime Pool Hall more frequently, once again trying to recapture the good old days with his buddies. Everything seemed to be going in circles for him, from one cocktail lounge to another. It was just easier to sit on a bar stool with his friends, have a few brews, and watch sports on the television set in the corner than face the reality that he was now twenty-seven years old and going nowhere fast. The prospects for an ex-con who had dropped out of high school in the Pleasanton area were minimal at best. All the new businesses were going high-tech, and Daveggio didn't have the proper skills and education. It must have made him feel even more alienated as the city of his youth changed from its working-class roots to a Yuppie bedroom community. The Pastime became more and more like a bastion against all those outsiders who were now depriving him of even his home turf. The complaints of his buddies matched his own— basically, how the city was changing and for the worse. The new people were snobbish; working-class people were looked down on by the new arrivals. It was a hell of a way to treat "old-timers," of which they now counted themselves.

Within its smoky walls, the rumors drifting around Frog once again began to percolate. It was no secret what he had done to Janet Stokes in Tracy, and when he had too much to drink he hinted at other dark things he had done as well. The shy, friendly smile would disappear and his brilliant blue eyes become harder, taking on a more dangerous edge. As one of his old-time buddies at the pool hall said, "There seemed to always be two sides to Frog. Normally, he was quiet and polite. But give him a few drinks and he began to brag. The things he bragged about made you wonder. Was he just making this shit up, or had he really done some of the things he said he did? I mean fucking women against their will. I thought it was just the booze talking, but when I found out later what went on, I just don't know. Maybe he really was trying to tell us something. It's hard to say if he really wanted to be helped, or he was bragging, after all. I don't know if that thing about multiple personalities is true. But with Frog he seemed to have at least two personalities. The quiet, friendly one, and the angry, loudmouthed one. There's no doubt in my mind what triggered the angry one. It's what comes out of a bottle. Without that booze, I don't know if he would have ever hurt anyone in his whole life."

Even though Daveggio was a registered sex offender, who knew the consequences if he deviated again, the cravings for illicit sex were still there in the back of his mind. Like monsters in a child's nightmare, they were always hiding beneath the bed in a darkened room. Pleasanton was becoming stifling now and too reminiscent of failure. Most of the people in town, except for his buddies at the Pastime Pool Hall, didn't give a damn whether he lived or died. He had to break out before he became like one of the nut cases who inhabited "the Creek" area, babbling all day long to himself and drinking cheap wine from a bottle in a paper sack.

Perhaps hoping for a fresh start, he, Deta and her eight-year-old daughter moved to Carmichael, a suburb of Sacramento, in 1988. The one thing Daveggio could not leave behind were those inner demons that would plague him more than ever once he reached that Central Valley city.

Chapter 12

Trouble in River City

Sacramento, California, goes by several nicknames: "Sac Town," "The Big Tomato," and "River City." This last one takes note of the two rivers that dominate the city—the Sacramento River on the west side of town, and the American River that cuts straight through its center. Often in winter, fog rolls out over the entire town and blankets the streets with a dense covering of white. James Daveggio's own life became lost in a sort of fog of rumors and innuendo during his stay in Sacramento from 1988 through 1997 when it emerged again into new and terrifying light.

He had moved to Sacramento, perhaps because he felt he'd just about used up all his good luck in the Bay Area. And for a time it did seem as if he truly would try to reform. The little family of James, his new wife, Deta, and her daughter moved out to a suburb of the city known as Carmichael and settled down on Gunn Road to a longed-for try at domesticity. The house was just across the street from a day care center and even though Daveggio was a sex offender, he didn't let authorities know about his new address. His usual response to authority was to ignore it if he could.

He couldn't ignore his past life, however. It kept intruding on him whether he liked it or not. In May 1988, only a month after he married Deta, his ex-wife Donetta served a modification order on him concerning child support for their daughter, Deborah. On July 20 she and her lawyer, and Daveggio and his lawyer, met in the courtroom of Judge William McGuiness in Alameda County. When all was said and done, James Daveggio was ordered to pay $200 on the first and fifteenth of every month for child support. His already tight finances were strained more than ever now. He began to wonder if not following through on his class at the diesel engine school was such a good idea.

Deta became pregnant by August, only four months after the wedding. Daveggio reacted to the news just like he had when his previous wife had informed him of her pregnancy—he went out of his way to sow his wild oats. Whatever his home life may have been, the demons in the back of his mind kept urging him on to more excesses. Not content with a sex life that included only Deta, Daveggio reverted to picking up other women in bars and restaurants. He had a shy, warm manner when he didn't drink to excess, and many women found it endearing. Rumors even circulated among his friends that he was dating a teenage girl. No amount of wanting to have a normal family life with a new wife and son seemed to restrain him for long. He still had to catch up to his dad in marriages and girlfriends.

He must have been particularly horny on the morning of September 30, 1989, because at 11:50 A.M. he was arrested by Officer McGee of the Sacramento Police for trying to pick up a policewoman posing as a prostitute at the corner of Boxwood and El Camino Avenue. Already half drunk, he was also cited for disorderly conduct.

When he was hauled before Judge Kobayashi's court, the formal charges read: "James Anthony Daveggio did willfully and unlawfully solicit another person for an act of prostitution." Daveggio's court-appointed lawyer, Steven Cohen, advised him to plead nolo contendere (acknowledging guilt), and he complied, paying $292 in cash for his fine and court fees. As part of his plea he signed a document stating:

1. Would not hitchhike or pick up hitchhikers.
2. Would carry identification when outside his residence.
3. Will not loiter for the purpose of soliciting an act of prostitution.
4. Would not rent a room under an assumed name.
5. Would not utilize services of a massage parlor or escort service.
6. Would not loiter in known prostitution areas around Auburn Boulevard from Marconi to Watt Avenue, Del Paso Boulevard from Arden Way to El Camino Avenue, the area bounded by 14th to 19th Streets, D to Q Streets, the truck stop at Stockton Boulevard and Mack Road, Stockton Boulevard from Broadway South to 47th Avenue.
7. Would comply with an AIDS test and get counseling.

Whatever lessons the counseling taught seemed to have no more effect on him than the AA meetings had. Daveggio stayed true to his nature, drinking and chasing women. But at least he stayed out of going back to prison, even though he was a registered sex offender and still technically on probation from his Tracy, California, rape conviction.

The Daveggio household was in pure chaos now. Half the time Daveggio didn't even try to hide what he was up to. Deta did the best she could to raise their boy and restrain James from his wilder aspects, but things only seemed to get worse. There was not only their son to contend with, but James had all those daughters, who kept being thrown into the mix. His children were scattered all over the area, often coming to live with him and Deta, costing him even more money. One thing became very evident, he didn't want any more children.

In 1993 Daveggio decided on an operation that would baffle law enforcement agents five years later and temporarily throw them off track. He opted to have a vasectomy. Seeking advice about the operation at a San Jose Planned Parenthood Clinic, he had the procedure performed on December 15, 1993. Six weeks later he had no more discernible sperm in his ejaculations. No sperm meant that not only would he have no more children, but also that he could not be traced in that manner by a DNA test.

The good years in the marriage to Deta lasted about as long as the others had. His last chance at having a "nice little family" was slipping away like a rain puddle in the desert. So was all his pretense at social responsibility. Daveggio decided if he was going to be wild, he might as well pull out all the stops. He bought himself a purple Harley, dyed his short-cut hair purple to match, and joined a local motorcycle gang known as The Devil's Horsemen.

In keeping with his biker brothers, who went by names such as "Thumper," "Stick," "Little Bill" and "Cowboy," Daveggio became known once again only as "Frog" or "Froggie." He added new tattoos to his arms, back and chest to go along with the others, becoming a walking tattoo gallery. He grew a "bad boy" goatee to round out his tough-guy image. He began to look just as rough as any other member of the group. With his muscled arms and 220-pound frame, Frog was not someone you wanted to mess with. The Devil's Horsemen, in some strange sense, became the family he was always looking for.

Their "clubhouse" on Stockton Boulevard in South Sacramento was something to behold. Built like a bunker and displaying a large Confederate flag, the place was open to outsiders by invitation only. One girl named Karen, who had recently moved to Sacramento from Florida, said, "Oh, man, it was far out. The [place] was like one of those militia places. You know, lots of Rebel stuff. It was built like a bunker. They were a bunch of hard-ass guys. They had lots of tattoos and were real tough. But they were fun too."

Daveggio enjoyed the camaraderie it brought. He often went on motorcycle runs up into the Sierra foothills, Lake Tahoe or down the Valley with his brothers. If one of them got into a fight, they all pitched in. They also hit the bars along Stockton Boulevard pretty frequently, but unlike the others, Daveggio still retained his soft-spoken ways with women. It just blew them away—the aspect of this tough-looking biker with a sweet personality and shy demeanor. Lizzy Bingenheimer, who was part owner of Lizzy B's Bar in South Sac, fell for Froggie.

Bingenheimer was no stranger to a rough life. One of her old neighbors remembered her as a girl on the south side of town. "I guess she didn't have a very good upbringing," he said. "She often would come knocking at the door and ask for something to eat. We always gave her something. I guess her own folks were too drunk or something to feed her. She wasn't real bad or anything. But nobody was really raising her. She had to raise herself."

An elderly woman neighbor concurred. "Elizabeth was basically a good girl who kept picking the wrong guys. She was nice to me. Kept me company 'cause I'm an invalid. But that new boyfriend of hers [Daveggio], he wouldn't speak two words to me."

Not all of the neighbors, however, were enamored with Bingenheimer. Peggy Morton, who lived nearby at the time, but has since moved, remembered Lizzy as a problem child from an early age. "She just got into drugs early and then it was on to motorcycle gangs. It became a real mess over there. People in and out all hours of the day and night. I think there was a lot of drug dealing going on. She hung out with a bunch of lowlifes."

Morton remembered James Daveggio in particular. "He was a mean son of a bitch. He got into it one time with my nephew, who made a casual remark about his stupid purple motorcycle. Frog, as they called him, came over and knocked my nephew right off his bike. It was totally uncalled for. I saw the whole thing from my front window and went outside. 'Hey,' I said, 'what's going on here?' I was going to discuss this whole thing with him like two adults. But that Frog came right up to me and pushed his finger in my face. He said, 'Bitch, I'm gonna kill your ass! Or maybe I'll let my motorcycle gang do it.' I'll never forget the look in his eyes. All the girls said what beautiful blue eyes he had, but all I saw was the look of a mean, crazy madman."

Peggy Morton went back in the house and called the police. They came, but all they did was talk to

Daveggio. Police cars on Vista Avenue became a common sight in what one man, Wray Tibbs, had once called Geritol Row. "Most of us were old and retired," he said. "But that place [Lizzy's house] was Rancho Notorious around here."

As Daveggio saw Deta and his son less and less, he began to stay over Bingenheimer's house more and more. But his old patterns had not changed. Polite and flattering when sober, he could be mean and dangerous when drunk. Morton witnessed Daveggio slap Bingenheimer around more than once. One time in particular caught her attention. "James owned a fancy pickup truck at the time and Lizzy drove it without his permission. When she came home, he gave her a good beating right there in the street."

But it wasn't always one-sided abuse. Lizzy Bingenheimer on occasion could give as good as she got. Morton remembered one comical incident. "James was drunk and trying to climb into a side window. Lizzy began beating him on the head with a broom. He kept saying, 'But, honey, I love you!' He finally staggered out to his pickup truck and passed out."

Once Daveggio came into Lizzy Bingenheimer's life, it wasn't long before he became a part of Lizzy B's bar in the capacity of a bartender and unofficial bouncer. If his size and height weren't enough to calm a rowdy customer, it usually didn't take any more than a word that he belonged to The Devil's Horsemen to quiet the malcontent. Anyone with even a bit of sense did not look forward to taking on the whole gang.

Deta Daveggio had to just keep on suffering with all his philandering. There came a point where she couldn't stand to be around him anymore and moved out of the area. But for Frog, life was about as good as he could have hoped for in the mid-1990s. He had an ersatz family, even if they were a rough pack of bikers; a son to carry on his name; and a girlfriend who loved him, according to her own standards. She liked to jump on the Harley, behind him, and go for a ride down the curving levees of the Sacramento River. With the wind in her hair and the sunset falling over the languid waters that looked like a scene out of bayou country, Lizzy fell in love with Frog.

In some ways it was even more exciting to take the twisting mountain roads up to Lake Tahoe. The cool air was bracing and the scenery beautiful. One service station attendant at the "Y" particularly remembered Daveggio coming in there quite a bit. It was evident he was no stranger to Tahoe and knew his way around even its backroads. With its casinos, Lake Tahoe became a kind of Mecca for Daveggio. So did the prospect of ogling all the nice young girls in their bikinis as they sunned themselves on Tahoe's warm, sandy beaches in summertime.

As time passed, Lizzy Bingenheimer allowed Daveggio to move into her home on Vista Avenue in Sacramento, but she and her neighbors got a lot more than they bargained for. It wasn't long before The Devil's Horsemen started showing up too, at all hours of the day and night. Drinking, yelling, swearing, the roar of motorcycles streaking down the street, became a part of everyday life on the once-quiet avenue. The tree-lined neighborhood of modest homes became wrapped in a state-of-siege mentality between the neighbors and the Horsemen.

One neighbor who lived a few doors down was a retired navy man, and he made no bones about what he thought of Frog and his buddies. "Never did like the guy," he said. "I thought he was a hustler and a no-good SOB!"

Another neighbor, a few houses up the street, who did not want to be identified, said, "It still makes me mad when I think about that guy. This used to be a nice neighborhood. But when he moved in with that gal, everything went to hell. I wanted to kill him. But then I figured if I killed him, I'd have to kill them all. The whole gang, I mean."

Another neighbor said, "I used to go to church and pray that they would move or get killed. I know that's bad, but I really hated them."

Despite all the turmoil, Daveggio was having the time of his life. For once, he wasn't the outsider. He was at the very heart of the action, even if it was a strange life. He was in such a good frame of mind that he often passed out small pins made in the shape of frogs to female patrons at Lizzy B's. Lizzy thought it was cute, just one more sign of what a really nice guy he was.

But she should have been looking a little more closely. Pins weren't the only thing he was displaying at Lizzy B's. Once in a while, when Bingenheimer wasn't around, he would coax some young woman down to the end of the bar, unzip his pants, and expose himself in front of her. Some girls were turned off and never showed their faces in the door again; others didn't mind at all. Lizzy B's was that kind of place.

So despite the fact that James Daveggio had it about as good as he ever wanted, there were still demons scratching on the inside, gnawing to get out. Just how deep-seated they were can be detected by a statement made by one of Frog's acquaintances named Dave. Dave sometimes frequented Lizzy B's, and he also patronized another bar up the street

that Daveggio would know all too well in the years
to come. In a rare moment of truth, Daveggio related to Dave that he sometimes inflicted wounds
on himself, either by cutting or burning. He had a
three-inch burn on his back. One story goes that
he got it from a childhood accident. Another that
he did it to himself. Either way, he seems to have
created self-inflicted wounds at some point in his
life. He didn't know why he did these things. But
he felt compelled to do them. This one brief
glimpse of the inner turmoil afflicting Daveggio
paints a picture of a deeply troubled man, unsettled
by terrible memories and urges even at this point
in his life, which should have been the most satis-
fying emotionally. At some level the brotherhood of
the biker gang wasn't enough, nor was Lizzy. Daveggio had a cold, dark void at the center of his life
that needed filling, and he knew no other way to
fill it except by excess. More drinks, more women,
more violence.

The women came first. Daveggio began seeing
other women behind Lizzy's back. Carla Pelfrey, a
diminutive, pretty patron of the bar, related that
Frog started dating her teenage sister, even though
he was already thirty-five years old. Daveggio was
able to keep the demons in check enough to still
come off as a good guy when he wanted.

"Froggie was a nice guy then," Pelfrey stated.
"He never talked dirty to my sister or slapped her
around the way some of those other biker guys did
with their girlfriends. Once in a while he would
bring over videos and pizza and stuff, like on a Saturday night, and he would pay for it all. He was
very generous. He just liked to kick back and watch
the TV. He was really into movies a lot. Sometimes
he even brought his son, who he got on weekends.
He was actually a lot of fun to be around. You'd

have never guessed he was a rough biker if you had seen him then. I never guessed about all that other stuff."

But there always was the "other stuff" with Daveggio, no matter how many wives he went through or how many girlfriends he had. They were never enough—not compared with the thrill of taking some terrified woman against her will into a dark place, unzipping his pants, and forcing her to go down on him. All the Annettes, Donettas, Detas, Lizzies and dozens of others just couldn't match the excitement of one Janet Stokes, taken at gunpoint into the orchards at midnight and forced to do whatever he wanted.

But if Daveggio had taken the time to read the Bay Area newspapers, he might have discovered a cautionary note in their pages concerning his old buddy Michael Ihde. Ihde had also surrendered to those same urges and finally run out of luck. He'd dug a hole for himself, dark and deep, and a Bay Area prosecutor, with the improbable first name of "Rock," was going to bury him in it for good. Little could Daveggio guess at the time that Rock had an extra "shovel" lying around for him as well. In the late 1990s Rock Harmon would bury Daveggio just as deeply as he was about to do with Michael Ihde.

Chapter 13

The Interrogation Room

With Mike Ihde it all went back to a morning in February 1986. He had moved up to Vancouver, Washington, with his girlfriend, Rachel Piazza, looking for greener pastures. They had given their baby up for adoption and were both unemployed, and living in their car, in flophouses or with friends.

They eventually found an apartment just as run-down as their old place on Ashland Avenue in San Lorenzo. It wasn't pretty, but at least it was cheap. And there was a nearby Denny's, where they could eat for inexpensive prices. Piazza wasn't much of a cook, and they liked hanging out at Denny's.

But Ihde just couldn't stay out of trouble. One afternoon he decided that it might be "fun" to steal the PLEASE WAIT TO BE SEATED sign from the restaurant while he thought no one was looking. He and Piazza spirited the sign out of the Denny's and back down the block to their house. But they were so inept in their theft that they were spotted and soon caught.

Brought before a judge with at least a nominal sense of humor, Ihde was admonished that he would be let loose on his own recognizance if he wrote 5,000 times: "I will not steal the Wait To Be Seated sign." Too lazy and not even attempting to follow the judge's lenient orders, he turned himself in at the county jail the following day, saying he just couldn't do it.

The court clerk was astounded. She said, "You fool, if you'd have written it only a hundred and fifty times, the judge would have probably let you off!"

So instead of a little lesson in handwriting, Ihde got to spend the next forty-eight hours in D block of the county jail, sleeping under the phones because of overcrowding. Rachel Piazza had also been taken into custody on the theft, and a warrant on earlier unrelated charges kept her behind bars longer than Ihde.

With Piazza still in jail, Ihde went wandering around in a Vancouver neighborhood not far from his latest address on 102nd Avenue when he was released on February 22, 1986. He stopped in at the Spot Tavern and bummed some money off an acquaintance there. It wasn't long before the money was going down his hatch in the form of a few beers at the bar. Wanting to make the money go as far as he could, Ihde left the bar and went to a nearby Safeway supermarket where he bought two forty-ounce cans of Schlitz beer that cost less than the tavern beer. He took the cans out to a picnic table behind the store and proceeded to get thoroughly drunk. It reminded him of his old times at the freeway overpass near the railroad tracks in San Lorenzo when he used to hang out and get drunk. It also reminded him of spotting Lisa Ann Monzo and his attack on her. That had been almost too exciting for words—the fact that she had come right to him as if in a dream. He just couldn't keep from thinking about those kinds of things.

It began to rain, turning into a downpour, and Ihde sought shelter under the awnings of the shopping center. Waiting out the rain, he spotted sixty-nine-year-old Ellen Parker returning to her car after buying some medication at the Hi-School Pharmacy. To Ihde's mind it was just like Amador County all over again. His mind quickly switched gears from the attack on Lisa Ann Monzo to the one on Gloria Hazelwood.

Ever the opportunist, Ihde ran up to Parker and used the same ploy on her that he had used on Hazelwood. He begged for a ride to his home. It was raining hard and Parker was a good-hearted woman. She let Ihde into her car.

Ihde directed her to a condominium complex that was under construction. There was no one around at the time. And it was there that things turned ugly. He hit the terrified woman in the face and forced her into an unfinished condo. There he kept punching her until she was completely cowed. Pushing her to the cold concrete floor, Ihde pulled her sweater and blouse up and undid her pants. She struggled, so he bit her face so hard that it left teeth marks in her cheek. Then he hit her in the head again. He forced Parker to copulate him orally. To complete his menu of sexual deviancy, he had anal sex and vaginal sex with her as well.

After Ihde finished with her, his hands sprang to her neck, just as they had done with Lisa Ann Monzo, and choked the life out of Ellen Parker. When he was sure she was dead, he dragged her body to an unfinished laundry room and hid it under some building material. He stole $120 from her purse and ditched it in a Dumpster a few blocks away. His concealing of Parker's body was so effective that workers didn't even discover it until two days later.

Ihde kept an eye on the local newspapers and was relieved to see that the police weren't even close to discovering that he was the culprit. He breathed a huge sigh of relief and thanked his lucky stars. The whole thing hadn't even been planned; it had just happened on a spur of the moment, like with Hazelwood and Monzo, because he couldn't control those urges.

Mike Ihde let things cool down for five months. He was married to Rachel now and she was pregnant again. But performing sex with her just didn't have the same excitement as raping a complete stranger. It was the victim's terror and the sense of total control that he had over her that turned him on. He also enjoyed beating and strangling them. In some ways it felt even better than the sex.

By August 9, 1986, he was on the prowl again, this time at Hank's Tavern in Vancouver, chatting up Lori Lynn Smith at the bar. After a few drinks Smith admitted he was kind of cute, and he coaxed her to her car in the parking lot so they could "talk" in a quieter place. Ihde climbed behind the wheel and asked her for her keys so that he could turn on the radio. Without an argument she complied.

After a few minutes he started the engine.

"What are you doing?" Smith asked, beginning to get nervous.

But Ihde was all soothing charm. "I want to go somewhere more private," he answered, "where we can be alone."

With some misgivings she agreed.

He found somewhere more private—an isolated spot in the parking lot of the Quarterdeck Tavern, not far from where he lived. It was dark and deserted in the parking lot.

Once Ihde stopped the car, he lost little time in

fondling Lori Smith's breasts and opening her blouse. But when he pulled down her jeans and attempted to do the same with her panties, she resisted. As soon as he started to pull down his own pants, Smith pulled hers back up.

This made Ihde furious. He grabbed her around the throat and pointed at his crotch, yelling, "You see this! You see this!"

Unable to breathe, Smith fought hard, managing to open the car door, tumbling to the ground. Ihde scrambled right out the passenger door after her and climbed atop her, tearing at her clothes and punching her.

Everything was repeating itself in his mind. Here was one more "bitch" he was going to have to rape and then strangle. All these bitches had it coming to them!

But fate intervened. Unseen by either Ihde or Smith, a passerby had stopped when he heard all the yelling. The man grabbed a flashlight and rushed over to investigate. When he shone his light on the pair, he yelled, "Hey, what's going on!"

Mike Ihde had finally been caught right in the act. He quickly pulled up his pants and ran away. But as he did, witnesses along his route saw him running straight back to where he and Rachel were staying at the time. And one more thing was about to trip him up for good—stupid, arrogant, unlucky Michael Ihde had dropped his wallet on the floorboard of Lori Lynn Smith's car during their scuffle. It contained his identification, including his address. As soon as the police found the wallet, they immediately went to the address, with Smith in tow, and found Ihde cowering there. Smith identified him as her attacker and they arrested him on the spot.

With the arrest of Michael Ihde, authorities in

Clark County, Washington, where Vancouver is located, began to look back at old unsolved crimes in the area. Detective Pat St. John and Detective David Trimble of the Clark's County Sheriff's Office noticed the similarity of Ellen Parker's rape and murder to the case of the abduction and rape of Gloria Hazelwood in Jackson, California, years before. But they were going to have to move fast. Ihde had already been convicted for attempted rape in the Lori Smith case during the summer and was set to leave Clark County on September 26, 1986. With only a few days to go, the sheriff's department took an imprint of Ihde's teeth.

Then with only one day left before Ihde's departure, Detectives St. John and Trimble contacted Ihde at the county jail at 2:20 P.M. They took him downstairs to the Criminal Investigation Unit to conduct an interview concerning Ellen Parker's unsolved rape and murder eight months before. What took place was set down on paper by Detective St. John; it gives an enlightening glimpse into the troubled mind and soul of Michael Ihde.

Detective St. John wrote:

"This interview began at 1437 hours and was conducted in an interview within CIU. Present were Ihde, Detective Trimble and I. At the beginning of this interview Ihde requested cigarettes and was provided them by Detective Trimble. At the beginning of the interview Ihde was advised that we were conducting an investigation into another matter than the Quarterdeck incident [Lori Smith case]. As such, we told him that we were interested in his whereabouts following his release from jail on February 22, 1986. Ihde was reminded that he had served two days on a Theft III convic-

tion [The Denny's sign]. Initially, Ihde stated
that the best he could recall was that he went
straight home. . . . Detective Trimble then advised Ihde that we were involved in a murder
investigation, and as such were questioning
him in regards to that. We asked Ihde if, on
the day of his release from jail, he recalled getting a ride from a little old lady in a red car.
He was advised that this ride would have been
from the area of the parking lot of Hi-School
Pharmacy on Andersen. In response, Ihde
stated that he did not recall getting a ride the
day that he was released from jail. I then
showed Ihde several photographs of Parker's
vehicle parked in front of the condominiums
where her body was found. I asked Ihde if that
car looked familiar or if he had seen it before.
Ihde studied the pictures and denied any
knowledge of the vehicle or having seen the
vehicle before. Ihde was questioned if he may
have seen the vehicle in the parking lot of the
Hi-School Pharmacy, and he was reminded
that on that date it had rained heavily. In response, Ihde stated that he did not believe he
got a ride from anyone on that day. I then
asked Ihde if he would like to see a photo of
the woman who owned the vehicle. In response, Ihde stated that he did not think it
would do any good because he had never seen
the car before. I then showed Ihde crime scene
photographs of Parker's body at the crime
scene. It was noted that when these pictures
were placed in front of Ihde that he glanced
at them for just a fraction of a second and
turned away. He stated that the pictures were
gross and that he did not want to look at them.
We questioned Ihde further about his knowl-

edge of the vehicle or the woman and he denied seeing either of them prior.

"We then talked with Ihde and attempted to explain to him that if he had any knowledge of this incident that it was best to tell us about it. He was advised that if he had a problem that it was best to get it off his chest. During this time we discussed evidence that had been collected from him two days prior [the teeth impressions]. He was advised that it would be compared with evidence recovered from the crime scene. He was advised that it would only be a matter of time until we knew if he was involved or not, based on evidence. We discussed these points with Ihde for approximately fifteen minutes. We told Ihde that the victim had been bitten and that is why we took his dental impressions. During this time Ihde looked at the floor and avoided eye contact and did not respond to any of our statements.

"Detective Trimble then asked Ihde if he had been drinking the day that he had been released from jail. Ihde stated that he did not remember. We then discussed Ihde's previous conviction in California [the Hazelwood rape]. On this subject Ihde perked up and adamantly denied his involvement in the crime that he had been convicted of, and adamantly maintained his innocence of that crime. Ihde stated that he had been railroaded. Ihde was asked if fingerprint evidence had been used against him in the California case. Ihde stated that he was aware that a fingerprint had been recovered but he did not know the outcome of it, and stated that it was not a point of the trial.

"Ihde then asked us if we could arrange a contact visit with his wife. Detective Trimble advised Ihde that those visits had been arranged in the past and could possibly be arranged this time. He advised Ihde, however, that we wanted to discuss the homicide further. Ihde stated that a contact visit had been previously requested because of his going to the penitentiary. He also stated that it may have some bearing on what we were discussing. Ihde asked us if when his wife came to the office that we not say anything to her regarding our investigation.

"At this point in the interview it was approximately 1558 hours. Without further questioning Ihde started crying and stated that he had hurt so many people. He continued to cry almost uncontrollably and did not talk with us further. At this point it was obvious that Ihde was extremely upset about something. I asked Ihde what his biggest worry or concern was and he stated that his wife was pregnant and he was afraid that she may miscarry. He stated that this was 'pretty heavy.' We advised Ihde that if he needed to talk to his wife that we could bring her in to talk with him.

"At this point in the interview it was 1606 hours and Ihde made the following statement, 'I know . . . I don't remember too much about the incident.' Unsure of what Ihde was talking about, we asked him to tell us what he did remember. He stated, 'I remember . . . being in the car. I remember her saying that I was a nice young man.' Detective Trimble asked Ihde if he had asked for a ride. Ihde replied, 'Yah.' I asked Ihde where this occurred and he stated, 'Kmart.' Ihde then stated, 'I know enough about forensics, I know you're good at your job, I know what it was . . . I don't remember biting though.' Ihde was asked if he remembered struggling with her. He replied,

'No, not any of it.' Ihde was then asked if he remembered where he took her. He replied, 'I know the place was behind the mall.' Ihde was asked if he had told her he lived there and he replied, 'No.' Ihde at this time was crying and stated, 'I didn't think I killed the poor woman. I don't know what happened to me.'

"At this point in the interview it was 1610 hours. Ihde was crying uncontrollably. Detective Trimble left the interview room in order to get Ihde some Kleenex and a glass of water. During that time I stayed with Ihde and asked no further questions. Ihde made the following statements at this time, 'I'm sorry for her family. When I left the garage, when she wasn't moving I got scared. I thought about leaving; maybe there is a chance I won't get caught. Something inside said I needed to get caught.'

"Detective Trimble returned two minutes later at 1612 hours and gave Ihde a cup of water and box of Kleenex. . . . Based on the statements made by Ihde, he was advised of his Miranda warnings. Following each advice of rights, I asked Ihde if he understood it. He nodded affirmatively and stated, 'Yes.' Following the advice of rights, he was read the waiver of rights. Ihde signed the form which is also signed by Detective Trimble and me. The form was signed at 1613 hours.

"Following the advice of rights, we asked Ihde to start at the beginning of what happened. Ihde stated that on that night [*sic*] it was raining and that he had gone to the Safeway store to get out of the rain. He stated, 'She looked like a nice lady. I asked for a ride. She said, sure. She said I looked like a nice enough young man. I had no right to do that.' Ihde was asked what occurred next. He stated, 'I told her I lived in those condominiums; I don't know why . . . no intentions, don't know why. Then the next thing I remember we were both in the garage. . . . I don't know how we got in there. . . . She was lying there, not moving. . . . I ran. I got scared.'

"Detective Trimble then asked Ihde where he sat in Parker's car. He stated that it was on the passenger side. He asked Ihde if Mrs. Parker did the driving and he replied, 'Yes.' Detective Trimble then questioned Ihde about the route taken from the Safeway store. Ihde stated that they drove down Fourth Plain and then drove back on Vancouver Mall Drive. He asked Ihde what type of conversation he and Parker had during this time and he stated they did not talk. I asked Ihde if he recalled what Parker was wearing and he stated that he did not remember.

"Ihde was then questioned in more specifics about what had occurred at the condominiums. Ihde stated that he had told her that she could pull in front of the condominiums and turn around without having to drive all the way in. He was questioned as to what happened next and he stated, 'Like I say . . . the next thing I know, we are in the garage.' Ihde was told that it was important for him to remember exactly what occurred next. Ihde was then asked if he hit Parker while they were still in the car. He replied, 'No.' He was asked how Parker got out of the car and he stated that this is what he was trying to remember.

"At this point in the interview it was 1629 hours. A short break was taken while Ihde was taken to the restroom at his request. During this time arrangements were made to notify the Prosecutor regarding the status of the investigation, and arrangements were made to bring Ihde's wife to CCSO [Clark County Sheriff's Office]. The interview resumed at 1636 hours. Detective Trimble asked Ihde if, and when, he was aware that Parker's body had been found. Ihde stated that he did not know about it and that he had not read the newspaper stories. Ihde was then questioned further as to how he got Parker into the garage of the condominiums. We advised Ihde there had to be a reason for taking her in there or a way that he did it. Ihde replied, 'I must have pulled her out of the car.' He was asked if he had done anything to Parker by this point, and we advised him that Parker had some bruises or abrasions on her head. Ihde stated, 'I remember pulling her into the garage. . . . She fell down. I stumbled.' Ihde was asked if he hit Parker in the head. He stated that when she fell that she fell pretty hard. He was asked if Parker was knocked out. He replied that she was not moving too much and then stated, 'I remember, so no one would see her, I pulled her through the garage into a little room . . . then I left.'

"Detective Trimble asked Ihde if he recalled having sex with Parker. In response Ihde stated he remembered being unclothed. Ihde was then questioned further about sexual contact with Parker. I showed him a picture of the hair stuck between Parker's teeth and asked him if he had oral sex with Parker. In response Ihde stated that he didn't remember. Detective Trimble then told Ihde that Parker had trauma in her rectal area and asked if he had any recollection of that. Again, Ihde stated, 'I don't remember anything about that.' Detective Trimble then asked Ihde if he had inserted an object into Parker's rectum and he replied, 'No.' He then stated, 'You guys are telling me all those things I don't remember. . . . That's pretty sick.' Ihde stated, 'I don't know how I can love my mom and wife like this and do this.'

"Ihde was then asked how long he spent in the garage with Parker and he stated that it was approximately ten minutes. Ihde was asked what type of things he did to Parker's car before leaving, and he stated that he had wiped down the top of the doors for fingerprints. Detective Trimbel asked Ihde what he had used to wipe the door down and he stated that he had taken his shirt off and used it. He also stated that he had wiped down any area of the car that he may have touched. When asked why he wiped the car down for fingerprints Ihde stated that he knew his fingerprints would be on file from his previous arrests.

"Asked again about the condominiums, at this point Ihde was crying and then made the statement, 'She was so nice to me, she was a nice lady.'

"Ihde was then told that it was very important that he remember the exact details of what occurred when arriving at the condominiums. Ihde stated that when he got out of the car that he told Parker to wait a minute and that he remembered pulling her out the car. I asked Ihde if he walked around to her side of the car and pulled her out the doorway. He nodded his head affirmatively. Ihde then stated, 'I don't know why the change.' Ihde was then advised that Parker had marks on her face and he was asked if he hit her. He replied, 'No.' He did state that he forced Parker to walk to the garage. Ihde was asked how he forced her and he stated that he grabbed her and pulled her out of the car. He was asked to explain further how he did this and he stated that he grabbed her by her clothing. Detective Trimble asked Ihde if he grabbed Parker by the hair or choked her and Ihde stated that he had wrapped his arm around her neck and was holding her clothing as he walked her to the garage. Detective Trimble asked Ihde if Parker appeared to be struggling to breathe. He replied, 'She may have. I stumbled in the garage. She fell. I fell to the side. She didn't move.' Ihde was asked what occurred next and he stated, 'When she wasn't moving I took her clothes off.'

"We then told Ihde to tell us what he did next. He replied, 'I remember raping her.' Ihde was asked how he raped Parker and he stated, 'I took off her clothes, dropped my pants, got on top of her.' Detective Trimble asked Ihde if he was talking about vaginal intercourse and he replied, 'Yes.' When questioned further about oral and anal intercourse Ihde stated that he did not remember doing that. He was then questioned about biting Parker, and in response stated that he did not remember. However, Ihde did ask if Parker had been bitten on the face. We asked Ihde why he asked that, and he stated that the other night, while lying in his cell, that he could see Parker's face with tooth impressions.

"He was then asked, following the rape, what he did with Parker. He stated that he put his head on her chest to see if she was alive. We asked Ihde what he heard and he stated, 'Nothing.' Detective Trimble asked Ihde if he thought Parker was dead and he replied, 'Yes.'

"Ihde was asked what else he did with Parker

or her property before leaving. He stated that when he took her purse to the dumpster that he opened it and found $120.00 inside. He stated that he took the money and then went to the theatre at Vancouver Mall and called a taxi cab. Ihde was questioned about the taxi cab and he stated that he knew the driver as Bob S. He stated that he took the taxi to Sunrise Bowling Lanes and stayed there until closing at approximately 2:00 AM. When questioned about what he did after that, Ihde stated that he returned home. Ihde was asked if he ever returned to the scene of the homicide and he stated that he never had.

"At this point Ihde stated that he knew from the start that we would find out. He then told us that he was glad that we stayed with him and that we did not believe him when he denied any knowledge of the homicide.

"Ihde then stated that he wished that his wife could leave the Vancouver area, and stated that this was going to hurt her real bad. I then asked Ihde if it was a possibility that the incident at the Quarterdeck Tavern [with Lori Lynn Smith] could have ended up the same way as Parker did. In response he nodded his head yes. He then stated that he thanked God every day that the guy walked up, referring to the witness from the tavern.

"At 1815 hours I contacted Ihde's wife, Rachel Ihde, in the visiting area of the County Jail. I advised her that her husband was downstairs. I took her to the CIV unit where she contacted Ihde in an interview room. I was present during Ihde's contact with his wife, during which time he told her that he killed Ellen Parker. Ihde told her that the money that he had given her, that he said he got from a subject named Dan, actually had come from Parker's purse. Ihde's wife was extremely upset and crying. In response to her questions of why he had done it, he stated that he didn't know why, and added that he did not even know her. Rachel Ihde stated that this was very hard to believe and she did not know what to believe about him. In response, Ihde stated, 'This is the truth. This is the truth.' Ihde then continued and stated to her, 'When they asked for the test [on the teeth marks] I knew it would come out. I subjected myself to it. I couldn't carry it anymore. I had to get rid of it.' "

Chapter 14

King David's Sins

It was obvious both to Michael Ihde and his lawyer after this admission of guilt that things did indeed look bleak for him. He'd already been convicted in the Lori Smith case. Now with the possibility of the death penalty looming on the horizon, Ihde decided to plead guilty to the Ellen Parker rape and murder charges in exchange for life imprisonment without possibility of parole. He was taken to Washington State Penitentiary in Walla Walla, Washington, and believed that he would spend the rest of his life there.

But fate was not quite through with Michael Ihde just yet. If he thought he had beaten the executioner's lethal injection, he was wrong. There were still those Bay Area, California, cases that had gone unsolved—Lisa Ann Monzo and Kellie Poppleton. In particular, Lisa Ann Monzo's ghost was still out there like a vengeful spirit and it was about to come back and haunt Ihde in a way he couldn't even imagine. From beyond the grave, Monzo's DNA and the DNA from Ihde's own semen were finally going to send him to hell.

It all started in 1987 in the dayroom at the Washington State Penitentiary. Mike Ihde had become friendly with another convicted killer named Richard Danielson. Danielson had lived a very violent past. He had killed a man with as little remorse as if he'd killed a cockroach. Danielson and Ihde were in continuous contact, being in the same unit. They saw each other every day in the prison school, at meals, in the dayroom and the yard. During the course of their conversations Ihde related to Danielson that his wife, Rachel, had moved to Portland, Oregon, and it was there that his new baby had died.

Danielson remembered that incident. "Mike was disturbed over it really bad. I think it was SIDS. [Sudden Infant Death Syndrome]."

As Danielson gained Ihde's trust, Mike began to open up to him more and more about his life. The repentant Ihde so evident at the Clark County interrogation room was again replaced by the cocky, arrogant Ihde of old. He began to tell Danielson about some of the seamier aspects of his former life on the outside. One day in particular stuck in Danielson's memory. It occurred in the Unit 5, Protective Custody Dayroom.

Mike Ihde described a date back in the early 1980s in a Bay Area city in California when he had been drinking by some railroad tracks. A girl had come walking toward him and she looked very pretty. He had grabbed her, he said, muffling her screams with her own clothing, just before he did her. Then he had strangled her to death and covered her up with some dirt and leaves. Ihde smirked that the cops had never caught him on that one. He also related that he had committed another similar rape and murder in California and they'd never caught him on that one either. He wasn't as specific about this one as he was about the girl at the railroad tracks, but Danielson got the impression that it had taken place in northern California. Ihde spoke of the whole thing as if it were a particularly good meal he had once enjoyed.

While Ihde told his story, he had no way of knowing that his listener was no longer the stone-cold killer that he had once been. Richard Danielson had found religion in prison and was a changed man. Danielson went back to his cell after their conversation and dwelled upon what he had just heard. The weight of it preyed more and more upon his mind until he could find no peace within himself. He knew the unwritten prison code about what other cons did to snitches. But he also now had a sense of justice.

As he said later, "Because after Mike shared with me the crimes, I just kind of kept it to myself for a couple of years and I was having a problem with that. I just pushed it back. And then I thought somebody innocent might be charged in the case or might have already been charged and I thought about the victim's relatives and family members. And what they might have went through and my spiritual walk with the Lord, I was just prompted forward to share it."

By the fall of 1992 Richard Danielson and Michael Ihde were no longer in the same prison facility. But it wasn't distance that prompted Danielson to do what he did next. He could no longer keep Ihde's story to himself. He wrote a letter to the Alameda Sheriff's Department detailing Michael Ihde's tale. It landed like a bombshell on the desk of the Alameda Headquarters on 150th Avenue in San Leandro.

The detectives there reviewed his letter, and after weeks of analyzing it, they deduced that the "girl" Ihde had been talking about to Danielson must be

Lisa Ann Monzo. Many of the things Danielson had related were so similar. On June 12, 1993, they sent Sergeant Detective Monte De Coste and Sergeant John Reasoner up to the Washington State Penitentiary to speak with Danielson in person. What he told them was compelling. He related what Michael Ihde had told him in the dayroom: "He was drinking near some railroad tracks and this girl was coming toward [him]. She had light brown hair and nice breasts. [He] decided to do her. [He] took her underneath a bridge and up against the slanted part."

Danielson then said, "I believe that there was some type of clothing used to keep her quiet. I don't know whether it was used to strangle her or what. I believe she was between the ages of sixteen and nineteen."

Lisa Ann Monzo had been eighteen at the time.

When Danielson sketched a map for them about the area that Ihde had described to him, he might as well have been drawing the detectives a blueprint of the murder scene in San Lorenzo. After nine long years, the Alameda Sheriff's Department was finally zeroing in on Lisa Ann Monzo's murderer— Michael Ihde.

Danielson, for all his faults, did have a certain sense of honor. He was transferred to a special witness protection area in another facility and there he could have kept quiet about the whole proceedings. But he wanted Michael Ihde to know what he had done. He wasn't willing to just sit back in the dark in anonymity, never taking responsibility for his actions. Via his sister, Danielson sent a letter to Ihde, who was now at another prison in Washington State. He later told the Alameda detectives it contained these elements: "I believe it was the right thing to do in front of the Lord. I had confessed my own sins in a similar manner and felt better for it. I mentioned the part [to Mike] about a passage of the Bible about King David, an offense he committed. [Referring to King David's illicit affair with Bathsheba and the intentional death of her husband by King David's orders]. And I mentioned that because of what Mike was hiding and stuff. Maybe that's the reason why some things had gone wrong in his life."

After Richard Danielson's confession, things were to go very wrong in Ihde's life. With the evidence in hand, Sergeant Reasoner approached Sharon Binkley, the criminalist with the Alameda County Crime Laboratory who had taken such scrupulous evidence at Lisa Ann Monzo's murder scene. She had kept all the items in storage, especially the vaginal swabs she had taken from Monzo's body. Since 1984 a new and powerful scientific tool had come on the scene in law enforcement forensics—DNA testing. First used in a double murder case in England during the late 1980s, it had been the key element in solving those crimes. Since then it had gained wide acceptance in the United States after several bumpy years of legal wrangling in the various court systems of individual states.

Binkley had kept up to date on the latest findings in the area of DNA testing, and she had the credentials and expertise to handle the detailed process. She was using a technique called RFLP testing, which got very good results from DNA. It was a slow and laborious process, but Binkley was nothing if not meticulous. She had a no-nonsense manner and took her job very seriously. She knew that her findings would later have to stand up in court by a judicial system that was still skeptical of forensic DNA evidence.

In conjunction with this new tool, she also was an expert in trace evidence, mastering the ability to magnify very small items, such as human hairs and other fibers, under the lenses of powerful microscopes. With these she could trace the items back to a crime scene with a great deal of accuracy.

She and Detective Reasoner won a court ruling that Michael Ihde must produce blood, pubic hair, semen and saliva samples. Sharon Binkley already knew from the Gloria Hazelwood Amador County case in 1978 that Ihde was a nonsecretor, and this factor also applied to the Monzo case. When the samples arrived from Ihde, they clearly corresponded to samples that had been in storage and had come from Monzo's body. The pubic hair from Ihde matched one that had been lifted from Monzo's pubic area. And the semen stains on the vaginal swabs were a direct match with the semen samples from Ihde.

Nine years after Lisa Ann Monzo's brutal murder, the DNA crosshairs had clearly lined up right in the middle of Michael Ihde's back.

Chapter 15

The Rock

The reopening of the Lisa Ann Monzo case brought Michael Ihde into the orbit of a man who would become his worst nightmare—Rockne Harmon, Alameda County senior deputy district attorney. Better known as "Rock," Harmon had already made a name for himself in the new field of forensic DNA analysis. A reporter from the *San Jose Mercury News* had termed him "a walking encyclopedia on DNA testing." The reporter went on to say, "If Rock Harmon didn't exist, someone would have to invent him—probably a scriptwriter."

In 1993 Harmon was forty-seven years old, married, and a Vietnam veteran who had earned the Purple Heart. After his military service he graduated from the University of San Francisco School of Law and joined the Alameda County District Attorney's Office. And despite his driven personality and intense respect for the law, he still managed to take his three small children to a local swimming pool every weekend. He was just as fanatical about his fitness as he was about the judiciary, working out daily in an Oakland gym and taking a couple of jogging laps around Lake Merritt near the Alameda County Courthouse.

In the courtroom he was more like a force of nature than a mere prosecutor. He had tried successfully one of California's first DNA-related cases, and Peter Keane, chief assistant San Francisco County public defender, said, "Harmon comes out swinging, no matter what the arena is. It's almost like he's on a mission on all this stuff. A quest for the Holy Grail. Anyone who doesn't believe [in DNA analysis] is a heretic and should be burned at the stake."

Tom Orloff, the Alameda district attorney, the man who had once worked on the Kellie Poppleton case as an assistant DA, told a *San Francisco Chronicle* reporter, "If bombs were going off all around, while everybody else would be running for cover, Rock would be trying to figure out how to get back at the guy who's dropping the bombs."

In fact, Harmon had become involved in an Oakland triple murder case and had used a primitive precursor to DNA profiling back in 1988. By 1989 the technique had been refined and Rock Harmon used semen stain DNA analysis to win a rape conviction. He started writing and speaking on the subject all over the state, becoming one of California's lead prosecutors on DNA. In the process he began to question the costly hearings California required before DNA evidence would be admitted into trial, whereas other states had already resolved that issue. He became so adamant in his resolve that he actually issued a blistering attack on an appeals court justice who handed down an adverse decision on DNA.

Every time prosecutors wanted to introduce the results of DNA testing in court they had to argue the validity of the technique all over again. The cost could come to $50,000. For small counties this process was such a financial burden that they often ignored DNA tests altogether. Harmon made it a crusade to change this inane and costly judicial procedure.

"We don't have to argue that fingerprints are unique to each person," a confederate in his cause, Lane Liroff, Santa Clara County deputy district attorney, said. "Literally, any tissue or any cell in the body that has a nucleus has DNA and can be used for testing. Scientists can test semen from the body of a rape victim; spit that has been used to lick a stamp; tears; earwax; vomit; or skin cells found beneath the fingernails of someone who has fought off an attacker."

By 1994 Rock Harmon was making his presence felt in the California judicial system, and the appellate courts began issuing a string of rulings that all favored the use of DNA testing as evidence. A panel of experts convened by the National Academy of Sciences made a report to the courts that stated, "DNA analysis is one of the greatest technical achievements for criminal investigation since the discovery of fingerprints. The technology has advanced to the point where its admissibility as evidence should not be in doubt."

As for those who doubted the validity of DNA tests, James McWilliams, an Alameda County deputy public defender, related that "Rock once called a defense DNA 'expert' at home and chewed him out as though he were a prostitute scientist."

Harmon's expertise on DNA evidence was so profound by 1995 that it brought him to national prominence in the O.J. Simpson case. Along with San Diego prosecutor George Clark, he joined Marcia Clark's "DNA evidence team" and took on the formidable defense duo of Peter Neufield and

Barry Scheck. It was a time of microscopic scrutiny by the media, and Marcia Clark had put together a team of experts for the prosecution.

Marcia Clark noted in her book *Without a Doubt,* "We were all nervous on the morning of May 24, when Collin Yamauchi took the witness stand. Collin had done the first PCR (DNA) testing at the LAPD lab—the lab the defense had taken to calling the cesspool of contamination. . . . This time he'd really gotten his act together. Under Rock's direct Collin calmly explained how he'd begun his testing by opening a vial of Simpson's blood and placing a small drop of blood on what is called a Fitzco card. . . . Collin went carefully over the procedure he'd followed in dealing with those samples. He'd even used a fresh knife after cutting each swatch. Pretty damned careful."

Rock Harmon methodically tied O.J. Simpson to the murder of Nicole Brown Simpson and Ronald Goldman by the analysis of O.J.'s blood, hair and tissue. He even managed to bring the technical terms down to a layman's understanding by inserting references to basketball players as part of his delivery.

The not guilty verdict did not deter Rock Harmon from his quest. He believed just as strongly as ever in the validity of forensic DNA evidence.

Tom Orloff, Alameda district attorney, said of Harmon after the Simpson trial, "Rock's a very aggressive trial attorney. He knows the law, and he'll push it as far as he can. If I committed a crime, I wouldn't want him prosecuting me."

Michael Ihde certainly wished Rock Harmon wasn't prosecuting him. By the winter of 1996 all the DNA evidence concerning him had been admitted into an Alameda court of law. His lawyer, Judith Browne, had tried to stymie Ihde's return to an

Alameda courtroom, citing that his testimony could be transmitted from the Washington State Penitentiary. But the penitentiary administration flatly refused, stating that any television cameras would compromise security. They won their case. Michael Ihde would have his day in court back in the Bay Area.

It was there that he came face-to-face with the ghost of his murder victim Lisa Ann Monzo. As the Monzo case commenced in September 1996, Rock Harmon came out swinging. He had eighty-four People's Exhibits for the jurors to view: everything from a close-up of Lisa Ann Monzo's dead body, to a photo of the murder scene area, to a map drawn by Richard Danielson that particularly zeroed in on the murder scene, showing the overpass, the railroad tracks and the pillar where Monzo had been raped and killed. But the most damning evidence of all was People's Exhibit #44, an analysis of a semen stain from Monzo's vaginal swab that matched Ihde's own semen analysis. A thin thread of the strand of life, DNA, was about to hang Michael Ihde for good.

Expert witness Martin Buoncristiani of the California Department of Justice DNA Lab took the stand. He stated that he had worked for the California Department of Justice DNA lab for the last 3 1/2 years. He had a science degree in molecular biology from San Francisco State University and a forensic science degree from the University of California at Berkeley. He had worked on twelve murder cases prior to the Lisa Ann Monzo case and definitely knew his business.

When the Alameda County Sheriff's Office had sent him vaginal samples from Lisa Ann Monzo and blood and semen samples from Michael Ihde, Buoncristiani first did a PCR test to determine if the more precise and complicated RFLP testing was necessary.

Rock Harmon asked him, "How would you describe those results in terms of whether you consider Mr. Ihde to be a possible source of the sperm that was on the vaginal swab?"

Buoncristiani answered, "Yes. He would be included as a source, a possible source for the sperm."

Buoncristiani was then asked to describe the RFLP test and its results.

"For the six loci tested, the profile that was abstracted would be seen in one in 398 billion blacks, one in approximately 90 billion Caucasians, and one in approximately 32 billion Hispanics," said Buoncristiani.

To double-check, the same samples had been sent to an independent laboratory, Cellmark Diagnostics. They came up with the same results—there was only a one-in-90-billion chance that the sperm found on Monzo's vaginal swab came from someone other than Ihde.

For every objection and alternate theory that Ihde's attorney, Judith Browne, came up with, Senior Deputy DA Rock Harmon had a plethora of "irrefutable evidence." There were no escape hatches for Ihde this time, no deals he could make. He'd already seen to that by pleading guilty to Ellen Parker's rape and murder in Vancouver, Washington. Harmon sought the death penalty on charges F187 (A) Spec pc and F261 PC 4 PRS in the rape and murder of Lisa Ann Monzo.

On November 5, 1996, at Alameda County Superior Court in Oakland, the jury took all the evidence in for deliberation. They weighed Michael Ihde's guilt or innocence all through Monday and into Tuesday afternoon. By 1:15 P.M. they had their verdict. He was escorted back into the courtroom and listened as the jury pronounced judgment upon him: "Guilty on both counts."

Ihde broke down at his penalty phase as Gloria Hazelwood from Amador County was once again placed on the stand to relate her tale of terror. She described her rape and near death at his hands while he reached for tissues to blot back tears. But the jury had no sympathy for him as they sat riveted by Hazelwood's testimony. "I was terrified," she said. "I thought for sure I was going to eternity."

Even his lawyer's pronouncement that Ihde had "found God" in prison and turned over a new leaf fell upon deaf ears. Instead, the jury was absorbed with every outraged word of Lisa Ann Monzo's maternal aunt, Ms. Brodie, who vented her anger upon Michael Ihde.

"He is a despicable creature. And I use the word creature because I do not, I cannot, believe he is human. I listened to garbage testimony about what a great guy he is. How he's such a positive force in this life, a positive light. If he ever was a positive light . . . that light was extinguished totally and irrevocably on the night he committed his first act of brutality against another human being. Not only was that testimony repulsive to me, but it was an insult to Lisa's memory. Lisa is and will always be deeply missed by so many good, good people. Her death left a huge void in this world, but when he dies, no one will miss him. No one will grieve for him. He will not leave a void.

"I still have trouble believing that I have to live in a world that does not contain Lisa. I still sometimes wonder how the world can keep spinning and spinning without her. But when he's gone, I will rejoice in a world that does not contain him. So when he meets his maker, Satan, because I believe he's a creature of the devil, I hope and pray that he rots in hell forever!"

Michael Ihde's appeals to escape the death sentence have systematically been denied. Even as this is written, he awaits a lethal injection at San Quentin in California in accordance with Code 3604. He'd come down a long and terrible path since he used to hang out with his buddy James Daveggio on Pleasanton's Main Street in 1977. His career in rape and murder was coming to a close just as Daveggio's criminal career was about to go into high gear. But one unsolved case still hung over both of them like a dark cloud that would not go away—the rape and murder of Kellie Poppleton. It remained to be seen in which direction her spectral finger would point as to who was her murderer.

Chapter 16

Bobby Joe's

If there was one constant in James Daveggio's life, it was that he was always drifting somewhere. Drifting from town to town. Drifting from girlfriend to girlfriend. Drifting from job to job. As his relationship with Lizzy Bingenheimer deteriorated in the mid-1990s, he drifted farther down Stockton Boulevard in Sacramento to a roadhouse called Bobby Joe's. The exterior walls of the unpretentious tavern were painted with whimsical cartoon characters of Pepe LePew, Hekyll and Jekyll, and Andy Capp, the tippling Cockney, beer mug in hand, being chased by his irate wife with a rolling pin. Andy wore a smug smile on his face, always just one step ahead of his incensed mate. Perhaps it was a feeling more than one patron of Bobby Joe's knew all too well after returning home late from the tavern.

Just like Daveggio, there had been waves of other drifters moving through South Sacramento—immigrants looking for the first rung on the ladder of the American Dream. Mexicans, Filipinos, East Indians, Vietnamese, they all washed through South Sac like a flowing and ebbing tide. Each group created their own taverns and cocktail lounges to ease their nerves after a hard day's work, often for minimum wages. They sought a convivial place to forget the harsh realities of life for a while, a place to escape the Boulevard.

Predating all the others was the initial wave of drifters who had washed ashore here in the 1930s—the Dust Bowl Okies. Looking for a place to just barely stay alive, they camped out in what had once been the orchards and farms of the area, eking out a bare existence by knocking almonds, picking tomatoes and tending to ranches. Slowly as conditions improved, they moved into shacks around the area that would become South Sacramento. In 1948 when the Campbell's Soup Company opened on Franklin Boulevard, they rushed in to fill the jobs, creating the first real stability in their lives. The work was still hard, but now they could at least put down roots and obtain the foundation of their dreams, a house of their own with a small front lawn and an automobile in the driveway. The orchards of South Sac slowly gave way to their modest but pleasant homes, as new waves of immigrants washed all around them, with different-colored skins and strange languages.

Like all the others, the Dust Bowlers, and their children when they grew up, needed a place to relax and unwind over a drink. Bobby Joe's became their place. Entering through windowless heavy front doors, they were greeted by a long, low rectangular room with curving dark-oak bar, cushioned bar stools, concrete dance floor, green-topped pool table and jukebox. Soft, glowing neon signs advertised various beers, and a few posters of country-and-western singers adorned the walls. Nothing fancy, but then they would have been put off by something fancy. This was their place, just as rough-hewn and simple as themselves.

The main bartender in the 1990s certainly fit the

image. Ted Williams (no relation to the famous baseball slugger) was an unpretentious, stocky man with a friendly face, graying hair and walrus mustache. Not given to flamboyant speech or actions, he nonetheless would serve up a drink with an ease that most patrons found reassuring. They weren't in Bobby Joe's to discuss the trends of Wall Street, California cuisine, or the latest art film. They were there to feel relaxed and be at home. Williams was their kind of bartender.

Janet Williams, Ted's wife and occasional bartender, on the other hand, was an effusive and extroverted blonde with a gift of gab and a friendly smile. Able to spin stories with the best of them, she could hold her own with anyone. She knew all the regulars by name and it wasn't long that anyone remained a stranger with Janet. Like her husband, she had seen just about everything in Bobby Joe's over the years, and nothing was too wild to startle her. After all, their tavern wasn't a monastery, and on an occasion or two, customers might find themselves heading for the parking lot to settle "their differences." But nothing in their wildest imaginations could have prepared the Williamses for what James Daveggio would eventually bring into their establishment and their lives.

It certainly started innocently enough. Daveggio drifted into Bobby Joe's one day in 1995 and ordered a few drinks. He was polite and talkative, speaking of his own days in bartending. He hit it off quite well with Ted and Janet and they immediately liked the young man. Although he looked pretty rough with his tattoos and motorcycle paraphernalia, he had such deep blue eyes and a polite manner that they couldn't help but like him. The very contrast of his looks and manner made him interesting.

One visit by Daveggio led to another, and before long he was asking the Williamses for a job at Bobby Joe's. There were no positions open for a bartender at that time, but they took one look at his six-foot, 220-pound frame and offered him a job as a bouncer. He took it without hesitation. He was still living with Bingenheimer and hanging out at Lizzy B's bar, but as time went on, he found Bobby Joe's to be his kind of place. It catered to an even "rougher" crowd than Lizzy B's, perfect for bikers such as The Devil's Horsemen.

Connie Jackson, another bartender at Bobby Joe's, was less sure about Daveggio. She was at a biker party in Sacramento where he was obviously drunk. He was rowdy and waving his sex offender paperwork above his head as if it were a winning lottery ticket.

She later told *Contra Costa Times* reporter David Holbrook, "He was flashing it around and I thought, 'Do we really want to hire this guy?' "

She also saw how he treated his women once he was past the "nice gentleman" stage. "He used his women like slaves, ordering them to clean his house and do his bidding."

Jackson did admit, however, that "James did have a nice bike. He was in a club and that's what women liked about him."

James Daveggio swiftly became a viable part of Bobby Joe's scene, taking on the more familiar name "Froggie" to those who knew him best. They were fascinated by his association with The Devil's Horsemen and his unexpectedly polite and quiet manner. Young women especially found it endearing. It was just such a contrast. Expecting some filthy language to come pouring out of his mouth, they instead were treated to a courtly kind of flattery. In echoes of Janet Stokes's comments, just before she was raped, they, too, thought, "He was a nice gentleman."

He even burnished his "nice guy beneath the rough exterior" image more by playing Santa Claus at a local hospital during the Christmas season and riding his bike on toy drives.

Although Daveggio was still living with Lizzy, he began taking out women from Bobby Joe's bar. His status improved even more when a bartender position came open and he was able to serve the ladies drinks. Two waitresses in particular, Anna and Jean, from a nearby restaurant called Eppie's, remembered him well. They often stopped by Bobby Joe's after work for a few drinks. Jean Sidener, a cute, dark-eyed, petite woman, remembered, "Frog used to always come by Eppie's for some food. He'd joke around and cut up with me. Nothing ever dirty. He was fun to be around. He was very soft-spoken and actually polite. He did have kind of a raspy voice, but that just added to his charm. It was funny, though, if you ever complimented him he would become all embarrassed. He just didn't know how to handle it. Especially from women. He was like a big, shy teddy bear."

Anna, a reflective young woman, agreed. "Froggie was as nice as he could be. Even though he looked pretty rough, he was usually pretty quiet. You never got the sense that he would hurt anyone. He was just this gentle giant. But then I guess you never know. He must have had a Jekyll and Hyde personality. Because there was this one incident around Christmas in 1995. It's something I can't be sure of. But when I think of it now . . ."

What she remembered was Daveggio being overly nice to her and Sidener. He had bought them stuffed animals for the holidays and they were touched by his thoughtfulness. Just around New

Year's Eve at Bobby Joe's, she remembered getting quite tipsy and the bar slowly emptying of customers near closing time. Frog seemed to be pouring very little orange juice and a lot of vodka into her mixed drinks. She was beginning to feel very woozy. To the left of the bar was a walled-off patio area, now totally deserted of other customers. She barely remembered being lured toward the patio by Daveggio.

Luckily for Anna, her friend Jean was there that night. Intrinsically more skeptical and wary than Anna, Jean felt there was something wrong. She quietly, but insistently, steered Anna away from Frog and out the front door. In doing so, she probably saved Anna from becoming Daveggio's next rape victim.

But as time passed, that incident was forgotten, and Daveggio's tenure as bartender at Bobby Joe's proceeded without further incident. Even to Anna and Jean, Frog seemed to return to his old, friendly, polite self in the new year. Plenty of other women and girls went out with him and one in particular caught his eye. He was now thirty-five years old and she was still a teenager, but they started dating, even though he was still living with Lizzy. Everything went fine until he had a few drinks too many and he slapped her one evening in the presence of others. She was young and small and he probably thought he could get away with it. But it wasn't the girl he had to be worried about, it was her mother.

In the words of Janet Williams, "That teenager had a big lesbian for a mom. A real bull dyke. When she found out what Frog had done to her kid," Janet chuckled, "she hauled him outside of Bobby Joe's into the parking lot and kicked his ass. It was one of the funniest damned things you ever saw."

For perhaps the first time in his life, Daveggio

found out what it was like to be on the receiving end from an enraged woman.

But as 1996 progressed, bull dykes would become the least of James Daveggio's problems. An exotic redhead in her midthirties was about to walk through the doors of Bobby Joe's and nothing in her life or James's was ever going to be the same again.

PART III
FROG AND MICKI

Chapter 17

Michelle

There are various versions of how James Daveggio met Michelle Michaud. One of the most compelling versions comes from Janet Williams. According to her, Michaud sashayed into Bobby Joe's one day in 1996, took one look at the blue-eyed, muscular Daveggio behind the bar, pointed her finger at him and announced loudly to a friend, "I want that!"

Michaud usually got what she wanted.

A different version comes from Michelle Michaud herself. It happened right around Halloween 1996. "When I first met him," she said, "I was introduced to him through some friends at their house. He was there to help with a mutual problem his friends and I were having with our daughters. He asked me not to take care of it myself but to let him have the opportunity to talk to this gentleman."

What Daveggio had in mind was probably a lot more than just a "talking" to the gentleman in question. He generally had rougher solutions than that.

Daveggio became interested in Michaud, but she warned him that she didn't like men. She was a prostitute and she'd seen the worst that men could dish out. She told him, "I think they're pigs because of the way they treat women. They generally piss me the fuck off! I'm a ho, a hooker, a prostitute, and have been for twenty-two years of my life, and I'm not changing."

Despite the warning, they continued to see each other, and against all expectations, she began to fall for him. Even though he had no upper front teeth by now, and only four bottom teeth, she found his manners "charming," just as many other women had done. She fell in love with his "striking blue eyes" and muscular build. It was nice to be treated as a lady, even though he knew her background. Somewhere deep inside, Michelle Michaud always craved acceptance. When she didn't get it, she would put on a front of foulmouthed worldliness and biting sarcastic humor. But when she was treated with respect and affection, she could return the same.

A case in point was when James Daveggio stuck up for her when some of her family members gave her a rough time about her lifestyle. "He's the kind of man who demands respect for you from your family," she said.

He also stuck up for himself when those same family members told Michaud that he wasn't good for her. They soon sensed that Daveggio might mean a lot of trouble for her. But she wouldn't listen to their advice, much as Daveggio's second wife, Donetta, didn't listen to her friends' warnings. Michaud said, "He stands up to your family and doesn't let them chase him out of your life. He's been nothing but good for me."

Unlike Daveggio, who could sometimes be shy and tentative around women when first meeting them, Michaud was brimming with self-confidence and had an attitude that no one in the world was

Victim Vanessa Lei Samson, 22, was found dead in the snow by the side of the road two days after she was reported missing. (*Photo courtesy* Tahoe Daily Tribune)

Samson at 18 in 1993.

Samson was kidnapped from this corner in Pleasanton, California on December 2, 1997.

Police blocked off the area to search for clues
in Samson's disappearance.

Family members leaving the church after memorial
service for Vanessa Samson.

Arrested on December 3, 1997, Michelle Lyn Michaud, 39, would be convicted in May 1999 for the abduction and rape of Juanita Rodriguez. (*Photo courtesy* Tahoe Daily Tribune)

In 1977, Michaud, 17, dropped out of Elk Grove High School in California before graduating.

Michaud worked as a prostitute at the Mustang Ranch during the 1980's.

After being arrested in a January 1991 police undercover operation, Michaud was found guilty of prostitution. (*Photo courtesy Sacramento, California Police Department*)

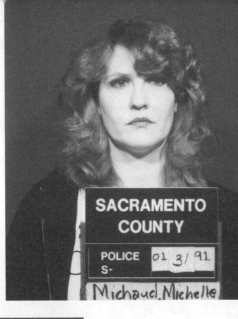

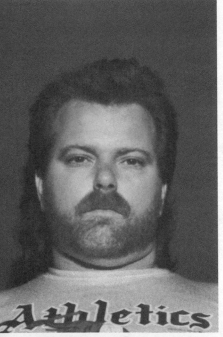

In 1989, Daveggio pled guilty when charged with soliciting a policewoman posing as a prostitute. (*Photo courtesy Sacramento, California Police Department*)

Daveggio was enrolled at Foothill High School in Pleasanton, California in 1977.

Michaud and Daveggio probably met in 1996 at Bobby Joe's, a roadhouse they both frequented in Sacramento, California.

James Anthony Daveggio, 37, was convicted on May 19, 1999 for the abduction and rape of Juanita Rodriguez. (Photo courtesy Tahoe Daily Tribune)

The rear seats of Michaud's green minivan had
been removed and rope restraints added.
(*Photo courtesy Federal Bureau of Investigation—Reno Office*)

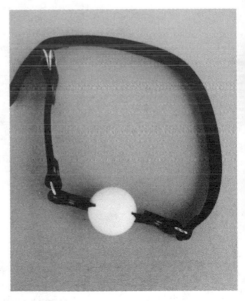

Police found this type of
ball gag in the minivan.

Salesclerk at this sex shop testified to an Alameda County, California Grand Jury that Daveggio and Michaud had purchased a ball gag.

Juanita Rodriguez, 20, was abducted from this corner in Reno, Nevada by Daveggio and Michaud on September 29, 1997.

In 1996, DNA evidence collected in November 1984 from the body of Lisa Ann Monzo, 18, helped to convict Ihde of her rape and murder.

Daveggio's friend Michael Ihde, 28, was convicted of raping Gloria Hazelwood in 1986.
(*Photo courtesy Detective Patrick St. John*)

After being raped and sexually tortured, Rodriguez was let go at Clipper Gap, close to where serial rapists Gerald Gallego and his wife had attacked their first victims.

Daveggio and Michaud at their November 1999 arraignment for the murder of Vanessa Samson. (*Photo courtesy* Contra Costa Times)

Assistant District Attorney Jim Anderson (*second from left*) with the Samson family at the arraignment.

Assistant District Attorney Rockne Harmon intends to use DNA evidence to convict Daveggio and Michaud the same way he used DNA to convict Ihde. (*Photo courtesy* The Oakland Tribune)

Detective Desiree Carrington took statements from Rodriguez about her ordeal, was with her when she identified Daveggio as her attacker, and was the first person Michaud spoke to in her confession about her crimes.
(*Photo courtesy Detective Renee Carrington*)

On May 10, 1991, Jaycee Lee Dugard, 11, was abducted while walking to a school bus stop in South Lake Tahoe, Nevada.
(*Photo courtesy* Tahoe Daily Tribune)

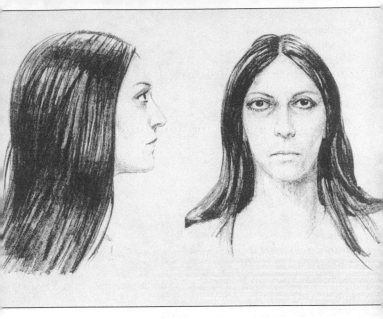

Police sketch of one of Dugard's abductors.
(*Photo courtesy* Tahoe Daily Tribune)

Dugard link investigated

By Christina Proctor
Tribune Staff Writer

Investigation of possible links between the Sacramento couple suspected of killing a Pleasanton, Calif. woman and the 1991 abduction of Jaycee Lee Dugard has been described by authorities in routine.

They are being considered just like any lead would," said Sgt. Jim Watson of the El Dorado Sheriff's Department. Watson is one of the lead investigators on Dugard's case. "We will definitely look at them and try to establish, or rule

Samson

The 22-year-old reportedly was abducted Dec. 2. Her body was discovered Dec. 4 in Hope Valley.

woman and the Dec. 2 abduction and killing of Vanessa L. Samson, 22, from Pleasanton, Calif.

Terry Probyn, Dugard's mother, has been bombarded in recent days by media representatives asking her to make a connection between Michaud and a police sketch of the woman who took her daughter

Michaud's resemblance to the woman in the police sketch was reported in newspapers when Michaud was arrested in 1997, but no evidence has been found yet to link her to the still-missing girl.
(*Photo courtesy*
Tahoe Daily Tribune)

Kellie Poppleton, 14, of Fremont, California, died in the emergency room after having been found strangled and sexually molested on December 2, 1983.

The 1983 decision to cremate Poppleton's body so she could rest with her maternal grandmother has unwittingly prevented present-day police from using modern DNA evidence to identify her killer.

better or more potent than herself. She had a huge chip on her shoulder and the determination of someone who could walk right through a brick wall.

At first the two of them seemed an unlikely match. Michaud always dressed well and used proper English when she felt like it; Daveggio was more likely to be sporting greasy jeans, T-shirt, beat-up biker boots, and his English was more often than not grammatically incorrect. She was a champagne and mixed-drink aficionado; he would mainly stick to beer. She carried herself with a certain self-confident ease; he often slouched and seemed vaguely uncomfortable. And most glaring of all, Michaud spoke of her sex life in the most graphic of terms to anyone who would listen; Daveggio would barely discuss his love life at all. When approached by most women, he would turn off rapidly and the charm would disappear. He did not like being the object of their lusts. He liked to be in command.

But there was definitely something about Michelle Michaud that secretly turned him on. If not her body, which was still in good shape at the age of thirty-seven, it was her mind. She was sharp, sarcastic, irreverent and provocative. She spoke of things she had done sexually, and things she wanted to do, that he had only dreamed about. She could spin the most outlandish stories of carnal delight beneath the soft glow of Bobby Joe's neon lights. She was an explicit Scherazade with 1,001 nights of depraved sexual fantasies. Buying drinks for everyone at the bar from her prostitution money, Michaud would regale the crowd with stories of her liaisons on the seamier side of town. As she delivered her soliloquies of lust, it was an incredibly surreal scene. Michaud never dressed suggestively, looking more like a secretary from one of the uptown businesses out for a break. But the filthy words pouring from her mouth hovered around her like tiny demons, betraying another darker side to this well-dressed, well-coiffed mother of two.

"You never knew which Michelle would show up," Janet Williams said. "The proper lady or the foulmouthed slut."

There was no doubt about it—Michelle Michaud had always been a very pretty girl. She was blessed with long red hair and deep green eyes that made heads turn. Everyone who met her commented on her striking good looks. Born in the exotic locale of Casablanca, Morocco, she had traveled around the world with her military father and family, bouncing from one location to another. At the age of fourteen she finally settled down in South Sacramento in a normal middle-class neighborhood of green lawns and two cars in the driveway. Her family, by all outward aspects, came to enjoy just an average California life.

But Michaud was not only blessed with good looks, she also possessed a keen intellect and an incisive memory. Perhaps she was too intelligent and too emotional for her middle-class surroundings. She didn't join any school organizations and she generally found the other students dull and too immature. School life in the mid-1970s became a joke to her, especially when the other students gushed in the yearbook about "Earth shoes, overalls, socks with toes in them and the various dances such as the bump and the hustle." Even more ridiculous to her cynical nature was something called CHANGES, a program that meant "Community Happenings and New Growing Educational System." It was pure 1970s. One of the teachers tried to validate it by saying, "We wanted to erase the idea that everyone here were burned-out vegetables just getting credits. Most classes offered were college preparatory." But in retrospect it's hard to keep a straight face when learning there were also courses in Pyramid Power and The Beatles.

By the age of fifteen Michelle Michaud was going through her own changes and she was starting to rebel in a big way. No amount of arguing or punishment of the girl seemed to work. Things got so out of control that she was adjudged to become a ward of the Juvenile Court. Before she graduated from Elk Grove High School in 1977, she dropped out and her school days were over. She hooked up with a wild boy named Danny Logan, who had already had a few scrapes with the law. To Michaud he was fascinating in a dangerous and exciting way. Michaud didn't end her school days with any formal announcement—she simply quit.

But she wasn't cut out to be a fast-food waitress or maid like other high school dropouts her age. She was too precocious and pretty for that. Even at that tender age she realized she had been given "unusual" good looks and a brain to go along with them. She intended to capitalize on them as best she could. She knew herself, and she knew what men wanted. Through Logan she met a Sacramento man, Charlie S., who ran a couple of massage parlors. These were in reality only a front for prostitution. Michaud began working at one and it wasn't long before she was hooking for top dollar, trading her now mature body for security and wealth.

In her early twenties she moved to Moundhouse, Nevada, just outside of Carson City, to work at the Kit Kat Ranch, a collection of wide mobile homes grouped together behind a high wire fence, where prostitution was legal. The surrounding scenery was

less than romantic—treeless, scrubby mountains of
the famous Virginia City silver district, a large agricultural plumbing outfit next door, and a collection
of auto junkyards. Michaud's living space consisted
of only a small room with a large bed, sink and
toilet. Like the other girls at the ranch, she spent
most of her time in her room when not busy with
a customer. She had brought in her own posters,
audiotapes and knickknacks to make it feel more
like home. Her days and nights saw an endless parade of tourists, truck drivers, businessmen and cow-
boys as she lined up with the other girls in the
lounge area when the bell at the front gate rang.
She was very young and pretty at the time and more
often than not Michaud was picked over the others.

At least there was Lake Tahoe, just over the
mountains about twenty miles away, to distract her
from the hours of boredom and frequent assigna-
tions with johns. With its pristine waters and blue
skies, Tahoe became a kind of haven for Michaud
away from the endless round of "servicing" customers. She became familiar with its streets and byways,
especially The Lakeside Inn at Stateline. Perched
right on the eastern shore of the lake, it was a hang-
out for the locals and perennially voted the number
one casino by them. It had a laid-back atmosphere
and a certain camaraderie, especially at the long
central bar where many of the locals gathered. It
was here that they could drink beers for a dollar
and forget about the rat race of catering to tourists
for a while. With its easygoing charm, The Lakeside
Inn must have seemed like a haven from the intense
confines of the Kit Kat Ranch.

After a few years at the Kit Kat Ranch, Michaud
moved up to the more famous and larger establishment of the Mustang Ranch brothel near Reno,
Nevada, world-renowned for its sexy ladies of the

night. Michelle fit right into the mix of high-class call girls with her good looks and intelligent, sarcastic style. She was nobody's fool and had a fairly clear picture of who she was and what she was doing. During her stay at the Mustang Ranch, her working name became "Ruby."

Joseph Conforte was a legend in his own time in Nevada. He had been a cabdriver in Oakland during the 1940s, then moved to Nevada where he started a bordello, the Triangle River Ranch, in Wadsworth in 1955. Its location had just one problem; it was at the junction of Washoe, Lyon and. Storey Counties, and prostitution was not legal in any one of them at the time. Conforte spent the next several years playing tag with the police by moving his trailers that the girls worked in back and forth across the county lines. He also tried to "influence" police and politicians by presenting them with cigars that had been wrapped with currency. According to him there was more than one policeman, judge and district attorney who accepted his cigars.

But one man he couldn't influence was the Washoe County district attorney, Bill Raggio. In 1959 Conforte attempted to set up Raggio with a young woman. According to Raggio, "Conforte told me [that if I didn't cooperate] I would be publicly accused of furnishing liquor to a minor girl and that I would be further accused of having been intimate with such girl unless I agreed to dismiss the criminal charge pending against him."

But Conforte's scheme backfired. Instead of caving in to the demands, Raggio filed extortion charges, and when the young woman pleaded guilty to perjury in front of a grand jury, Conforte was found guilty as well. He ended up serving twenty-two months in jail. Meanwhile, Bill Raggio had a great time standing in front of the cameras as his team burned the Triangle Ranch to the ground.

In 1967 Joe Conforte built a legitimate trailer park in Lockwood, Storey County, next to a railroad siding known as Mustang. It also had the advantage of being a few miles outside of Reno right alongside new Interstate 80. The residents of the trailer park benefited by Conforte's cheap rent and they saw fit to return his favor by voting in prostitution as legal in 1971. The following year Conforte, surrounded by his girls, made the cover of *Rolling Stone* magazine under the title "The Crusading Pimp, Joe Conforte's Fight to Keep Nevada Clean."

Conforte made sure the media knew that he contributed to the poor, helped rebuild historic buildings and supported county sports programs. Some of the prostitutes had good things to say about Joe Conforte and his Mustang Ranch. One, who called herself "Cookie," told a *Reno Gazette* reporter, "We girls got pretty close, covered for each other. For many of those girls it was the closest thing to home and family they would ever know."

The girls kept half the take, minus a couple of hundred dollars a month for doctor bills and kickbacks to the staff and cabdrivers who brought customers in from Reno. The house kept the other half. To make sure the girls weren't cheating them, the manager could hear right through the heating vents of the girl's room when the customer made an offer for services to be rendered.

Another prostitute, "Mistee," told the same Reno reporter, "A lot of the girls were head-cases—bad backgrounds, abuse, drinking, welfare. They were cast-off people, throwaway people. For them the life made sense."

Michelle Michaud wasn't quite a cast-off person yet. She was young and pretty with a nice body and above average intelligence. She could have gone to college or business school and earned a respectable living. Instead, she chose "The Life" and in the process became chummy with Joe Conforte and, according to her, was "one of his girls. There were three of us who were his favorites."

Despite the good money and steady stream of customers, Michaud became homesick, and just like James Daveggio, who always gravitated back toward Pleasanton, she opted to move back to Sacramento, California, in the mid-1980s. Still disdaining a workaday life, she hooked in massage parlors, calling herself "Micki." She even hooked in her own home. In fact, she had become so homesick that she moved into a house right across the street from her parents on MacFadden Drive and not far away from her younger sister, Misty Michaud. She was great friends with her mom at this time and called her every day on the phone. Somehow her rebellious youth had been forgotten or at least not discussed. Despite daughter Michelle's unorthodox lifestyle, they often went out shopping together like any other mother and daughter.

The rent for the house was soon paid for by a man in his seventies who was smitten with Michaud. He was an ex-career army man who was now retired. But he got a part-time job just to help keep her in style. He adored Michaud so much that he wanted to marry her. Though she liked him, Michaud often rather harshly referred to him not as an individual but as a "business." There was no doubt in her mind that his main function was to supply her with money. Her main function was to supply him with sex. He not only paid the rent but bought her thousands of dollars' worth of expensive furniture, elegant meals and took her on vacations. But he wasn't the only one. A middle-aged gentleman also became one of her regular sugar daddies. Before long she was living quite comfortably off these two and making extra money hooking on the side.

Along the way she had two children out of wedlock, a boy and girl, by two different men. Her daughter was a dutiful and quiet child who needed little supervision. But the boy was something else again. He was hyperkinetic and had severe emotional problems. He needed constant supervision and help. Before long Michaud's prostitution money was being siphoned off to provide a psychologist for her son.

By her late twenties Michelle Michaud was a strange combination of high-class hooker and caring mother of two. Despite all her rebellious ways, she was quite settled down. Neighbors remembered her as friendly and a good mom. It would be easy to write her off at this point in her life as a slightly interesting and good-looking hooker who masked her nightlife with a middle-class facade. But Michaud was much more complex than that. She had unexpectedly developed a devout spiritual side, which found free outlet at a nearby Catholic church.

Monsignor Edward Kavanagh, a native of Ireland, had moved to America in 1948. A kindly loquacious man, used to dealing with all sorts of people from different cultures and walks of life, he was a great storyteller. He could recount incidents from all fifty years of his service on Franklin Boulevard, and inserted them in his stories when it seemed appropriate. With a diverse congregation of nearly 1,600, he had helped many a troubled young person trying to come to grips with life, turning them toward becoming happy and productive adults. It was with a great deal of hope that he wished Michelle Michaud to become one of these.

Naturally wary of all people, especially sanctimonious ones, Michaud nonetheless came to trust and admire Father Kavanagh. He spent countless sessions with her emotionally disturbed son, always patient, always willing to help, and for this she was immensely grateful. For possibly the first time in her life, Michelle was determined to serve others. She became interested in the Altar Society and helped them in their duties. She even volunteered to become a crossing guard for schoolchildren on busy Franklin Boulevard. One parishoner remembered her standing on the busy street with a red stop sign like the most caring suburban "Soccer Mom." It was if Michaud had rounded some emotional corner in her life and was ready to turn over a new leaf.

Monsignor Kavanagh said of her at this time, "If you talked to her and really got to know her, she struck you as an intelligent and reasonable person."

Michaud was lucky in another respect during this time frame. She had a very nice neighbor named Marie Ward, who loved Michaud's children. "They became almost like my own kids," Ward remembered. "I took care of the boy from the time he was very young. He had his problems with Michelle, but he got along very well with my husband and me. When he and the girl were old enough, I began to take them to church. Then one day Michelle asked if she could go along. We were great friends from that time on."

It was Ward who got Michaud interested in the Altar Society, a group of churchwomen who supervised bake sales, cleaned up the church after various functions, and sent items to the thrift store. Michaud got into it so much, in fact, that she was allowed to be the hostess of an interchurch society luncheon at one of Sacramento's major hotels. Anyone who didn't know her would never guess this well-dressed, well-spoken woman was leading a double life as a prostitute. She carried off the whole luncheon with a great deal of success.

Michaud became so religious that she asked some church members to come and bless her house. She listened to them very seriously when they told her that the statuette her daughter owned of the witch in *The Wizard of Oz* had to go, as well as her son's poster of Darth Vader from *Star Wars*. These were items connected with satanism, they said. Michaud listened to their advice and dutifully complied.

She was even open to other people's religions besides Catholicism. Marie Ward related that when a couple of Mormon missionaries stopped by they were so taken with Michelle Michaud's sincerity that they decided to paint her house for free. She, in return, fed them good meals for the service they rendered.

Michelle Michaud was a good cook. When neighbor Marie Ward became very ill with a kidney problem, Michaud taught Ward's husband how to cook.

"He couldn't even cook oatmeal," Marie Ward laughed. "But Michelle showed him how. Pretty soon she had him cooking all sorts of things."

Michelle Michaud visited Marie Ward every day in the hospital and kept up the visits when she returned home.

"She was very sweet," Ward confided. "Very caring and attentive. I knew about her lifestyle, but even prostitutes have hearts. And Michelle had a very good heart back then. She would come over every morning and have coffee with me. Then she would return in the afternoon, watch her favorite soap opera, *Days of Our Lives,* and we'd chat.

"She even helped care for my mother, who was nearly ninety at the time. She used to go over and comb her hair and rub her legs. My mom had terrible arthritis and Michelle used to rub her legs to ease the pain and get the circulation going.

"Her kids had a nice home. Always clean and tidy. She couldn't stand a mess. She was a good mother to them. Like I said, she didn't try to hide the fact that she'd been a prostitute. But now she was trying to do good.

"I liked Michelle very much. She was a real live wire. I remember one crab feed the church put on. She coaxed Father Paul out onto the dance floor and pretty soon they were dancing like kids. It was so funny to watch."

It did indeed seem for a time in the mid-1980s as if the cynical, tough call girl might find a gentler side to her nature. By this time she was also making large sums of money from hooking and had two regular sugar daddies who were paying her, according to a friend, large sums of money "for services rendered." The older one even went so far as to buy her a green Dodge minivan, which he registered in his name and hers. It was hard to give up this lifestyle, even if it entailed selling her body for loveless gropings in the dark. The emotional balancing act between hooker and altar girl was becoming harder and harder to maintain. She began to frequent neighborhood bars, spending large sums of cash and laying down twenty-dollar tips for the bartender for a single drink. And she spun tales of sex and debauchery to anyone who would listen.

Michaud especially began to frequent a bar called The Rustic on Stockton Boulevard, which was right down the street from Lizzy B's. One bartender at The Rustic named Collette recalled that Michaud mainly drank champagne while she was there. She remembered, "Beer just wasn't good enough for her. It had to be champagne. Once she began drinking, she just wouldn't keep her mouth shut. Some of the things she said were totally outrageous. She liked to throw in a lot of swear words. She particularly ragged on men. How they were pigs and treated women like shit. She made no bones about it that she preferred women over men. And I mean sexually. She even came on to me one time."

Then Collette laughed. "But I turned her down."

Michelle Michaud was a boiling sea of contradictions: she was an intelligent, well-spoken single mother of two, and a guttural, filthy-language whore. By the time she reached thirty-two, the tightrope act between the sacred and profane had reached a point of unbearable strain. It only needed one slight shove to knock her off—and in January 1991 it came, pushing her over the edge into further darkness.

Chapter 18

Bad Day at Maxine's

January 31, 1991, should have been a day just like any other for Michelle Michaud as she turned tricks at Maxine's Studio in Sacramento. This establishment billed itself as a "relaxation business," but there was a lot more than just relaxation going on behind its closed doors. The Sacramento Police Department was pretty sure that prostitution was taking place in the establishment and on that particular day they sent in one of their undercover vice officers to find out.

At exactly 1:26 P.M. a vice officer entered Maxine's and was met by a pretty red-haired hostess, Michelle Michaud. Unaware of his real intent, she informed him that he could have forty minutes of massage for thirty dollars. The undercover officer answered that the price seemed fair and gave her forty dollars as payment. She escorted him to a room with a bed on the floor and told him to make himself comfortable and she would be right back with his change.

The officer proceeded to undress completely and was sitting on the bed when Michaud returned, giving him the ten dollars she owed him. With a smooth-talking routine he now went into his act. "My neck feels pretty stiff," he told her, and she told him to lie down on the bed as she began to rub his neck, back and buttocks. While she massaged him, he said, "A friend of mine has been here and one of the girls treated him very nice, gave him a massage and took care of him."

"What do you mean by 'took care of him'?" Michaud asked, her natural wariness now alerted.

"Oh, you know. He got laid." And then the officer quickly added, "I just won a football pool for two hundred fifty dollars. My wife doesn't know about it and I want to spend it before she finds out."

Perhaps it was this lure of easy money that now caused Michaud to disregard her normally suspicious nature. There was something not quite right about this guy. But she shook it off and instructed him to roll over on his back as she began to run her hands lightly over his chest and legs while she pulled her black skirt up. She wasn't wearing any panties underneath.

The undercover cop reached over and pulled up her T-shirt, revealing her bare breasts. He said something to the effect of, "You have nice tits. I want you." He began to fondle her breasts and kiss them; according to Michaud, he made more vulgar comments.

In one last clever ploy to mask a direct solicitation of money for sex, Michaud gazed up at a fan on the wall and asked, "How much would you pay for a fan like that?"

He answered, "Eighty dollars."

"That's a price we can 'dicker with,' " she said.

The officer laughed. "Nice play on words. That's exactly what I want to do with you. I'll give you eighty dollars and a nice tip if everything is good."

"All right," Michaud agreed, and her last chance at escape slipped away. She reached over to her purse on a nearby nightstand and pulled a condom out. He then got off the bed and took eighty dollars from his wallet, saying, "I'll give you the extra ten you gave me if everything turns out all right." He started to hand the bills to Michaud, but she said, "Put it on the nightstand," perhaps thinking that if he didn't directly hand it to her, no prostitution could be charged.

She was wrong. As soon as she started to place the condom on his penis, he said, "I'm a police officer. You're under arrest."

Michaud was inwardly furious. How could she have been so stupid? She'd felt something was wrong with this guy from the very beginning. But she said with as much composure as she could muster, "Okay. I'll cooperate and won't cause any problems."

He then looked in her purse and asked if thirty of the thirty-one dollars inside was from their first encounter at the door.

"Yes," she answered.

Michaud was taken down to police headquarters and booked into the jail for less than twenty-four hours. The charges against her—647 (b), solicitation for prostitution—was only a misdemeanor. Her mug shot photo was in stark contrast to the happy teenager who beamed at the camera for her high school yearbook. Instead, it shows a Sacramento County placard propped up in front of her with the date 01/31/91 and the name "Michaud, Michelle" penned in. Her face is a mask of barely controlled hostility. One can catch signs of anger, frustration and outrage beneath her tightly clamped jaws. It's the look of someone who intends to get even with her tormentors by any means possible.

If the city of Sacramento thought Michelle Michaud would take her arrest lying down, they were sadly mistaken. They didn't know how fired up she could become when she felt she'd been wronged. And in her own estimation of this incident, she felt badly abused by the undercover cop. Michaud was a fighter at heart, and despite advice from her attorney, Bradley Wishek, to accept the misdemeanor charges, she fired him and took her case to trial.

On August 19, 1991, Michaud got her chance to argue her case before a jury in Judge Tani Cantil's courtroom. The jury consisted of a legal secretary, elementary school teacher, real-estate broker and custodian. Some of them were quite willing to believe the story the now prim and proper Michelle Michaud presented of police entrapment. Not only had the undercover officer been crude, but in her own words, she said, "He was vulgar, acted way out of line and exceeded the professional boundaries of a police officer." She was particularly upset that he had fondled her breasts, and according to her, had placed his fingers in her vagina, all while perpetrating the elaborate ruse.

Some of the jurors tended to agree that the sting operation smacked of entrapment, and as they deliberated, they asked to review comments the police officer had made. But in the end the assistant DA's photo of the opened condom wrapper and the judge's directions that "a police officer can provide opportunity for the commission of a crime, including reasonable, though restrained, steps to gain the confidence of suspects," proved to be vital.

They found Michelle Michaud guilty of prostitution.

She was forced to take an AIDS test, pay a $120 fine, be on probation for three years, and told not to frequent known prostitution areas, such as lower Stockton Boulevard near her home. She complied with all of these, not raising a fuss, just as she had promised.

Terrible things were now bubbling to the surface in her mind. She felt used beyond endurance by society as a whole, and other people were going to be paid back in kind. Michaud was at an invisible crossroads where the delicate juggling act of high-class call girl and pious churchgoer could no longer be performed. She now hated men and used them as they used her. She even said to a friend, "I like to beat up on men. Literally. Wait until they're drunk and then kick their ass. Dare them to get back up."

Within this mixture of heat and anger a curious incident occurred between Michelle Michaud's arrest in January 1991 and her trial in August of that same year. It happened in Lake Tahoe, a place that both she and James Daveggio knew well. Its ramifications would echo down the years and haunt them both in the waning days of 1997.

Chapter 19

Vanished

On the morning of June 10, 1991, pretty, blond-haired, blue-eyed Jaycee Lee Dugard of South Lake Tahoe got ready for school. The eleven-year-old girl gathered up her books and lunch and was glad that spring had finally arrived at her home of 6,200-feet elevation. Except for a scattering of snow on surrounding peaks, winter was over—a vast relief in this region where "winter" can be seven or eight months long. She lived in a typical neighborhood of modest homes on Washoan Boulevard. Almost every driveway held a Subaru station wagon, Toyota 4x4 pickup or some other form of four-wheel drive vehicle, ready to take on the long snowy season and icy roads. And the yards were filled with children's bikes and toys, attesting to the fact that this was a young family neighborhood. On cool mornings like May 10, the pungent smell of woodsmoke from fireplaces drifted through the neighborhood, giving it a pleasant woodsy smell.

Dugard tied her long blond hair into a ponytail, put on a white T-shirt, pink stretch pants and pink windbreaker before she left the house. Then she said good-bye to her stepfather, William Probyn, who was working in the front yard. She walked down Washoan Boulevard toward her school bus stop on the Pioneer Trail, a route once used by the Pony Express riders. The morning was cool under the dark shadows of the tall Ponderosa pines and Jaycee Lee hurried her steps to ward off the cold.

It was 7:50 A.M.

Probyn puttered around in the front yard, his mind still not quite fully in gear, when he suddenly heard a squeal of brakes and a loud scream down the street. Looking in the direction of the commotion, he stared in stunned disbelief as a two-toned 1970s or early '80s American sedan flipped a U-turn right in front of his stepdaughter. The vehicle screeched to a halt as Jaycee Lee stood frozen in shock. In the next instant a woman with long dark hair leaped from the car and swept Jaycee Lee into the vehicle, the girl screaming in terror. Before Probyn could even react, there was a screech of tires and the car was off, roaring down the street in the opposite direction with his stepdaughter inside.

In one terrible moment eleven-year-old Jaycee Lee Dugard vanished right in front of her stepfather's eyes, on one of Lake Tahoe's supposedly "safe streets."

It took only a moment for the shock and disbelief to wear off before Probyn ran to a nearby bicycle, hopped on, and began pedaling furiously down the street toward the departing car. His legs pumped in fevered haste and it felt as if his lungs would burst as he skidded around the corner onto the Pioneer Trail, searching everywhere for the vehicle. But it was already too late. The car and his stepdaughter inside were already gone. Worst of all, he had never caught a glimpse of the driver or the license plate. As far as he knew, the car could have been carrying California, Nevada or some other state plates.

He knew that further pursuit of the car would be fruitless and he pedaled back to his home and called the El Dorado County Sheriff's Department.

At forty-seven years old Sergeant Detective Jim Watson of the El Dorado County Sheriff's Department looked every bit the outdoor Tahoe type. With sandy brown hair and windburned complexion, he had deep lines around his eyes from so much time spent out in the Sierra sun and wind. He was soft-spoken and serious, in the Gary Cooper mold, and his staff and superiors admired him greatly.

Detective Watson was just taking his wife to Meyers Elementary School when he learned about the Jaycee Lee Dugard kidnapping over his radio. Rushing back to his office, he became the coordinator for the entire operation, and he put everyone available on the case. The situation demanded urgency.

Almost immediately an all points bulletin (APB) was issued for a four-door American sedan carrying a dark-haired woman and a blond-haired girl wearing pink clothing. Detective Watson knew that they'd been lucky when the girl's stepfather spotted the car and abductor. In most stranger abductions this was not the case. They were lucky in another instance too: the Tahoe Basin had very few blacktop roads that led elsewhere. All of them funneled down to a few easily patrolled bottlenecks that the police knew very well. In a very short time the El Dorado Sheriff's Department was joined by the South Lake Tahoe Police Department, Douglas County Sheriffs Department, California and Nevada Highway Patrols, Forestry Service rangers and even CalTrans roadworkers. Within the hour local radio stations KRLT-FM and KTHO-AM were broadcasting descriptions of the car, Jaycee Lee Dugard and the woman abductor. It seemed like it would be only a matter of hours before some officer or local citizen would spot the vehicle.

But all of this didn't take into account one critical factor, the maze of back roads and dirt trails, hardly more than tracks, that snaked in all directions from the Pioneer Trail back into the wilderness. Branching through thick forest and rocky terrain, they wound everywhere with no seeming purpose or direction. Many had been logging roads, others were the work of off-road enthusiasts, and it would have taken an army on foot to scour every square inch of this region. Despite the big call out, the authorities at work on the case were more of a scouting expedition than a full-sized army at this point.

One officer who well knew the ruggedness and complexity of the dirt roads was Deputy Randy Peshon of the El Dorado Sheriff's Office. He had once been a backcountry ranger in the wilds of Canyon Lands National Park, and he knew just how "lost" someone could get if they wanted. When he got the call about the Dugard abduction, he was working the west side of Lake Tahoe in Tahoma, where he was the only resident officer. Quickly jumping into action, he began scouring the "Wild West Side," driving down its twisting hidden lanes, going door to door, canvassing the area, doing vehicle searches and looking for witnesses. He went forty-eight hours straight without sleep, doing every thing humanly possible to find the little girl, until the intensity of the experience burned itself into his very soul. He was eating, breathing, living the Jaycee Lee Dugard case. This kidnapping had happened in his backyard, and he took it personally. As he said later, "No cop likes it when something bad happens on their watch. Especially if the bad guys get away. One thing was for certain from that day on, I would never give up trying to find out what happened to Jaycee Lee."

Detective Jim Watson had this dedicated officer and a dozen others like him on his team. And even though the hours were ticking away, he still felt confident as the afternoon of May 10 wore on. A special kidnap hotline number was set up and calls were coming in at the rate of one every five minutes about possible sightings of the girl and car. It seemed as if all of Tahoe was awake and searching for one of its own this day, alerted by word of mouth as much as anything else on the invisible mountain grapevine. Dozens of late '70s and early '80s two-toned American sedans were spotted by investigators all over the Tahoe Basin and checked out. A particularly exciting lead popped up at 3:30 P.M. A man and woman were seen driving a sedan on a remote road in the Fallen Leaf Lake area, about five miles northwest of Dugard's home, with a girl wearing pink clothes in the backseat. This was a region of log cabins set so far back in the woods that they could hardly be seen from the dirt road, a perfect site for kidnappers to hide out while things cooled down.

The police and sheriff's department officers descended on the area in a wave, scouring the woods and cabins for any clue. They spread out through the trees and wild tangle of boulders, searching through the maze of cabins and shacks. Every parked car was checked out, every possible hiding place among the shrubs and tiny crawl spaces too. But in the end the car and the girl were just as elusive as ever.

The calls kept flooding in, coming from farther and farther away. The car had supposedly been seen in Placerville, sixty miles to the west. The girl had possibly been seen in Carson City forty miles to the east. A combination of both had been spotted in Sacramento, in Reno and in San Francisco. Someone was sure they'd spotted Jaycee Lee four hundred miles to the south in Los Angeles. Calls came from as far away as Minneapolis, Minnesota. Nothing was too outrageous or too fantastic to be discounted.

The FBI was now involved too, and Albert Robinson, special agent in charge, asked people to think back one or two weeks and try to remember any suspicious people who might have been hanging around school yards or their homes. He explained in the *Tahoe Daily Tribune,* "Even though it may seem trivial, what may seem trivial (to you) may fit into our puzzle."

Hikers, cyclists, mountain bikers, and just plain sightseers were asked to keep on the lookout for the girl or the car. Once again a particularly promising lead surfaced on May 12. A car matching the description of the vehicle was found parked on Pine Avenue near the Stateline casinos with a pair of pink sweatpants inside. But further investigation proved that the pants could not have possibly been worn by Jaycee Lee. Later that same evening, police in Vacaville, California, a city 120 miles away to the west, sprang into action as they ran down a sighting of the missing girl. But in the end it proved to be just as ephemeral as all the rest.

Slowly but surely, Detective Watson knew that the good luck of William Probyn's sighting of the abduction was slipping away. Every hour past the first twenty-four decreased the odds of ever seeing the young girl alive again. He was not giving up hope, not by a long shot, and he was still the dynamo at the heart of this massive manhunt. But Sergeant Detective Watson was also a realist. He could plainly see the clock on the wall ticking away.

So could Jaycee Lee's mom, Terry. She bounced erratically between sheer panic, terrible anger, tears and despair as the hours became days. Although surrounded by friends, neighbors and family, there was now an invisible barrier between all of them and herself. No one else could plumb the depths into which she had been cast. The only one who could even vaguely glimpse that gulf of despair arrived on the afternoon of the twelfth. She was Trish Williams from San Jose, a director of Child Quest International, a missing children's hot line center.

In her own quiet way, Trish Williams talked with the distraught mother, getting to know her and calming her down. She decided the best way to do that was to keep Terry busy. "We wanted to get her out of the house and doing something. Something positive."

In that regard they soon found a useful outlet. Thousands of posters bearing Jaycee Lee's likeness, a police sketch of the two-toned car and composite of the woman William Probyn had seen, were being printed and distributed. The depiction of the female abductor revealed a woman in her thirties, front and profile, with shoulder-length dark hair, parted in the middle. Her face was thin with arching dramatic eyebrows, and she had dark eyes. The nose was long and slightly ridged in the center. The expression she wore was one of deadly seriousness.

These posters kept Trish Williams and Jaycee Lee's mom busy at St. Teresa's Catholic Church in South Lake Tahoe as a flood of volunteers came by to distribute them. The posters popped up on walls of mini-marts, cafes, liquor stores and motels all over the Basin until it seemed a person couldn't go anywhere without seeing a depiction of the smiling eleven-year-old girl or the dour dark-haired woman. These posters even spread over the mountains to

Carson City and Reno, Nevada, in the east, and Placerville, Auburn, and Sacramento in the west. Within weeks Jaycee Lee Dugard's face was seen in almost every state of the Union.

Some local had the bright idea of placing pink ribbons around Tahoe as a reminder of the girl, not that anyone was likely at this juncture to forget her. Pink had always been Jaycee Lee's favorite color, and in a duplication of the yellow ribbons that had sprouted on light poles around the United States to remember the American Embassy hostages in Tehran in the late 1970s, pink ribbons began to spring up all over Lake Tahoe like a profusion of alpine wildflowers. Slowly blowing in the breeze, they evoked a sense of caring and commitment that this community would never forget its lost daughter. For in a strange way, Jaycee Lee Dugard had become a daughter to them all now.

But spring turned to summer, and summer faded into fall. With it so did the ribbons. And so did hope.

Chapter 20

Fire and Gasoline

By 1996 Michelle Michaud's attention was riveted on James Daveggio and their strange relationship at Bobby Joe's.

With Daveggio ensconced behind the bar, Michaud would relate tales of sexual contortions and lewd encounters with sex toys of all shapes and sizes. She not only delved into the descriptions of them, but also where they were used and when. She had seen it all and done it all; she had been with truck drivers, businessmen, car dealers, ranchers, and—as she liked to point out—even cops.

According to Jean Sidener, "Michelle never kept a black book of her johns; instead, she knew all their names and their secret desires by heart." And she wasn't above relating to the patrons at Bobby Joe's about her johns' sexual prowess or lack thereof. Sidener remembered Michaud telling of the different men's "endowments" she was familiar with, much to the amusement of the gathered clientele.

While Michaud held forth at the bar, Daveggio stood by, hardly uttering a word. "Frog was shy about such things," Sidener said, and Anna agreed.

"Froggie was uncomfortable talking about sex. He never spoke about his own love life, even though he always had plenty of girls and women. He would be embarrassed even if some woman paid him a compliment."

Daveggio must have been terribly conflicted about Michaud. Certainly, he had never met anyone like her before, even though he'd been married three times, had numerous girlfriends and even a few "conquests," who just happened to have been raped, though he didn't quite see it that way. But Michaud was something else again—a woman with a vast array of lusts and sexual desires just as twisted and depraved as his own. Where he kept all of his yearnings bottled up inside, she announced hers to perfect strangers. She was both fascinating and repellent, a little Catholic altar girl/whore. Daveggio was innately cautious around such strong women; bit by bit, Michaud wore him down by her sheer force of will.

Why she wanted him remains even more of a mystery. With her good looks and charm she had already gained two sugar daddies who supported her high-living lifestyle. The one who had bought her a green Dodge minivan even lived with her now and paid rent for a room in the house that he was renting for her. All he expected in return was a sexual favor once in a while.

She could have easily enticed some of the most respectable and wealthy businessmen around town if she'd put her mind to it. Michelle Michaud did have flair and knew how to cater to men's egos as well as desires. She could act the part of salacious slut or innocent schoolgirl. But for some reason she wanted Daveggio, this multi-divorced, convicted rapist, for her own. Perhaps it was the dangerous man who lurked behind that shy charm that lured her

on. For she had already perceived that he was a
dangerous man underneath all that quiet polite-
ness. Michaud had a way of sizing people up very
quickly. Days and nights in the bedroom had seen
to that. It might have been just a very complex
game with rules of her own devising that enticed
her to Daveggio, somehow attuned to his own unorthodox desires that so closely matched her own.
For whatever reason she chose him; the combination of the two of them was like gasoline and fire.
Separately, they were dangerous. Together they
were lethal.

Daveggio and Michaud began spending more
and more time together, feeding off their mutual
unseemly lusts. So many of the things she had done,
and still wanted to do, he had only longingly
dreamed about. What thin veneer of civility he still
possessed for respectable society was torn away by
her unbridled carnality. It wasn't long before Daveggio got his wish for a threesome—two women, one
of them being Michelle, and the other a prostitute
friend of hers. That was just fine with her. She now
preferred sex with another woman rather than with
men. Michaud had been bisexual for a long time,
but the lesbian side of her nature was coming more
and more to the fore in 1996.

One smoky night drifted into another beside the
long bar at Bobby Joe's, with the soft click of billiard
balls in the background and country-western music
playing on the jukebox. Somehow welded together
by an innocuous, interchangeable third woman for
their sex games, James and Michelle became an
item. They became Frog and Micki to the regular
clientele of Bobby Joe's.

Soon after the inclusion of the first prostitute in
their sexual games, they were picking up other
women at the bar for their "sessions." Frog always

made sure that a few drinks were poured down the hatch of the ladies involved, helping ease things along. More often than not, Micki would do the picking. She had an eye for such things and was very attuned to people's psyches. Whenever some young woman was ambivalent, naive or had tendencies that way, Michaud was sure and confident in her approach. It was no rare sight to see Frog and Micki "working on" some woman at the bar, convincing her that the thing she had always desired most was a sexual encounter with a man and a woman at the same time.

Afterward Daveggio would rarely talk about it; Michaud, on the other hand, would go into the most graphic detail about everything. It both excited her and gave her pleasure to see the incredulity and amazement of other tavern patrons as she recounted her exploits. The more uncomfortable the listeners became, the more turned-on she would become. She was recounting the one great lesson she'd learned in life: at rock-bottom level, everyone had secret desires that they dare not even look at for fear of what they might find. She looked long and deep, and forced Daveggio to look there too.

It was about this time that Daveggio's relationship with Lizzy Bingenheimer fizzled. The threesomes with Michaud had struck such a nerve that he could rarely become erect anymore without the presence of a second woman to spice things up. He really enjoyed it when some half-drunk woman at Bobby Joe's could be coaxed into bed. He was much less happy when Michaud picked out some fellow prostitute for their playmate.

"Frog would get really mad at times when Michelle picked out a call girl for him," Janet Williams related. "He liked to be in control of the situation. But Michelle usually called the shots in everything. She had enough moxie for two people."

In early December 1996 Frog moved in with Michelle, and her sugar daddy moved out. Daveggio brought with him the chaos that had reigned on Vista Avenue. Much to the consternation of the neighbors on MacFadden Drive, the street was soon filled with roaring motorcycles and partying bikers. Moses Baldizan, a man who lived a few houses down the street, took up the complaints where Wray Tibbs of Vista Avenue had left off.

"Things started to go downhill when that guy [Daveggio] moved in. Before, it had been pretty quiet here. But now, late-night parties, drunken brawls, motorcycles everywhere. What a mess."

The Devil's Horsemen arrived on the scene with roars of engines, poppin' wheelies, drunken shouts and laughter that cascaded down the suburban street like a wall of noise. The siege mentality that had bedeviled Vista Avenue was now in force on MacFadden Drive. The Horsemen's advent brought booze, loud motorcycles and one more key thing that stripped the last vestiges of sanity from Michaud's mind.

Methamphetamines.

"Michelle was a tweaker [one who uses meth] from that time on," Jean Sidener said. "God, she lost a lot of weight and her cheeks became sunken and everything. She used to be pretty good-looking, but it started fading fast when she started doing crank."

What at first was only an adjunct to booze soon became a mainstay of her existence. Meth clouded everything she did. Michaud, who had always been interested in the supernatural, now began to believe in it more and more as her grip on reality loosened. Lost in a haze of alcohol and meth, she began to consort with a prostitute friend whose street name was "Fawn." Fawn was heavy into spells, witchcraft and black magic. She studied books on the subject and used spells of her own devising to try and alter the world around her. Michaud soaked up the lessons from Fawn the way she was now doing with crank. It seeped into everything she did until the nerve-racking roar of motorcycles and inebriated bikers in the background were placed on another plane of consciousness than the one she inhabited. Not very keen on bikes in the first place, she rarely went for a ride with Frog on his purple Harley anymore. Instead, she did drugs, performed sex for money when she had to, and slipped into a dreamworld that echoed like sounds beneath the waves of an inland sea.

Just like Fawn, Michaud began to concoct potions and devise enchantments of her own design. She lit candles and went into trances to try and reach some spiritual plane beyond the norm. In one of her most bizarre dabblings with witchcraft, she one day found a dead frog on a neighbor's porch. Certain that it concerned Froggie Daveggio, she placed a rosary around the dead frog along with a candle and strands of Daveggio's hair. Long gone were the days when she had thrown away her daughter's statuette of the witch in *The Wizard of Oz*. If anything, she now identified with that witch. There no longer seemed to be a blessing on the house, bestowed by loving members of her church. In fact, she had all but stopped going. Whenever her old friend and neighbor Marie Ward tried to phone her now, she said she couldn't talk. Whether Daveggio was influencing this, Ward couldn't say. But she knew something was wrong with Michelle. "All the brightness seemed to be gone from her life," she said. "And I blame it on that man."

Michelle Michaud became ill through much of early 1997, a victim of her own excesses. She was now thirty-nine years old, having endured twenty years of booze, sexual extravagances and meth. She might have been able to handle the booze, but methamphetamines were another story. Just what she was up against was graphically described by Dr. Alex Stalcup of Contra Costa County's New Leaf Treatment Center. Contra Costa County has the most prevalent meth problem in California, and Stalcup knew what he was talking about. He told a *San Francisco Chronicle* reporter, "The meth on the street now is between four to six times more potent than the speed in San Francisco in the '60s or the Methedrine injected in the '70s. This new drug, when it interacts with the brain chemistry, permanently injures it. Some will develop true psychosis, with the dominant theme being wild paranoia."

He noted that the key ingredient in the meth of the '90s is ephedrine, an over-the-counter cold remedy that is mixed with substances such as hydrochloric acid, Drano and strychnine. He also related that meth has become pervasive in the suburbs where many of the local doctors are not equipped to deal with it. Known on the street by various names—crank, speed, ice or meth—the drug comes in an array of colors, but a yellowish crystal or rocklike chunk is the norm. It can be smoked, snorted, injected or taken orally by the user. Increasingly in the hectic '90s, it became the drug of choice for women. One of the reasons was its appetite-suppressing capability. More than one woman trying to keep a slim figure became addicted to meth. Another factor was its ability to allow the user to stay awake and alert for long periods of time. With the use of meth, even the most tedious and repetitive of tasks can seem easy and enjoyable.

But the downside to the users can be extreme, sending them into a deep depression or bouts of paranoia. They carry a dread that even friends and family members are out to get them. Sometimes they become quite violent due to their psychotic behavior. Dr. Stalcup has had more than one meth user attack him in the course of trying to cure the addict.

Meth operates deep in the brain where natural biochemicals known as neurotransmitters shuttle between gaps in the neurons. The neurotransmitter most associated with pleasure and well-being is dopamine. Too little can result in depression; too much can propel the individual into a manic state. Meth keeps dopamine in the brain in continuous circulation. Once addicted to meth, the user must take larger and larger doses to reach and sustain the highs.

Life Education International backed up Dr. Stalcup's findings with a report of their own on the short-term and long-term effects of methamphetamines. Short-term effects included loss of appetite, agitation, insomnia, paranoia, hallucinations, aggressive behavior and convulsions. Long-term effects included weight loss, severe depression, lowered resistance to illnesses, liver damage and possible brain damage. Michelle Michaud had faced many tough obstacles in her life and beaten the odds. But she wasn't going to be able to beat meth.

As her looks began to go, the big money from prostitution was quickly ebbing away. One of her sugar daddies quit contacting her and Daveggio had all but driven the other one out of her life. By now Daveggio was totally hooked on threesomes. Michaud both loved and hated him at this point. On more than one occasion she would stride out of Bobby Joe's, mad as hell, and then return hours later as if nothing had happened.

"Micki used to burst out of here a lot by the summer of '97," Janet Williams related. "She'd just get pissed off by something Frog did or said. She'd take off in the van and drive around for hours. Not really going anywhere. Then she'd come back sweet as pie."

Even with her iron will slowly breaking down beneath these assaults, it was still Michaud who got things done. Williams related, "If there was food to buy, or a woman for their threesome, or drugs to be purchased, it was Michelle who got it done. Sometimes she was so blitzed she could hardly stand up straight. But Michelle wasn't your normal person in any respect. At times she looked about as possessed as the witch she pretended to be."

Into this volatile, anarchic madness James Daveggio added one more lethal element in the summer of 1997—his growing interest in rapist/serial killers. He was fascinated by all of them: Ted Bundy, Charles Manson, John Wayne Gacy, Jeffrey Dahmer. But one pair of killers in particular grabbed his attention, the man-and-woman team of Gerald and Charlene Gallego. They, too, had owned a van, which they used to kidnap young girls. Who better for him and Michelle to emulate?

Chapter 21

The Devil's Apprentice

By chance, Gerald Armand Gallego happened to have been another Sacramentan. In the summer of 1979, right about the time Michael Ihde was raping his first victim, and Daveggio was getting married to Annette, Gallego became determined to live out his deadly sexual fantasies. In the pursuit of these sick perversions, he had an unlikely accomplice, his girlfriend, soon to become his wife, Charlene Williams.

Charlene was a petite blonde who was twenty years old at the time and looked about fifteen. She was cute, bright and madly in love with Gallego. So in love, in fact, that she was willing to do anything for him, even if it meant luring young girls to be his "love slaves."

James Daveggio knew all about the Gallegos and the way they picked up girls for Gerald's sexual torment and rape. Their depredations in Reno, Nevada, particularly caught his eye. They occurred on June 24, 1979. Gerald and Charlene Gallego had gone to the Washoe County Fairgrounds in that city and cruised the carnival area, checking out the young girls in their tight jeans and slinky tops. Then

Charlene went into her "work mode." She moved among the crowd while Gerald went back to his van and waited. Charlene had a knack of mixing with teenage girls, hardly looking more than a teenager herself. She soon convinced fourteen-year-old Brenda Judd and thirteen-year-old Sandra Colley that they could help her pass out flyers around the fairgrounds for money. She had the flyers right back at her van, she said.

Totally unaware of what awaited them, the girls all too willingly followed her, only to experience the same fate as Kippi Vaught and Rhonda Scheffler before them. This time, faced with a loaded .44 in Gerald Gallego's hand, they didn't even emit a sound as they were forced into the van. Once it was rolling eastbound on I-80 past the Mustang Ranch, the lure of that place must have aroused Gallego's "urges." He had the young girls strip off all their clothing, and as Charlene drove toward Lovelock, he didn't even bother waiting for an isolated location. He raped them repeatedly as they drove down the interstate.

After he was through with them that evening, Gallego had Charlene drive to an isolated spot in the desert. With the cold moon shining down, he dispatched each girl with a shovel blow to the head. Then with that same shovel he dug their graves and buried them in the wasteland. James Daveggio wasn't sickened by Gerald Gallego's exploits. In fact, they excited him. The thought of snatching young girls off the street was intoxicating. If Gerald Gallego could convince Charlene to help him in these matters, why couldn't he convince Michelle Michaud to do the same?

* * *

By the end of summer 1997, Michaud could no longer make big money at hooking because of her drug abuse and deteriorating looks. She was rail-thin from meth use and her cheeks had a gaunt starved look about them. As her main sugar daddy was no longer paying her rent, she applied for (ADC) Aide for Dependent Children and began to receive $538 a month from welfare. But it wasn't nearly enough. Desperate for money, she and Daveggio pulled her expensive furniture out onto the front lawn and sold it for dimes on the dollar. Still it wasn't enough.

Marie Ward remembered that yard sale. "It was pathetic to see all her nice furniture pulled out on the lawn and sold for a fraction of what it was worth. When somebody came up and paid her, she immediately gave the money to that guy James. I don't know what kind of hold he had on her. It must have been the drugs. She had totally changed from the woman I used to know. He absolutely ruined her life."

Nothing they did seemed to work. They were evicted on August 4 when Michaud could no longer make the rent payments. In disgust, Daveggio moved back in with Lizzy Bingenheimer, along with his two daughters; Michaud took to sleeping in her van or over at her sister Misty's house, along with her children. The move was a mere inconvenience for Daveggio, but it was devastating to Michelle. Her whole world had been wrapped up in that house so close to her parents and sister.

It brought back echoes of Amy Goldman's work about serial killers *The Time Before the Crime*. Therein she wrote: "A pre-crime stressor is an event that happens right before the serial killer begins killing. Often this is a loss of a job, a financial issue, or about to lose his place to live. The offender may not even realize he is actually reacting to events. . . . The offender may not ever realize the full extent of his motivations or fail to see the issues behind the stress. . . . whether his disposition is an already aggressive one or his reaction to what you and I might consider 'a run of bad luck,' is violent. This person cannot deal with it. He, at this point, becomes a killer."

In desperation for more money, Daveggio, never one to adhere to loyalty, turned on his motorcycle brothers. On a "poker run" the gang had collected $1,500 and put the proceeds into their safe. Daveggio knew the combination. Sneaking into the office, he took all the money for himself.

It didn't take a rocket scientist to figure out how Frog, who had been nearly broke only days before, was now spending cash like it was going out of style. Vowing a good "ass-kicking" on their former motorcycle brother, the Horsemen took off after him. It fell to Daveggio's loyal patrons Ted and Janet Williams to save his skin. They hid him from the bikers as they searched for their former "brother" in vain. Realizing that he might have quit the area for good, the Horsemen simply took his beloved purple Harley and called things even. Only then did Daveggio come out of hiding—minus one motorcycle, but with his head still intact.

Daveggio thanked his benefactors, the Williamses, in typical fashion. By stealing from them. Totally engrossed in his fantasies to become another Gerald Gallego, he stole some industrial-strength rope from Ted Williams's garage. It was so strong, in fact, that it could withstand immense pressure beyond the flexibility of normal rope—especially if used on some trussed-up victim.

According to Janet Williams, he also stole Ted's "come along," a mechanical device with a handle that could pull rope tauter than any man could by arm strength. These would come in handy someday if he decided to construct a rack for torturing victims, just like a medieval torture rack.

Daveggio's stay with Bingenheimer only lasted a couple of weeks. He missed Michelle Michaud and he especially missed the threesomes she would arrange. According to Michaud, "In early September, he and Liz split up, and I got a page to come over there. His daughters and himself put all their things in the van."

At this point Daveggio wanted to visit his mom. She was now living in Manteca, a town about forty miles east of Pleasanton. According to one relative, there was a family get-together that day and James Daveggio and Michelle Michaud arrived all cranked up and extremely agitated. As the other people sat around and talked, Daveggio and Michaud couldn't sit still for anything. It was obvious to even the most casual observer that they were high on something. Daveggio in particular rambled on and on about some dark and mysterious thing he had done. The relative thought it had to do with either his rape conviction back in the 1980s or something with a motorcycle gang. He had no way of knowing at the time that it might be an event that he was planning. As Daveggio rambled and strode around the house, he showed his pistols off, even in front of the children. There was just no calming him down and it was a relief when he went outside and did something to the interior of the van.

Daveggio and Michaud soon dumped the daughters off at ex-wife Annette's house and discussed where they might go next. Now living in the van or with friends, they found their possibilities were endless. But first there was one more ignominy to visit on the Williamses, their kind friends and benefactors. According to Janet, while she and husband Ted were out of town, it was to their house that Michelle Michaud drove thirteen-year-old victim Nancy Baker for the drug use and molestation. It was in the Williamses bathroom that Baker later testified Michaud made her disrobe at gunpoint and attempted to make the girl fondle her breasts. When the girl demurred, she dragged the naked girl in front of Daveggio, and they soon cornered her in the bedroom for Daveggio to rape while Michaud pleasured herself. It was also here that Michaud produced the pistol after they were done with the girl and told her, "If you tell, I'll personally kill you!"

Michelle Michaud at one time had dreamed of taking care of other people's children as a nanny, and had even enrolled at the California Nanny College in Sacramento. But after her arrest for prostitution, those plans had fallen through. Now instead of caring for people's children, she had dreams of molesting them. She was going to make others pay for having lost the last anchor of her stability in life—her home. Unlike Charlene Gallego, who had only wanted to please her man by supplying young girls for his depraved pleasure, and balked at joining in, Michelle Michaud was determined to be part of the action.

Despite all her financial troubles, there was one thing that Michaud never even considered selling—her minivan. By some similar dementia, Michaud's plans to strike back at the world that had treated her so roughly dovetailed with Daveggio's desire to live out his wild sexual fantasies. The outcome was to turn the harmless Dodge minivan into a mobile torture/murder chamber.

All the anger, all the fantasies, all the hatred,

were coming out now. With so many possibilities
and destinations to choose from, they faced the van
northeast and headed toward Reno, Nevada, home
to two of Gerald Gallego's victims. Daveggio was
eager and determined to follow in the footsteps of
his "patron saint" of murderous depravity. Reno
seemed like a good place to start.

Chapter 22

The Torture Chamber

James Daveggio was a volatile volcano of emotions when he and Michelle Michaud reached Reno, Nevada, on September 25, 1997. Being habitual gamblers, he and Michaud booked themselves into the Circus Circus Hotel and Casino using a credit card she had cajoled out of one of her sugar daddies. While Daveggio hit the slot machines and black jack tables day and night, Michelle holed up in the room with her meth, charging room service and pay-per-view movies. Even though she and Daveggio were not intimate at this juncture—he was sleeping in the bedroom and she on the living room couch—they constantly paged each other. They devised a code: 143 meant "I love you"; 401 meant "I'm sending love"; 422 meant "Undying love"; 42 meant "Forever." Their relationship had always been strange. But now it was downright surreal.

On the second day of their stay at the Circus Circus, one of Michaud's sugar daddies arrived for "an intimate moment," as she delicately put it, while Daveggio stepped out of the room to gamble.

After they had finished having sex, they went to dinner. Michaud convinced him that the van needed repairs and that's why she still needed to keep his credit card. He bought her pack of lies and let her keep the credit card.

Only when he was gone did Michaud page Daveggio to come back to the room. He spent some time watching movies with her, but his mind was really on gambling. He was able to maintain his almost nonstop gambling frenzy because he was cranked up on methamphetamines. In fact, they both were high as kites during their entire Reno stay. Michaud would admit later of this period, "We used meth like other people drink water."

Luck was not with Daveggio. The cash advances he had garnered from the credit card were quickly ebbing away on the green felt tables. Daveggio and Michaud took the expedient of buying jewelry with the credit card just to pawn it at a shop across the street. And still it wasn't enough. Michaud went down Virginia Street to the Cal Neva Club where her old friend and massage parlor owner from years before, Charlie S., was now tending bar. She talked about old times, had a drink and hit him up for fifty bucks. She even told him a strange story about a time in Sacramento when she had supposedly killed a man who had tried to strangle her while he had sex with her. She said, "I cut him and enjoyed it."

Like many others now, Charlie couldn't tell for sure when Michaud was telling the truth or when she was lying. Her world had become so warped that her grasp of reality became blurred.

When she returned to the Circus Circus, Daveggio took the fifty from her and lost it in no time. Michaud then called her mom in Sacramento for money and seventy-five dollars was wired to her via Western Union. This did not last long either. Finally, in desperation to earn more money for the tables, Michaud hooked on the street. She picked up a middle-aged Asian man and they went back to her room where he paid her money for sex. But she could no longer make the big money by prostitution. He only paid her fifty dollars. She turned the money over to Daveggio and he immediately lost it.

By the third day of their meth-induced madness, Michaud had maxed out the credit card and the front desk called their room telling them that they would have to leave. Michaud remembered, "James was angry and put off that we didn't have anywhere to go." The sexual fantasies à la Gerald Gallego, which he'd ignored in the midst of his gambling frenzy, were now back full force. He was determined more than ever to kidnap some woman in the area and force her to do whatever he wanted. At least this would give him the satisfaction in what so far had been a losing trip.

They looked up Charlie S. at the Sands Hotel and bummed twenty dollars' worth of gas money from him. With the cash they bought some gas, and had enough fuel to cruise around town looking for a likely victim. Michaud wasn't quite as into it as he was, not yet, but she didn't object either. Later she would claim that she didn't know what he was up to. But Michaud was not that stupid, and Daveggio was less than coy about his intentions. As he sat behind the wheel, motoring around through the downtown area, Michaud suddenly became aware that he was following a young woman who was walking down the street. She remembered, "We came through a tunnellike part by the railroad tracks, and there was a big parking lot on the right-hand side. There was a young lady he had spotted and he circled around again just as she walked to her small white truck. As soon as she got in the truck, he just drove right past."

Extremely angered and agitated that he had been thwarted in his plans to grab her, Daveggio was furious as they cruised back toward downtown Reno. Nothing had gone right on this trip—not his gambling nor his wish to emulate Gerald Gallego. At a little after 10:00 P.M. on the corner of Washington and Sixth Streets in Reno, not far from where he had wed his second wife, Donetta, he spotted a petite, dark-haired woman standing on the sidewalk alone.

James Daveggio had spotted Juanita Rodriguez standing on the corner, waiting for her boyfriend. Once he drove by, he stopped at the end of the block and told Michaud to take over the wheel while he climbed in back. As she circled around, he crouched down in the interior of the van, ready to strike. Just as the van came even with Rodriguez, he slid the door open and hurtled from the van, grabbing her by the hair and the backpack she wore. Even when he hit his knee on the curb, he didn't let go. This was one prize that was not going to escape his lusts.

The rest became a nightmare for Rodriguez. His forcing her to disrobe, sticking his finger in her anus and then forcing her to do the same to him. He made her suck his penis and then drew out in time to ejaculate on her face. Even then the sexual torture didn't stop. It continued for more than an hour as they drove through the darkened mountains on a winding road. The worst was when he kept singing about a person "who shot a man in Reno, just to watch him die." She was sure he meant to kill her after he was tired with her. It was only by the grace of the woman driver that she was sure that she escaped with her life.

After they let Juanita Rodriguez go, Daveggio became worried that she had seen his distinctive tattoos and that she would identify him by those to authorities.

"We've got to go back and cap her [shoot her] in the head!" he kept insisting.

But Michaud drove on and calmly replied, "It was too dark in the van. She didn't see your tattoos. Look, you have very prominent tattoos all over you. But she can't identify them. I'm telling you, if you ever get arrested, she can't identify them. It was too dark. She was traumatized and she was so busy talking and trying to save her own life. She wasn't paying any attention to any tattoos."

Actually, it had been light enough to have seen Daveggio's tattoos during several points in the trip. But by whatever means, Michelle Michaud had divined that Juanita Rodriguez would not remember. In fact, Rodriguez had been so traumatized by the events that she would not remember that Daveggio's eyes were blue and his hair was blond. (She thought both were brown.)

While FBI Agent Lynn Ferrin and his team and Washoe County criminalist Rene Romero were putting the pieces together in the Juanita Rodriguez abduction case, James Daveggio and Michelle Michaud were taking steps to throw them off the track. After leaving Juanita Rodriguez in the woods at Clipper Gap, they drove past Sacramento to Ceres, a small town in the Central Valley where Daveggio's wife Deta (they were never divorced) now lived. He went into the house while Michaud slept in the van. The next day Michaud helped him shave his head; she strategically tucked her own hair up under a baseball cap, put on men's clothing and wore no make-up. From a distance she was so unfeminine-looking now that she could pass for a man.

They added large silver striping on the exterior of the green minivan to alter its appearance and they removed the rosary from the rearview mirror. Daveggio did one more key alteration. He removed the rear captain's chairs from the van. But he wasn't just content to leave things that way.

Daveggio must have been remembering how exciting it had been to hold Rodriguez down and force her to do what he wanted. What if there were rope restraints built right into the floorboard of the minivan to tie his next victim down? He had the material at hand—the industrial-strength rope he had stolen from the Williamses' residence. He could do that right now. Later he could hook up the come-along that he had also stolen and he would have the ultimate mobile abduction/torture chamber. He'd be able to stretch out his victim for maximum sadistic pleasure and do whatever he wanted to her shackled body.

While Michaud stayed inside, Daveggio went to work with a methamphetamine-induced vengeance. He removed the rear captain's chairs so there would be no obstacles in the way now to throw the next victim into the van through the sliding side door. All that was left in the rear area was a long bench-like chair. He also added a mirror into the interior of the van—better to see his victims once they were trussed. At last he had a van his mentor Gerald Gallego would have been proud of.

While staying in Ceres, Daveggio sent Michaud back to Sacramento to see if the coast was clear with the old motorcycle gang and look for any indication that law enforcement officers were snooping around their former addresses. She did as instructed and returned saying that everything looked normal. He was still paranoid that Juanita Rodriguez had seen his tattoos, but she said, "Look, quit panicking, James. If we ever get stopped, what is she going to tell them? The first thing they'll ask her, 'How could you not notice his tattoos?' And she didn't notice the color of your eyes either. You have striking blue eyes. So relax."

She finally convinced Daveggio that they could return to Sacramento. Even though he was still nervous and edgy about the police, those feelings weren't as strong as his need for more victims. Both were too hyped up now on meth and lust just to lie low. In her drug-crazed madness, Michelle Michaud, however, did one incredibly stupid thing. While watching a news report on a local television station with her daughter and Nancy Baker, the thirteen-year-old she had helped rape in the Williamses' house, a story came on about the Juanita Rodriguez abduction in Reno. In the middle of the story Michaud blurted out proudly, "We [James and I] did that!"

She must have been counting on her daughter never snitching on her and she knew that Nancy, the thirteen-year-old, was terribly cowed ever since the incident with the gun in the bathroom. She must have figured she had nothing to worry about.

By October Michaud's and Daveggio's lusts pushed them on into abducting Michelle's daughter on a terror ride up to Klamath Lake, Oregon, on a trip filled with molestation and rape. This wasn't enough, so they did it to her again a week later on the drive to Santa Cruz, along with Nancy Baker. Everything was disintegrating in Michaud's world now. It was hard to tell at this point what was real and what was fantasy as far as she was concerned. She was hooked into meth so badly that her mind drifted in and out of reality. In early November she told her sister Misty's live-in boyfriend, Rick Bourne, that she had in years past fingered individuals for Hell's Angels members to kill. One incident in particular stuck in her mind. It happened in 1982, according to her, when she allegedly lured a Sacramento bail bondsman named Leo into a hotel room. There was a Hell's Angel member with a pistol waiting inside the room. While Leo was forced to kneel on the floor with the gun to his head, Michaud said, "Sorry, you fucked up"; then the Hell's Angel blew the man's brains out.

She also told Bourne that she was involved in some murder where "a Nigger was hung in a tree in Wilton."

Bourne knew that she often lied and embellished her tales, but with Michaud you never really knew for sure. There was always an element of truth to what she said.

In a last gesture to the past and a keepsake for the future, James Daveggio stole a tape recorder from the Williamses and recorded a rambling message on audiotape to his son, James Jr. On it he said he wanted forgiveness for what he had done and what he was about to do. Maybe no one would understand, he said, but he had to do it. The demons he was struggling with were too strong now. The tape was to be his last will and testament. He vowed he would not be taken alive if caught and he had a semiautomatic and a .38-caliber pistol to prove it.

He left the tape at the Williamses' residence and he and Michaud dropped off her children at her parents' house. Then they climbed into her minivan, Michaud at the wheel. The whole wide world lay before them that evening as MacFadden Drive receded in the rearview mirror. It was a world brimming with potential young women to be kidnapped and raped. And like a beacon, Pleasanton was calling James Daveggio home. He instructed Michaud to turn the minivan southward and they motored out of Sacramento, bound for the place where all the "urges" had first bedeviled him and another boy named Michael Ihde so many years before.

Chapter 23

"That's him!"

As would later be alleged before a Grand Jury, it was in Dublin, California, on November 3 that James Daveggio and Michelle Michaud met Patty Wilson working at the game arcade; her abduction and rape occurred soon after. Just like the Sacramento thirteen-year-old, Nancy Baker, they frightened Patty Wilson into remaining quiet. Like the gypsies they had become, Daveggio and Michaud then turned the van eastward and motored up to Lake Tahoe after raping Wilson. It was as if the Bay Area and high Sierras were dual homing beacons to their depraved desires.

They spent some time in a motel room at Stateline in the Tahoe region and helped paint the exterior for a free room. Then they took a room at the Horizon Casino and Hotel not far away. Always hard up for money, Michaud went to the Horizon Casino on November 8 and wrote $389.65 in bad checks. She was soon detained by a security guard and was booked later at the Douglas County jail for an overnight stay. The jail was directly across from the Lakeside Inn where she used to be a customer at the bar. It was her second bad mistake.

Unfortunately for the law enforcement agencies involved, there was still no concrete evidence about who owned the green minivan or who had been responsible for the rape of Juanita Rodriguez. Michaud posted bail and promised to appear for a court hearing in early December. Then she and Daveggio hightailed it back to the Bay Area.

Only ten days later, on November 18, the first significant clues to the depredations of Daveggio and Michaud became evident when the two Sacramento teens were picked up by Sacramento cops and spilled their stories about forced drug usage and rape. Nancy Baker was willing to tell everything, right down to the smallest detail. Even Michaud's daughter told Detective Willover when he spoke to her that she had been forced to take drugs at the hands of Daveggio and Michaud, and then molested. Michelle Michaud, who had been a good parent, no longer was the virtuous mother. She had slipped far indeed from her days as a crossing guard on busy Franklin Boulevard. According to one account, Michaud's daughter later told a reporter from the *San Francisco Chronicle* that she had said to her mother, "They told me to watch out for people like that. But I never guessed it would be you, Mom!"

Detective Willover made out a full report about Baker's rape and also the one concerning Michaud's daughter who had been raped on the drive up to Oregon. The Sacramento Police then informed the local FBI about James Daveggio and Michelle Michaud, and they, along with officers of the Sacramento Police Department, scoured the pair's old haunts all through the later days of November. One of the people they talked to was Peggy Morton, who lived across the street from Daveggio's old girlfriend Lizzy Bingenheimer.

"The FBI agent told me to call immediately if I spotted James or Michelle," she said. "I knew them both by sight—James because he hung out with Lizzy all the time and Michelle because I knew her from the Catholic church on Franklin Boulevard. The agent didn't tell me what they were wanted for, but I figured it must be pretty bad if the FBI was involved. I remembered what James had said to me, 'Bitch, I'm gonna kill yer ass!' I didn't doubt for a minute he was capable of doing it. His eyes were just crazy-looking."

Even though the Sacramento police and FBI agents canvassed the area, including Bobby Joe's and the Williamses' residences, Daveggio and Michaud were long gone. Even though they were living dangerously now, they at least had enough sense to steer clear of Sacramento. In a bit of luck for the fugitives, Detective Willover did not contact the Placer County Sheriff's Office about the Sacramento girls' testimony concerning Juanita Rodriguez until November 26, nearly a week later. The man he contacted was Detective Bill Summers, the same detective who had found the body of Gerald Gallego's last victim, Mary Beth Sowers. In a strange twist of fate, Bill Summers had just finished working on a murder case with another tie to James Daveggio and Michael Ihde. He had been working with Ken Hale of the California Department of Forestry—the same man who had been the first official to see Kellie Poppleton's battered body along Kilkare Road. The threads of all these different cases so far apart in time and distance were starting to come together at last.

Some media sources would later make a big deal of Detective Willover's weeklong delay in letting the

Placer County Sheriff's Department know about Daveggio and Michaud. But law enforcement agencies do not operate in a vacuum. There are other crimes to be solved, other disturbances to quell, and everything can't be dropped for one potential breakthrough in a case, especially when multiple agencies are involved. Real cases are not solved in the methodical and timely manner of television shows. Real cases unfold in murky depths, with interrupting phone calls, conflicting information and court dates on other cases. Everything has a priority. Unfortunately for everyone involved, Daveggio and Michaud had priorities of their own.

Bouncing back to the Bay Area on the day after Detective Willover informed the Placer County Sheriff's Department that a possible link existed between them and the Juanita Rodriguez case, the pair decided to spend Thanksgiving week at Daveggio's first wife Annette's house in Dublin. It was not destined to be a traditional Thanksgiving, however. Daveggio's sixteen-year-old daughter was supposed to get her driver's license the next day on Friday, so he convinced her to come stay with him and Michelle at the Candlewood Hotel in Pleasanton overnight. The Candlewood Inn was located close to the Department of Motor Vehicles.

According to the Alameda County Grand Jury indictment, at around 10:00 P.M. on Thanksgiving, Michaud, Daveggio and his daughter checked into the hotel and Michaud immediately plopped down onto the bed and began to read a book. But Daveggio sat in a chair and began to ask his daughter all sorts of strange questions. One was "Would you like to torture people?"

She answered, "I don't know. I've never tortured anyone. But most people like to torture people to watch the fear in their eyes."

He agreed with her. "Yes," he responded, "that's the reason it would be cool to torture people. To see the fear in their eyes."

Then he asked, "Have you ever killed anyone? You'd never know if you'd like it unless you try. Would you like to go hunting with me?"

His daughter was getting scared now and asked, "What do you mean by hunting?"

"When you go and stalk someone to kill," he answered.

Now she was thoroughly scared and wanted to change the subject. She knew what kinds of books he liked to read. Books about serial killers.

He next asked her. "If I ever killed someone, would you hide me out?"

"It depends on the situation," she answered.

Daveggio grilled his daughter a little more with these macabre questions and then got up to take a shower. As the girl sat stunned from the conversation that had just ensued, Michaud quietly put down her book and absolutely floored her with the casual statement, "Your dad's going to have sex with you."

"No, he can't! He's supposed to be my father. He's supposed to love me."

Daveggio emerged from the bathroom wearing only shorts. Michaud went in to take a long shower as Daveggio sat down on the bed next to his daughter and began to fondle her.

"Please stop!" she cried. But he kept right on. As if justifying his actions, he said, "Michelle won't let me have oral sex with her, and so I'm going to have it with you."

He pushed her back on the bed and pulled down her pants and panties and forced his head between her legs. She remembered staring at the clock the whole time. The ordeal began at midnight and did not end until 1:00 A.M. Sometime around 12:45 A.M. Michaud came out and joined them. She began to give Daveggio a blow job as he continued oral copulation on his own daughter.

Afterward Daveggio went out to get orange sodas for them all as if nothing out of the ordinary had happened. Michaud said to the girl, who was suffering from shock, "Tomorrow is the busiest shopping day of the year and it will be the best day to kill somebody. Do you want to come along with us?"

"No!" the frightened girl responded.

Michaud became angry at her reply. Then she uttered a chilling comment the girl would not soon forget.

"Well, we'll have to do it sometime really soon."

After Thanksgiving Day, Daveggio and Michaud went to stay with a friend of his in Pleasanton until November 30. On that date they went to a Kmart store in Hayward to buy two Revlon curling irons. But they didn't plan to use them on Michaud's hair. They had other more diabolical plans in mind for the curling irons.

The next day, December 1, was "cruising day," sizing up the schoolgirls at his old high school, Foothill High in Pleasanton. Perhaps he thought about all the girls who wouldn't give him the time of day while attending that school. Now they weren't going to have any choice. He'd simply tie them up and take what he wanted from them and force them to satisfy him. Daveggio and Michaud stopped only briefly in the parking lot of Foothill High until a passing teacher frightened them away. Running low on money, they hit up James's long-suffering ex-wife Annette for some cash. Next they drove over to Valley High in Dublin where Daveggio had buddied around with Michael Ihde so many years before. They also stopped by Wells Middle

School where Daveggio had a daughter—the same school where Kellie Poppleton had been a lonely child. Everything was coming full circle now. The things he and Ihde had only dreamed about so long ago were all coming true.

James Daveggio and Michelle Michaud decided they would strike the next day. Pleasanton would be the target area, his old neighborhood of Clovewood Drive would be ground zero. It was the neighborhood that had seen fourteen-year-old Tina Faelz die a lonely death in a nearby drainage ditch.

But first they had a few more items they wanted to buy. At 6:17 P.M. they stopped in at Not Too Naughty No. 2 in Livermore, an adult sex shop and bookstore. Robert Maisonet was working behind the counter and he remembered a couple coming in that didn't fit the norm. As he recalled, "They weren't our typical customers. Our typical customers are couples in their mid-twenties, fairly well dressed. These people were somewhat not as well dressed."

He also noticed that the unusual couple made a beeline to what he termed—"the most extreme items" in the store—handcuffs, gagging devices and dildos. They picked out a green ball gag to be placed in a person's mouth during sadomasochistic sessions. It had attached elastic strings that were to be placed around the person's head. Daveggio also picked out an audiotape with two scantily clad girls on the cover. The tape was labeled *Submissive Young Girls*.

On December 1, 1997, Juanita Rodriguez was escorted into the Washoe County Sheriff's Office one more time by Detective Desiree Carrington and FBI

Agent Lynn Ferrin for a look at a photo lineup of possible assailants. The information about James Daveggio and Michelle Michaud that the Sacramento Police had passed on to the Placer County detectives was finally being implemented. As Rodriguez flipped through the pages of photos, none of the men looked familiar to her. Suddenly, she let out a small gasp. A photo stared back at her from the page with the face of a man she would never forget. Her finger reflexively pointed at the photo.

"That's him!" she cried. "It looks like this one!"

It was a photo of James Daveggio.

The news was passed on to Daniel G. Bogden, assistant U.S. attorney at the Federal Building in Reno. A young man with the Organized Crime Drug Enforcement Task Force, he issued a complaint against James Daveggio and Michelle Michaud. It stated in part:

"Count One, Title 18, United States Code, Conspiracy to Commit Kidnapping—Interstate Transportation—James Anthony Daveggio and Michelle Lyn Michaud—defendants herein, did knowingly and intentionally combine, conspire and agree to commit a kidnapping offense in violation of the laws of the United States, in that the defendants willfully kidnapped, seized and confined a twenty-year-old female Reno resident and then willfully transported the aforesaid victim in interstate commerce from the state of Nevada to the state of California, for some benefit, defendants alleged herein did further and specifically aid, abet, counsel, command, induce and procure the conspiracy within the meaning of Title 18, United States Code, Section 2."

U.S. Attorney Bogden went on to state:

"The whereabouts of both these individuals are not presently known. It is believed that both are still traveling together and may be in California or Nevada. Due to their unknown whereabouts, the Government is seeking the sealing of the Criminal Complaint in this matter. If the Criminal Complaint for defendant James Daveggio were to become public prior to his arrest, it is believed that the defendant and his accomplice would attempt to avoid arrest by fleeing the country or attempt to go into hiding. If allowed to complete its investigative efforts, the FBI and law enforcement can minimize or eliminate this flight possibility and keep the defendant and his accomplice from committing further criminal offenses. Therefore your affiant believes that good cause exists to seal the above-mentioned Criminal Complaint until execution of the arrest warrant by law enforcement upon defendant James Anthony Daveggio after which time this Order to Seal will expire automatically upon his arrest."

United States magistrate judge Robert McQuaid Jr. signed the arrest warrant and issued the order to seal it, eliminating any possibility that the media would somehow alert the pair.

Nearly one hundred miles away, Detective Desiree Carrington drove back to Auburn, California. She was busy too, filling out a Probable Cause Arrest Warrant. She wrote:

"Your affiant, Detective Desiree Carrington is employed as a peace officer for the Placer County Sheriffs' Department and has attached here to and incorporated by reference as exhibit an official report and records of law enforcement agency. These reports were prepared by law enforcement officers and contain factual information and statements obtained from victim, witnesses and others which established the commission of the following criminal offenses 207 PC 261 (a) (2) PC and 259 PC (kidnapping, rape and the use of a firearm).

"Person to be arrested: Michelle Lyn Michaud."

Law enforcement agents were at work in Sacramento as well. They contacted Michelle Michaud's mother, who told them that her daughter would soon be on her way up to Lake Tahoe for a court date dealing with the Horizon bad checks incident.

But one wish of Assistant U.S. Attorney Daniel Bogden to "keep the defendant and his accomplice from committing further criminal offenses" was not destined to be. Not only were James and Michelle contemplating further criminal offenses, they were upping the stakes.

As the wheels of justice got into high gear in Reno, Nevada, and Auburn and Sacramento, California, Daveggio and Michaud watched movies on the television in a Pleasanton motel. They took drugs and drank, and according to one source, they ate at a nearby Denny's restaurant. (This report differs from Michaud's own timeline.) One waitress who had seen Daveggio in years past vaguely remembered him. It was the same Denny's where Daveggio's long-suffering second wife, Donetta, had toiled to make a buck just so James could run up to Reno or Tahoe and lose it at the card tables.

"Yeah, I knew that guy," she said. "He used to come in here a lot. But I can't remember his name. He had some nickname. It was some kind of animal's name. I remember someone calling him that. He also had a real unusual voice. Kind of like an old man's raspy voice. He liked to order breakfast, sometimes even later in the day. And I remember his eyes. They're real blue. He was pretty talkative and friendly most of the time. But I hadn't seen him in a while."

She had no way of knowing what he had been up to recently or that there was a warrant out for his arrest.

As night closed down over the upscale city of Pleasanton, James Daveggio went out to the van and tested the rope restraints. He had picked his material well. They were strong and unrelenting.

Chapter 24

Over the Edge

Pleasanton has always been a haven for dreamers. It must have seemed like paradise to the few Yanquis drifting into the area after the Gold Rush. Certainly, it must have seemed that way to Charles Garthwaite who made the arduous trek from the eastern states in 1849 to become part of the wild rush to pan for gold in the Sierra foothills. After years of enduring the icy streams and rugged conditions, he decided to settle in the more hospitable climate of Amador Valley where Don Augustine Bernal had his *rancho*. Of all the places in California he could have chosen, he chose Pleasanton.

By the middle of the twentieth century, there were many more like him—people who could have moved anywhere in California, but chose Pleasanton. For instance, the Samson family, a clan of tightly knit Filipino Americans who lived near the racetrack that Don Bernal's sons had built in 1858, not far away from where Charles Garthwaite had chosen his last spot to repose in the San Augustine Cemetery. The Samsons were a family of go-getters who truly believed in the American Dream. They had a pleasant single-story home on a quiet court, with tidy lawn and neat landscaping. The father, Daniel, had instilled in his children the benefits of a good education, and mother Christina had nourished them with love. Both were proud of son Vincent, who was turning into a well-spoken and handsome young man, and daughter Nichole. But there was an especially soft spot in their hearts for the baby of the family, Vanessa.

Vanessa or 'Nessa, as friends and family called her, was a delightful young woman with a ready smile and friendly brown eyes. She had absorbed the easygoing suburban lifestyle of Pleasanton, as well as a belief in its work ethic. But she knew how to have fun as well and was often seen at football games on Friday nights cheering the home team. She always found time to make leis of candy for friends and family at Christmastime, join high school clubs, attend school activities. In short, she was immensely popular. There was a combination of the fun-loving and the studious in 'Nessa.

Her parish priest, Father Daniel Davidson, knew her as "an extremely happy child. She enjoyed group activities and social events. Vanessa never seemed to have the problems many teenagers go through. She was always upbeat and positive. She seemed remarkably well balanced for someone so young."

When Vanessa worked on the high school yearbook, it was stressful for all the staff, designing layouts and collating all the material. But staffer Kelly Amick remembered, "I was pretty involved in school activities and when I'd get stressed out, I'd turn around and Vanessa would be there smiling and saying, 'Need help?' "

Vanessa Samson had developed the maturity to deal with the stress and craziness of the yearbook project and still keep up her grades. As her senior

year drew to an end, she was captured forever on
the yearbook pages she had helped to create: she
appears beautiful and elegant in a senior prom
photo, hair done up, wearing a spaghetti-strap
gown, white elbow-length gloves and a big smile. Of
that smile, her friend Rob Smith said, "For me the
most striking feature was her smile. It said a lot.
She was caring and very lovable. She had a love for
life, friends and family and she wasn't afraid to show
it. Vanessa was a very strong person who spoke her
mind."

When she graduated from Pleasanton's Amador
Valley High School in 1993, she went on to obtain
a higher education in business at nearby Ohlone
College in Fremont. There she became secretary of
the Filipino Americans Student Association. Once
again she garnered accolades for her hard work and
always having an open ear to everyone else's problems.

After college she landed a job with S.C.J. Insur-
ance Company in Pleasanton, one of the many new
offices in the business park along Hacienda Road.
Shirley Lapp, president of the company, said, "I
know it's a cliché, but Vanessa was like the girl next
door."

Even though 'Nessa still lived at home, her one
big dream was to buy a car so that she didn't have
to walk the three quarters of a mile to work. Not
that she minded the exercise. The pretty young
woman weighed 120 pounds and was in good shape.

Her normal route to work was a pleasant walk
east on Singletree Way to Dorman Road and then
on West Las Positas Boulevard. It wound through a
combination of suburban homes and a small business district. On December 2, 1997, she left home
as usual about 7:00 A.M. and her mother remembered, " 'Nessa poked her head through a door to

say good-bye." She wore a three-quarter-length black nylon jacket, blue jeans and white tennis shoes. She was carrying a green Jansport canvas backpack and red Safeway nylon bag containing her lunch. It was a foggy morning in Pleasanton, as so many days were around there in early December. Just as she approached Singletree Way and Kern Court at 7:30 A.M., a dark green minivan came driving slowly down the street. The driver, a dark-haired woman, seemed to be eyeing her.

According to the Alameda County Grand Jury Indictment and Michaud's confession, on the morning of December 2, 1997, one day after a warrant for their arrest was issued in Reno, James Daveggio and Michelle Michaud were up early cruising Pleasanton for a new victim. Michaud was at the wheel and Daveggio remained tensed in the back, ready to spring at a moment's notice. Unlike the time with Juanita Rodriguez, Michaud was fully aware of what was about to happen. At seventy-thirty they were driving in Daveggio's old neighborhood near Clovewood Drive when they spotted Vanessa Lei Samson walking to work. Michaud moved the van forward, coming to a halt right beside the startled young woman. Daveggio was out the door in a heartbeat, grabbing Samson, who managed to get off one piercing scream before his large hand covered her mouth and his bulky 220-pound body dragged her into the van. She was no match for him as he threw her to the floor and gagged her. He slammed the door shut and Michaud slowly pulled away so as not to attract attention.

As Michaud drove toward Interstate 580 and entered that roadway, Daveggio was in a hurry. He lost no time in tying Vanessa Samson with the ropes, pulling her clothes aside and taking his own clothes off before climbing atop her. Then he satisfied himself in a manner that no sex with Michaud, or any other unbound woman, ever could. The abduction/torture van was living up to his wildest expectations.

Michaud motored east on Interstate 580 while Daveggio continued raping and sexually torturing his helpless victim. Michaud drove twenty-five miles to Tracy, where she pulled off the freeway to get gasoline. No one at the gas station knew anything was amiss in the darkened interior of the van. As they drove north, Daveggio used the curling iron with duct tape attached to torment Vanessa Samson, who was tied so securely to the floor by the ropes that she could do nothing to evade his depredations. This torment was visited on his trussed-up victim almost all the way to South Sacramento where they stopped to cash Michaud's $538 welfare check at about 10:00 A.M. at DBA Check Mart. Tanya Chinn handled the transaction, and in the process didn't notice anything unusual or suspicious in Michaud's actions or manners.

It was at this point that they decided to continue their journey up to Lake Tahoe. Michaud needed to show up for her court date concerning the bad checks she had attempted to cash at the Horizon Casino. They had become so bold now that it didn't even faze them to take a kidnapped victim right to the very doorsteps of where Michaud was wanted by the law. They deduced that if they had been able to secret Juanita Rodriguez right through an inspection station on the California border, then why couldn't they pull this off as well? Methamphetamines and arrogance were clouding their senses to an extreme.

Daveggio continued to molest Vanessa Samson all the way up the twisting mountain road of Highway 50. With the ball gag in her mouth and the rope restraints in place, Samson was helpless against all his sexual torments.

The trio arrived at the Sundowner Motel at about 11:30 A.M. It was a small, inexpensive motel that the manager, Mukesh Patel, had made more presentable over the last year by adding a hot tub and improving the grounds. Mr. Patel saw the green minivan drive up and a heavyset man with close-cropped hair come into the office. The man signed the registration form and paid for room 5. Mr. Patel didn't know how many were in his party. But it didn't matter since the room was just a single set price no matter how many people stayed. The customer named James Daveggio made a few innocuous comments and then drove the van over to room 5. The bulk of the van blocked Mr. Patel's view as to whether any more people got out of the van.

He did notice a little bit later when he went out to work on the hot tub, which needed repairs, that a woman with long dark hair got into the van and drove away for ten or fifteen minutes. She then returned and went into the room. He paid her scant attention. As far as he was concerned, they were just a couple more customers who had driven up from Sacramento. They probably needed a nap in the room after driving up from the Valley far below.

But the customers weren't taking a nap. They were both turning their attentions on the bound and helpless Vanessa Samson. It was then that the sexual torture began in earnest. They both assaulted her at the same time in the room, and according to some comments that Michaud later told another woman, the curling irons were freely used on their unfortunate victim in the rectal area. The evidence would show that they both wielded the curling irons at the same time. One up her rectum, the other against her buttocks. With the ball gag in her mouth, Samson's screams could not be heard. What torments she suffered at the Sundowner, God only knows. But her suffering was about to come to an end.

Tiring of their "sport" at last, Daveggio and Michaud quietly conferred about what to do with their victim. Later Michaud would contend that she didn't know what was about to happen; she thought Samson would just be let off by the side of the road like Juanita Rodriguez. But by that point Michaud was trying to save her own skin and her comments were self-serving. Even she would admit later in a slip of the tongue, "I knew things would be different this time."

By late afternoon they had decided they would kill Vanessa and dump her body in an isolated area. But they told Vanessa another story. Michaud promised they would let her go once they were outside the city if she behaved. Convinced of her impending release, Vanessa Samson weakly cooperated, though Michaud thought the unfortunate woman was "half dead" by this point. She was quietly hustled out of the Sundowner Motel and back into the van. Mr. Patel, the manager, never noticed anything out of the ordinary.

Just about the time the sun was going down on that cold December day, Michaud drove as Daveggio sat in the back of the van with Samson. Somewhere near the summit of Luther Pass on Route 89, Michaud stopped the van and Daveggio suddenly picked up a length of black rope and twisted it around Samson's neck. He pulled on one end while Michaud pulled on the other, in a pact to murder their victim in tandem, just the way they had sexually tortured her. Vanessa Samson couldn't have struggled for long against all their strength. She died about five miles from the spot where Jaycee Lee Dugard had been kidnapped six years before.

Daveggio and Michaud drove over the mountain on Highway 88 to a remote section of Hope Valley known as Crater Wash, in Alpine County. They dumped Vanessa Samson's body down into the icy ravine and hoped that the next snowstorm would cover her beneath a blanket of white. Or if they were lucky, animals would eat the flesh and scatter the bones. People disappeared in the Sierra wilderness like this all the time, only to be found as skeletons the following spring, if they were found at all.

But there was a reckoning in the wind now, even as they dumped the body into the snow-covered creekbed in isolated Hope Valley. They were arrogant and had evaded the law for so long that they now became extremely foolish. They went back to the Sundowner and cleaned it up as best they could. Instead of fleeing the area, Daveggio instructed Michaud to drive to the Lakeside Inn at South Lake Tahoe. It was an act of brazen audacity that bordered on madness. For this was the one area that law enforcement agents thought they might show up, hoping that Michaud would actually arrive for her court hearing the next day concerning the bad checks at the Horizon Casino. It was a long shot—but with these two one never knew. The law enforcement officials were right. Michelle Michaud intended to keep her court date at the Douglas County Courthouse right across the street from the Lakeside Inn.

Even though Michaud would later confess to what happened to Vanessa Samson, Daveggio to this day claims he has never killed anyone.

Chapter 25

The Bulldog

As James Daveggio and Michelle Michaud drove across town and booked themselves into the Lakeside Inn, Lake Tahoe behind them grew dark and quiet. Not once did they suspect that law enforcement agencies in California and Nevada were starting to close in on them. All the pieces of the puzzle were beginning to come together now, from the reported rapes of the two Sacramento girls, to the abduction and rape of Juanita Rodriguez in Reno, to the Dublin rapes of the teenage girls. Various agencies, including the FBI, were putting together a picture of a man and woman from Sacramento named James Anthony Daveggio and Michelle Lyn Michaud who were probably involved in one if not all these crimes.

Independent of all of these agencies, Police Chief Bill Eastman of Pleasanton was also having his force investigate the disappearance of Vanessa Samson. He had been frustrated by the inability to solve the Tina Faelz case years before, and he was pulling out all the stops on this case. The fact that the perpetrator had committed the crime in broad daylight near a busy interstate and simply vanished like a ghost galled him to no end. One salient characteristic Eastman possessed, however, was the mental tenacity of a bulldog. Large and muscular, at fifty-seven years of age in 1997, he had all the energy of a much younger man. He was known by his officers as a "cop's cop." He once told a *Tri-Valley Herald* reporter, "If you don't give the streets away, you never have to take them back."

He made no bones about the fact that he routinely called criminals "punks" and "idiots." He ingrained in his officers the need to be on the alert always, reasoning that crooks would go elsewhere if they saw a highly visible police force in Pleasanton.

He didn't compromise when it came to his hard-nosed style and posted memorandums throughout the department that stated, "Be committed, meet community needs, look to the future, get involved and make things better."

As Deborah Acosta, city manager, had said, "He created a reputation that Pleasanton is tough on crime." The statistics backed her up. Crime rates were three times lower in 1997 than they had been in 1981 when he took over as chief. In fact, there had not been a murder in Pleasanton for over two years. He'd started a local Drug Abuse Resistance Education program (DARE) in Pleasanton and instituted a K-9 program with trained police dogs. Under his command the police force had grown from thirty to eighty cops. The department headquarters on Main Street had been so outmoded when he first became "Top Cop" that pencils rolled off desks from the uneven floors, and the basement was a mass of exposed wiring. Eastman lobbied and got a new department headquarters on Bernal Avenue, where it became a leader in police work with computer-aided dispatch and records systems. He even got updated radios and new computers for the squad cars in town. He figured a city so tied to high tech ought to be safeguarded by the same use of technology.

But he also said, "Technology doesn't make a damn bit of difference if you don't have good people on the street. You can have a set of views, but if you don't get them where the rubber meets the road, it's over."

He was honest and plainspoken with a large dose of common sense, and his officers admired him for it. "I'm serious when I say my leadership style is no mystery," he once told a local reporter for the *Tri-Valley Herald*. "What you see is what you get."

What Pleasanton got on the morning of December 3, 1997, was full-court press from Bill Eastman to find one of its missing daughters, Vanessa Samson. Police Chief Eastman sent his officers in a sweep over the entire area. Friends, coworkers and relatives of Samson's were interviewed and two sets of flyers were distributed all over town. A canine tracking search was conducted along her usual route of travel from home to work while an aerial search was conducted from overhead. Residents and businesspeople were contacted along the route and a Teleminder computer called 324 residents and businesses in the area asking if they had seen the young woman on the previous day. Other law enforcement agencies all over the area were contacted and a "hit" was put in the California Law Enforcement System to be on the lookout for Vanessa Samson. Local radio, television and newspapers were contacted and before long Vanessa's face was all over the Bay Area. Police Chief Bill Eastman was leaving no stone unturned to find Vanessa Samson and her kidnappers. The last thing he wanted was another Tina Faelz mystery.

The tracks between James Daveggio, Michelle

Michaud and the law enforcement agencies had almost converged by December 3, 1997. Michaud was holed up in room 133 of the Lakeside Inn with methamphetamines while Daveggio once more tried his luck at the casino. If the ominous shape of the Douglas County Sheriff's Office and jail right across the road gave them any second thoughts, they never expressed them. Michaud was too far into her drugs and Daveggio too far into his gambling addiction by now to take any warning signals. She had already made her court appearance in the morning, and soon they would be back on the road. There were a lot more roads and a lot more potential victims just waiting out there—that the van worked as an abduction chamber had already been proved. They couldn't wait to give it another try.

Afternoon turned into evening and the winter sun began to go down over 9,000-foot Mount Tallac on Lake Tahoe's west shore. It angled right toward Tahoma where Detective Sergeant Randy Peshon had once looked for Jaycee Lee Dugard. He had never given up on that case and he had over 150 different folders concerning tips and leads on that kidnapping.

As the late-afternoon shadows crept down the canyons, and law enforcement agents spread out around the South Lake Tahoe area, a van matching the description of one owned by Michelle Michaud was parked right outside in the parking lot. Even the license plate numbers matched.

The local FBI agent, Chris Campion, phoned the Reno office and an electric shock went right through Special Agent Ferrin. At last—this was it! Rounding up Agents Bruce Wick and Mike West, he phoned Agent Kip Steele in Carson City, as well as Douglas County detective Tim Minister. The word

also went out to Placer County Sheriff's detective
Desiree Carrington—they were all to converge on
the Lakeside Inn at Lake Tahoe, ASAP. Time was
of the essence. James Daveggio and Michelle
Michaud might vanish at any moment like the foot-
loose gypsies they had become.

Chapter 26

The Arrest

Rounding Tahoe's beautiful east shore, which Mark Twain once described as "the fairest picture the whole earth affords," Lynn Ferrin and his team of FBI agents had no time for sight-seeing now. He laid out the general plan of attack as they drove along the curving road and through the dark tunnel of Cave Rock, sacred to the Washoe Indians as a place haunted by spirits. These spirits, known as "water babies," often brought down retribution on evildoers. If Michelle Michaud ever believed in such things, she should have believed in them now.

Agent Ferrin's plan called for the various agents to make a sweep through the parking lot, casino and restaurant, and cover as much area as possible at the same time, while closing off escape routes. They couldn't assume that Daveggio and Michaud were in room 133. They would assume, however, that both were armed and dangerous.

At 6:35 P.M. the FBI vehicles pulled into the parking lot of the Lakeside Inn. Agents Wick and Steele headed toward the casino area while the others, guns drawn, approached the door of room 133. Special Agent Lynn Ferrin had concocted a ruse to take Michaud by surprise. Under his orders, Agent Chris Campion knocked on the door and announced, "Mrs. Daveggio. Your husband is in the casino and very ill."

Michelle for once let her guard down. She bought it. She opened the door only to find several armed FBI agents waiting outside. She didn't put up any resistance as they burst into the room. Then she slumped back onto the bed, seemingly knowing that her spree of kidnapping, rape and murder was over.

There was only one problem. James Daveggio was nowhere in sight. It was now up to Agents Bruce Wick and Kip Steele to find him before he got wind of what was going on. The thought of a shoot-out in a crowded casino did not cheer either one of them. It was known that Daveggio was dangerous. Just how dangerous remained to be seen.

Moving through the main area of the casino, they passed rows of slot machines and the long central bar, where overhead televisions were tuned to sports channels. The casino area was not particularly crowded, but it was noisy with the clink of slot machines and televisions playing. Even more frustrating was the fact that the slots were laid out in a configuration that made the whole area seem like a maze. For a moment they were afraid that Daveggio had flown the coop.

Then suddenly they spotted a stocky man wearing a blue denim shirt, blue jeans and hiking boots, playing a slot machine against the wall in one corner. With his greying blond hair, mustache and blue eyes, he matched the photograph that both agents had seen.

"Mr. Daveggio," Agent Wick said in a firm voice as he approached the man.

James turned around, looking as if he half-expected their presence.

The agents' eyes were on his hands. Instead of reaching for a pistol, he merely clutched a handful of coins.

Responding to his name being called, Daveggio simply answered, "Yes."

"We're FBI agents," Bruce Wick said. "You're under arrest on a federal charge."

James Daveggio, despite all the bombast on the audiotape he had left for his son, James Jr., submitted without a struggle. He had left his loaded .25 automatic back in the room and the .38 in the glove compartment of the van. What he would have done if one of these had been in his waistband is anyone's guess. The audiotape to his son had stressed a shoot-out if caught, but now it was a moot point whether it was true or just a bluff.

Agent Wick put handcuffs on Daveggio and searched him for weapons. He located James's wallet, flipped through it and put some money that he had in his hand into his shirt pocket. Then unceremoniously Daveggio was walked across the casino to the small security office and placed in a chair. Within minutes the office was filled to bursting with FBI personnel Jerry Hill, Lynn Ferrin, Bruce Wick and Kip Steele. Daveggio looked somehow smaller and less threatening in their midst.

He wasn't Mirandized immediately, an oversight that would cause problems later. When asked about this by Ronald Rachow, U.S. assistant prosecutor, Agent Lynn Ferrin answered, "I knew that I probably had more information about the case itself and wanted to interview Mr. Daveggio at the FBI office rather than in a security office in a hotel or someplace in between."

Ferrin acknowledged that this was normal procedure based on his experience.

The whole time Daveggio was in the security office he barely said a word. Agent Ferrin did remember him piping up at one point and volunteering some information: "He said he was a 290 registrant [sex offender] and we asked him what that meant, and he replied. I think that he also spoke about having a motorcycle stolen from him at one point."

Even with all the trouble he was now in, Daveggio still stewed over the Harley his former biker friends had taken. It was the one possession he truly loved.

The agents stayed in the cramped security office until 7:07 P.M., at which point they escorted Daveggio to room 134 next door to where Michaud was under arrest.

Thirty minutes after the initial arrest of Michelle Michaud, Placer County Detectives Desiree Carrington and Bill Summers arrived on the scene and were allowed to take over the interrogation of Michaud, since they knew most about the Juanita Rodriguez abduction. Neither they nor the FBI agents connected Daveggio or Michaud with the Vanessa Samson kidnapping and murder as of yet. Detectives Carrington and Summers asked Michaud questions for about an hour, and for the most part she was cooperative, though evasive. She even went so far as to sign a form for Special Agents Lynn Ferrin and Mike McKinley that stated, "These agents are authorized by me to take from my vehicle any letters, papers, materials or other property which they may desire." She filled out a similar form for room 133, where she had been staying.

Chris Campion came into the room and snapped a picture of Michaud to compare with the sketch of the woman who had kidnapped Jaycee Lee Dugard.

Agent-in-charge Lynn Ferrin shuttled back and forth between the two rooms and noted some pretty interesting items in Room 133. In his report he wrote, "During the search of room 133, law enforcement officers located controlled substances, believed to be marijuana and crack cocaine, drug paraphernalia, a scale, pay and owe sheets as well as a loaded .25 caliber semi-automatic pistol."

He did not have anyone inspect the minivan at the time, wanting to do it at the Washoe County crime lab instead.

Carrington and Summers asked her more questions about the Juanita Rodriguez kidnapping and Michelle Michaud still tap-danced around the issue, not implicating herself directly.

Finally, after what must have seemed an eternity to Michaud, she asked for a bathroom break and was granted it by the detectives. When she returned, she said, "Shouldn't I have a lawyer? I think I need to talk to a lawyer."

Her initial interrogation was over.

Even while all of this was going on, James Daveggio was still not questioned about Juanita Rodriguez's kidnap and rape, or Mirandized. At 8:42 P.M. he was removed from room 134 without once seeing Michaud and placed into a Ford Explorer along with agents Wick, Duffer and Ferrin. Michaud, on the other hand, was merely escorted across the street to the Douglas County Jail and court complex.

During the trip to Reno, Daveggio hardly said a word. When he did open his mouth, it was only to say he had once lived on Vista Avenue in Sacramento. Perhaps he was thinking of better days when he had lived with Lizzy Bingenheimer. Not once during the entire trip did he mention Michelle Michaud's name.

It was 9:55 P.M. when Daveggio was escorted into the FBI office on Kietzke Lane and finally Mirandized by Agent Lynn Ferrin. Agent Ferrin pulled out a FD395 FBI form and advised Daveggio of his rights. Daveggio made no statement and refused to sign. Already he was digging in his heels. He might have blanched had he known that Michaud had a completely different course of action in mind.

Daveggio was asked about his height, weight, address and Social Security number. He was forced to take his shirt off and show his tattoos as well as the large burn scar on his back. During his stay at the FBI office, he did mention that he had lived for a while on MacFadden Drive in Sacramento. But he uttered not a word that Michelle Michaud had been his girlfriend.

After his brief stay at the FBI office on Kietzke Lane, Daveggio was hustled over to the Washoe County Jail. It was to become his first permanent address after having lived so long on the road. The inveterate gambler had indeed gambled big time and lost. At the time of his arrest, he had forty-five dollars in his wallet while owing $48,000 in back child support.

Michaud, meanwhile, was filling out her own forms at the Douglas County Jail, adjacent to the Lakeside Inn. Under the space marked employment, she wrote, "No." Told that if a no was indicated, give month and year of last employment, she wrote, "Unknown years." The next question was even more revealing: "Have you received within the past 12 months any income from a business, profession, or other form of self-employment?" She answered, "Welfare" and also wrote down one of the names of her sugar daddies. Perhaps in the back of her mind, Michaud wished she had stayed with him and never hooked up with Daveggio.

As for her dependents, she wrote, "Daughter, now with foster care," and "Son, lives with parents." Asked about debts and monthly bills, she wrote, "Been homeless for three months." At the very bottom she signed the document in a fluid, bold, still confident hand, "Michelle Michaud."

PART IV
THE RECKONING

Chapter 27

Witchy Woman

So far the FBI agents hadn't searched the interior of the minivan but they did haul it to Reno and obtained a search warrant, even though they already had a statement from Michelle Michaud that they could search the van. They weren't taking any chances on the legality. The following morning, December 4, in the crime lab garage of the Washoe County Sheriff's Department, Agent Lynn Ferrin supervised a specialized crew as it scrutinized the van's interior. The search revealed a plethora of incriminating material.

He wrote in his report, "[We found] a rosary style beaded necklace with crucifix, a roll of duct tape, audio and video cassette tapes, bedding, several pillows, eyeglasses, photographs, dangling earring with horse head, magazines, jewelry, a sleeping bag, controlled substances, and dark colored pistol with magazine."

The evidence was damning indeed. Juanita Rodriguez could identify some of the items, especially the rosary she had been looking at when repeatedly raped by Daveggio. Some of the other items were even more interesting. The title of the audiotape was *Submissive Young Girls.*

Agent Ferrin went on to write, "Further, due to the fact that there is probable cause to believe that the minivan contains fibers, hairs, blood, semen and fingerprint evidence, as well as other trace evidence relating to the kidnapping and sexual assault offenses, authority is also requested to allow the Washoe County Laboratory Forensic Investigation section to conduct a detailed search of the interior and exterior of the minivan and to obtain any fibers, hairs, blood, semen and trace evidence related to the kidnapping offense and sexual assault offense."

One of the main persons involved in the search of the van was Toni Leal, a forensic technician with the Washoe County Sheriff's Office, who did photography and processed film and latent work. She assisted the FBI as they went through the van and lifted hair samples and other small items by means of special adhesive tape and a thorough vacuuming of the entire interior with a powerful vacuum cleaner. She was in fact able to collect two small hairs consistent with those taken from Juanita Rodriguez. Amidst the immense amount of hair, lint and rubbish collected from the van, this was no mean feat. She also obtained a blood sample from James Daveggio that day and put it in a tube so that it could later be used by criminalist Rene Romero.

But one of the most interesting things Toni Leal found in Michelle Michaud's minivan was a curling iron with duct tape still attached. The cord had been severed from the curling iron. She also found several items wrapped up in a white towel: a green ball gag, yellow nylon rope, duct tape, tissue paper with a reddish stain on it and a large Revlon curling iron. In the front cup holder rack, she discovered a cassette case entitled *Submissive Young Girls,* and the tape itself was in the cassette player.

Amid all the trash in the van, Toni Leal picked up a couple of items that turned out to be important later as far as fingerprints were concerned: an AM/PM drink container and Diet Pepsi plastic bottle. She documented everything using the Washoe County Code system, which began everything with the letter Q. The Pepsi bottle became item Q12782, the AM/PM cup Q12780. Among all the debris she also found a book entitled *Dead of Night.* It was about serial killers.

Toni also requested a major case set of prints to be collected from James Daveggio and Michelle Michaud not only for the Washoe County Sheriff's Office, but for the California Department of Justice as well. A major case set of prints differed from a normal set of fingerprints in that not only the fingertips were rolled, but the side of the palm and the entire palm as well. Ms. Leal was taking no chances on these two.

A great deal of this material and information was soon sent to criminalist Renee Romero, who really went into her element. She obtained the vacuumed items and other small fibers from the interior consistent with the Juanita Rodriguez crime of September 29, 1997. Starting with a low magnification of about thirty mags to get a general idea of what she was looking at, she steadily increased the power to nearly 400 magnifications. She was now an expert with the stereomicroscope and could actually see the item in three-dimensional form, allowing her to analyze a single fiber to a remarkable degree of accuracy. One by one she noted fibers that came from clothes that Juanita Rodriguez had been wearing on the night of her abduction and were now picked up by adhesive tab at the lab. All of this added to the ever-growing amount of quantifiable evidence against James Daveggio and Michelle Michaud.

On that same day, December 4, 1997, another fateful event took place fifty miles southwest of Reno in Alpine County, California. At around ten o'clock in the morning, a motorist stopped by the side of the road on Highway 88 near Crater Wash and saw a "dark shape in the snow." Curiosity overcame his caution and he walked a little closer. What he saw next made him rock back in horror. The dark shape was the frozen body of a young woman.

The motorist quickly contacted the Alpine County Sheriff's Department and Deputy Everett T. Brakensiek was dispatched to the scene. Alpine County is the most mountainous county in California, and the least populated. With peaks jutting 12,000 feet into the sky and a population of less than 2,000, there are more bears, deer and raccoons in the county than there are people. Presiding over the whole area was Sheriff "Skip" Veatch, and he knew that the backcountry dwellers were an independent lot and sometimes at odds with the local law enforcement. But their crimes were usually petty in nature, consisting of shooting some game out of season, cutting firewood without a permit or pilfering road-crew equipment. Once in a while a mountaineer might come into the "big city" and county seat of Markleeville, population 200, on a drunken spree, but murder was practically unknown in Alpine County.

The body of the young woman was first put down as a traffic accident. But Deputy Brakensiek knew this section of Highway 88 like the back of his hand, and it soon became evident to him that this was no traffic accident. He scrambled down the snowy embankment and found the victim fully clothed in a

dark coat and blue jeans. He inspected her body
and discovered she possessed a checkbook, audiotapes, and wallet with cash still inside. The checkbook
and wallet revealed that she was a twenty-two-year-old
woman from Pleasanton, California, named Vanessa
Lei Samson. Beside her lay a long length of black
rope.

James Daveggio's and Michelle Michaud's luck
had held for months in eluding the authorities. But
now, they were in the land of chance where luck
often rides on the flip of a card or the roll of the
dice. The motorist had discovered her body after a
week of sunny weather. The next day it snowed,
obliterating all forms on the ground beneath a
cover of white.

Once Deputy Everett Brakensiek relayed his information to the Alpine County Sheriff's Office, a
phone call was placed to Police Chief Bill Eastman
in Pleasanton that Vanessa Samson's body had been
found. At 5:30 P.M. a policeman and chaplain arrived at the Samson household with the sad news
that their daughter had been found, but she was
not alive.

Everything was coming full circle very quickly. A
man named David Valentine came forward with a
bit of interesting news to the Pleasanton Police Department at about the same time that the chaplain
was visiting the Samsons. He had bought a house
on Page Court in Pleasanton near Kern Court, not
long before Vanessa Samson took her fateful walk
on December 2. Valentine and a co-worker, David
Elola, were up on the roof of the house replacing
shingles on that foggy, cold morning. Just about
7:50 A.M. they heard a scream from the street below
on Singletree Way. As David Valentine remembered,
"I heard a large, I mean super-loud, female's voice.
It was most definitely a scream. I thought something

desperate happened. But Dave had a better view and then he said, 'Hey, nothing happened. Nothing. Just calm down. It's probably a mom just getting her daughter into the car.' "

Unfortunately, David Elola had seen Michelle Michaud through the windshield of the van and had assumed that she was Vanessa Samson's mother. Vanessa was not a large girl and looked about high school age from a distance. Besides, not many people connect a woman driver with a kidnapping.

David Elola recounted, "I focused on the van that was slowly pulling away. And as it proceeded to go left, I focused in on the driver 'cause that's the first thing I wanted to find out, who was driving. I saw a female and she had long brown-black hair. She was looking forward. I could see just her profile."

The whole scene seemed to verify his initial thoughts that it was just some suburban mom getting her recalcitrant daughter to go to school and maybe they had some kind of argument. It wouldn't be the first time a teenage daughter screamed at her mom. Besides, the way the van slowly pulled away allayed his last bit of suspicion.

But David Valentine wasn't so sure, and the scream kept bugging him. As he said later, "I kept having a weird feeling in my stomach. I went back to the house two days later, to see how the roof turned out, and I don't know exactly what time it was, but I did see police officers passing out flyers, and that's when my heart completely dropped. So we notified the police officers immediately. And it happened so quickly that, you know, we talked about it, but then he [the police officer] said, 'If you have any questions, please page me.' So I went to bed that night and started thinking; I remembered looking at the license plate and the first number was definitely a three. And I paged him [the officer] and he called me at my parents' house. He said, 'Why are you calling?' And I said, I remember things and I did look at the license plate, and I know the first number is a three. And he said, 'Thank you very much,' and he started quizzing me, saying what color is the van, and I said, 'You know, I know it's a forest-green-color minivan.' "

Good luck was deserting James Daveggio and Michelle Michaud now like rats off a sinking ship. Vanessa Samson's body not only was found in the snow near where they had been arrested, but now there was a reliable witness who could put Michelle Michaud's minivan at the scene of the abduction at the time that it had happened.

The autopsy of Vanessa Samson's body came on December 5 in Auburn, Placer County, California, at the request of Alpine County. Alpine was a very small county and didn't have the facilities for such a major crime case. The autopsy was performed by Dr. Curtis Rollins, who had a degree in Anatomic Pathology with a subspecialty in forensic pathology, which concerned the determination of cause mechanism and manner of death in suspicious, sudden and violent deaths. He had a large audience that morning, including Deputy Everett Brakensiek and Officer Tom Nagel of Alpine County, Detective Desiree Carrington and Sergeant Bob McDonald of Placer County and two of their evidence technicians. Also there was a criminalist from the Department of Justice and FBI Agent Jeffrey Reed.

Following prescribed procedures, Dr. Rollins carefully opened the body bag and documented each piece of clothing as he took it off Vanessa Samson's body. He noted that her Calvin Klein jeans were unzipped and contained no belt. He also thoroughly searched for any trace evidence on her clothing. Then he carefully looked at her body for any external injuries. As far as that was concerned, it soon became obvious that she had a large bruise mark around her throat.

Dr. Rollins wrote:

"Cause of Death—mechanical asphyxia, due to a ligature strangulation. Mechanical asphyxia is essentially lack of oxygen, and mechanical lack of oxygen due to ligature strangulation which means that a ligature was placed around this person's neck and pulled tight enough to either cut off the air flow and all blood flow to her cerebral circulation or brain, resulting in death.

"In any asphyxial death there's several findings that you discover. Some of the classic findings of dying of asphyxia are the point above the ligature you get what's called cyanosis, which means basically that the blood can't get out because you've occluded venous flow, so it turns purple. You get cyanosis.

"Once the cyanosis stays there for awhile you get tardu spots or petechiae, which are darker spots within the blue. Sort of like pinpoint areas. You also get on your eyelids and on the sclera of your eye, petechial hemorrages which means, little busted vessels. The eyes protrude a little, so you get exophthalmos.

"[Vanessa Samson] had a furrow mark on her neck. That's just an area where the ligature was pulled tight enough and for long enough that it left a permanent sort of trench in the skin. It measured about a fourth of an inch wide. It was about ten and a fourth inches long. And it's an important thing about that ligature mark on her neck that it's horizontally oriented, which is not sloping upwards, which means she wasn't suspended. [Consistent with hanging, as in a suicide.]

"Over her left buttock region there was a cluster of individual bruises. On her right buttocks there's an area also of similar appearing purple or violaceous bruising."

Later when shown photographs of the curling irons, Dr. Rollins said, "The curling irons would be included in the group of objects that could have caused that injury."

When asked later by a prosecutor, "Assuming a curling iron was examined and determined to have fecal matter and blood that was Miss Samson's blood, would that be consistent with an item that was inserted into her rectal area?"

Dr. Rollins's answer was succinct. "Yes" was all he said.

Officer Chris Phelps of the Pleasanton Police Department was also there that day to obtain fingerprints from the dead woman. Because her fingers were no longer very manageable due to rigor mortis, he had to use a device known as a "spoon." A fingerprint card was attached to the spoon, and by rolling it over her stiff fingers and palm, he was able to pick up her prints. These fingerprints were very important indeed. They would be found on some items that came from Michelle Michaud's van.

The news of arrested suspects in the Vanessa Samson case and the Juanita Rodriguez case hit the television airwaves in the Bay Area, Sacramento, and Reno in time for the early-morning broadcasts on December 5, 1997. One of the most interested viewers was Michelle Michaud in the television room of the Douglas County Jail. She looked up at the screen and the image of her own photograph there sent her into a state of shock and panic. Up until this moment she believed the authorities only knew about the abduction and rape of Juanita Rodriguez. That was bad enough. But it was now crystal clear that they had also found the body of Vanessa Samson. Michaud knew that a conviction for the Juanita Rodriguez crime meant prison time. The murder of Vanessa Samson could bring the death penalty for her killers.

At this critical moment she decided to cut her losses. Witchy woman Michelle Michaud was about to start severing her ties with James Daveggio, one by one. What she would do next would have drastic repercussions not only for him, but for herself as well. Whether she misjudged, or panicked, or thought of what she was going to do as a well-conceived plan, only she knows for sure. But it would ultimately backfire on her as well as on Daveggio.

After the news report she called her father in Sacramento and told him the news about her was true. He was so stunned he didn't know what to think. He knew Michelle had problems, but nothing like this. One thing gave him scant comfort, she swore she hadn't killed anybody. About noon on the same day, a cellmate of Michaud's named Theresa Agorastos alerted the sheriff that Michaud had something to tell them about a murder in Alpine County, California.

Agorastos brought Michaud into the presence of Deputy Sheriff Doug Conrad. Both women were crying, but for very different reasons. Michaud of course for being caught, but Agorastos was crying because of what Michaud had just told her. She later told reporter David Holbrook, "I'd never heard anything like it. I was crying my eyes out. I told the deputies to get her the hell out of my cell. My God, the things they did to that poor woman! It was sickening."

Michaud finally spoke to the deputy and said, "I saw the newscast [about the discovery of Vanessa Samson's body]. I told Theresa I was scared. I was in trouble and I didn't know what to do. Theresa brought me up to the gate to see you."

Michaud said she had some information about Vanessa Samson's murder.

The Douglas County sergeant on duty placed her in an isolation cell and phoned Detective Kibbe in Pleasanton, who rang up FBI Special Agent Chris Campion in South Lake Tahoe. Detective Kibbe told Campion that Michelle Michaud wanted to talk about the Samson murder. Would Campion interview her? He didn't have to ask twice. Agent Campion was at the Douglas County Jail before 2:00 P.M., and along with him came Detective Tim Minister of the Douglas County Sheriff's Department.

They sat down with Michaud in an interrogation room and Agent Campion turned on a tape recorder. He said, "Michelle, we just started talking [indicating the tape recorder was turned on] and I just want to ask you to make sure that I'm clear that you want to talk to us, to me and Detective Minister here, about something that's obviously bothering you. You're obviously emotional right now and it's something that you need to get off your chest. Is that true?"

Michelle [crying]: "Yes. I have some information about the young lady who was killed a couple of days ago."

Agent Campion went over her rights again and she signed a Miranda form. Then he and Detective Minister questioned her for several hours and not only did she give information about the Vanessa

Samson kidnapping and murder, but she talked about the Juanita Rodriguez abduction and rape as well. She also talked about the trip up to Oregon with her daughter. She admitted that Daveggio had molested her daughter, but she denied having any hand in it.

At one point she told Agent Campion, "He's [Daveggio] been reading these books, and I have these books on serial killers. . . . He had a thing about the Charlene and Gerald Gallego book."

As far as the murder of Vanessa Samson went, she was still hedging her bets and not admitting to full involvement. She said, "Was she gone before? [Meaning was Vanessa already dead when she pulled on her half of the rope.] I'm not sure. No movement. Not sure."

Then Campion wanted to know if Michaud was involved with the Jaycee Lee Dugard kidnapping. She said, "No! I swear to God!"

Her testimony took up seven audiotapes.

The next day, December 6, Placer County detective Desiree Carrington was brought in and Michelle Michaud talked further about the Juanita Rodriguez case. This time it took up four audiotapes.

All the stress and terrible emotional strain was finally catching up with Michaud. On the way back from the session with Detective Carrington, she collapsed in her cell. She was rushed to a nearby hospital and placed in intensive care. When Agent Campion visited her there the next day, Michaud told him she had collapsed because of an imbalance in hormones caused by a recent hysterectomy. She said that Daveggio hadn't allowed her to take her hormone medication. But the nurse had another explanation. She told Michaud that people coming off a heavy dose of methamphetamines will often react in a similar manner.

Whatever the cause of her collapse, Michaud's hospital visit was short. By the next day, December 8, she was back in the Douglas County Jail giving more taped testimony. Once again she was asked about the murder of Vanessa Samson. Even though she once again tried to distance herself from that killing, she did admit that James Daveggio had placed her hands on the rope tied around Vanessa's neck and made her pull in tandem with him. Then, according to Michaud, he muttered, "Together, forever." This time six audiotapes were filled.

Michelle Michaud and James Daveggio were separated by more than just distance now. She was not subscribing to Benjamin Franklin's loosely translated adage "Hang together or hang separately." She didn't intend to hang at all. She would let Daveggio do it on his own. And as time went by, she would give the prosecutors the rope to hang him with.

But time would tell if her testimony was a clever attempt to put most of the blame on him while sparing herself or if indeed it was a tremendous loss of nerve on her part. One thing was for sure— Michelle Lyn Michaud was handing over on a silver platter evidence that might have taken months to uncover, or may have never seen the light of day at all. In her rush to put the blame on Daveggio, she forgot one thing. Juries are unpredictable things, often unwilling to convict on circumstantial and trace evidence alone. But with the testimony of an eyewitness, especially one involved in the crimes, they could destroy not only the recipient of the message, but the messenger as well.

Chapter 28

The Gathering

Pleasanton Police Chief Bill Eastman was overjoyed to have both James Daveggio and Michelle Michaud behind bars. Always frustrated by the inability to solve the Tina Faelz murder in 1984, he hadn't wanted the Vanessa Samson case to turn out the same way. Without the timely discovery of Vanessa's body by the passing motorist, it might indeed have had the same sour results.

But there was no time to think of past failures now. It was time to tell the media about the incredibly involved manhunt that had snared this murderous pair. At 2:30 P.M. on December 10 he and Alameda district attorney Tom Orloff held a news conference in front of a crowd of newspaper reporters and a bank of radio and television microphones and cameras. The bulldog tenacity that had been so in evidence during the search for Vanessa Samson was still showing in Bill Eastman's countenance.

He started out by taking the reporters back through all the stages of Vanessa Samson's abduction and the steps taken by the Pleasanton Police and other agencies to discover her whereabouts. He touched on Daveggio's and Michaud's abuse of Vanessa, their route to Tahoe and their arrests at the Lakeside Inn. Then he said, "I express our heartfelt condolences to the Samson family and I thank them for their assistance during their ordeal and our investigation. I would also like to thank the many law enforcement agencies who were of such great assistance to us."

It was a veritable laundry list of agencies:

South Lake Tahoe FBI
South Lake Tahoe Police Department
Placer County Sheriff's Department
Alpine County Sheriff's Department
Sacramento Police Department
Douglas County Sheriff's Department
Washoe County Sheriff's Department
Alameda County District Attorney's Office

Bill Eastman wasn't alone in his praise of the interagency cooperation. The Placer County sheriff told reporters, "The resolution of this case demonstrates the importance and value of cooperation and information sharing between federal, state and local agencies. Without the efforts of all agencies and peace officers, the suspects would have been free to continue their activities. The presence, manpower and coordination provided by the FBI greatly assisted the jurisdictional issues involved. The cooperative spirit and efforts between California and Nevada authorities is a marvelous example to the law enforcement community."

Amid all the praise, Police Chief Bill Eastman did issue one cautionary note: "A male and female together throw off public suspicion and certainly throw off witness perception." It had happened with Gerald and Charlene Gallego and now it had happened with James Daveggio and Michelle Michaud.

As roofer David Elola had said to his co-worker David Valentine when they heard the scream and saw Michelle Michaud in the driver's seat, "Hey, nothing happened. Nothing. Just calm down. It's probably a mom just getting her daughter into the car."

But all in all, the press conference was one of satisfaction of a job well done, tempered only by the somber realization that Vanessa Samson had not survived her ordeal.

Onto the point of Samson's murder, Alameda County district attorney Tom Orloff now took center stage. He disclosed that Alameda County would be prosecuting Daveggio and Michaud after they were tried on federal charges in Reno, Nevada, for the abduction and rape of Juanita Rodriguez, and that he would seek the death penalty. One of the key people trying the case would be none other than Michael Ihde's old nemesis Assistant District Attorney Rock Harmon.

The press was interested in James Daveggio and Michelle Michaud, not only in the Bay Area but up in the Sierras as well. Once Michelle Michaud's photo appeared on the front page of the *Tahoe Daily Tribune,* it sent shock waves through the community. Her mug shot eerily matched the police sketch of Jaycee Lee Dugard's kidnapper in 1991. Veteran crime reporter Christina Proctor ran a story on December 12 noting the similarities. The large headline DUGARD LINK INVESTIGATED was accompanied by photos of Michelle Michaud and Vanessa Samson on the front page. Christina brought Jaycee Lee's old detective Jim Watson once more into the news. He stated, "We will definitely look at them [Daveggio and Michaud] and try to establish or rule them out as suspects, but we have no smoking guns at the present time."

She also spoke with Jaycee Lee's mom, Terry Probyn. Terry had been through so many ups and downs for the past six years that she attempted to keep her emotions in check. She told Proctor, "I agree and so does Carl [nickname for William Probyn, Jaycee's stepfather and only witness to her abduction] that they [the photo and the police sketch of the woman he saw] are similar."

Everyone in the area was talking about the case, all of them noting the remarkable resemblance of Michelle Michaud's mug shot to the sketch of the Jaycee Lee Dugard kidnapper. The case had never left the community's consciousness completely, and posters of Dugard and a few faded pink ribbons could still be glimpsed around town. Jaycee Lee Dugard's abduction had as profound an effect on Lake Tahoe as the more publicized Polly Klaas kidnapping in Petaluma, California. Even when FBI spokesperson Carole Micozzi pointed out that Michelle Michaud looked much different in 1991, it still didn't quell the remarks about the similarities of the gaunt-looking woman in the Douglas County mug shot and the police sketch taken from William Probyn's eyewitness account. After all, Michaud could disguise herself when she wanted to, it was surmised. She had already done so after the Juanita Rodriguez kidnapping by making herself look like a man as much as possible.

In fact, Carole Micozzi's statement only led to a new and stranger wrinkle of speculation among the Tahoe locals. The new alternative theory concerned not Michelle Michaud, but James Daveggio. It was speculated that he came up to Tahoe in June 1991 with a dark-haired girlfriend and spotted Jaycee Lee

Dugard walking down Washoan Boulevard. Fuel was only added to this line of reasoning when it was learned that a man somewhat matching Daveggio's description had kidnapped a nine-year-old Hayward, California, girl in 1988. That girl had also been snatched off the street and into a four-door American sedan by a blond-haired stocky man who was about Daveggio's age and height at the time. It was noted that he had used a four-door American sedan in the abduction and molestation of Janet Stokes as well. The Hayward girl was blond, blue-eyed and could have passed for Jaycee Lee Dugard's younger sister. Even though James Daveggio and Michelle Michaud didn't know each other at the time, when it was learned how many girlfriends Daveggio always had, it was speculated that he had coaxed one of them into being his mysterious driver on the Dugard crime. He seemed to have a definite knack for talking people into doing things they might not have normally done without his insistence. In December of 1997 the rumors about James Daveggio's predatory activities were running rampant.

In 1997 the Jaycee Lee Dugard files at the El Dorado Sheriff's Department filled one complete wall. A few sightings and phone calls still came in, but nothing like the frantic hours of the first few weeks in 1991. Since then, every day had a leaden feel in the home where she had lived. The strain became too much in the marriage between her mother, Terry, and stepfather William Probyn, and they divorced. Terry, to fill the empty hours, became a full-fledged advocate on children's safety. She was the main speaker at the 1997 Soroptimist International meeting in South Lake Tahoe, dubbed "A Fighting Chance."

She told them, "It is really time to tell our children that, at the very moment that they are in the grasp of an abductor, it is important to free themselves. If a person tries to pull a child into a car, that child should try to run in the opposite direction from where the front of the vehicle is pointed. If a person tries to pull a child off a bicycle, the child should hold on to the bicycle as long as possible."

The program was based on real-life child abductions and stories of children who had escaped their attackers. The whole program was dedicated to Jaycee Lee's memory.

If Jaycee Lee's mother had to fill up her lonely hours with these sorts of experiences, things were even worse in some ways for her stepfather. On March 18, 1997, a team of detectives arrived at the home where he and Terry had once lived on Washoan Boulevard and began to dig around the front porch of the house. They didn't say what they were looking for, but the implication was clear. . . . They either thought William Probyn was either a liar or—even worse—part of the reason why Jaycee was missing. In a town as small and tight-knit as South Lake Tahoe, the word of the detectives digging soon spread. William Probyn had to suffer a new kind of indignity in addition to guilt and grief—humiliation. It became hard just to show his face in places that he had patronized for years.

He told a *Tahoe Tribune* reporter, "There is about one percent of Tahoe who think we had something to do with the kidnapping and this just gives them fuel for the fire."

Lieutenant Fred Kollar of the El Dorado Sheriff's Department explained, "We're going back and trying to put closure to some leads. Sometimes you want to have someone else come back and look at the case and have them satisfy their curiosity."

The detectives dug around and found nothing.

Jaycee Lee's mother, Terry, commented after the Sheriff's probe to *Tahoe Tribune* reporter Jennifer Ragland, "It doesn't bother me—I'm used to it. We never had any doubt that the family had nothing to do with it, but some people in town expressed concern that somehow the family was involved."

Then she defiantly added, "There's another answer out there, and I have as much hope as I did six years ago. It's hard to move on with life when you are still stuck in the past, but I am bound to this town until I find an answer."

The gossip that she and William were involved in Jaycee Lee's disappearance must have disturbed her more deeply than she first let on, but not as deeply as a bizarre incident that had happened next. On September 4, 1997, a parolee named Rick Tanksley was sentenced to five years in prison for attempting to obtain money under false pretenses and ten years for extortion. Supposedly, he had been collecting money that would be added to the Jaycee Lee Dugard reward fund. In truth, Tanksley was keeping all the money for himself. He even went so far as to claim that he would get assistance from South African leader Nelson Mandela to help in the effort. It was all an elaborate scam.

When Tanksley was brought up on charges, he insisted on representing himself in court. But the outcome was disastrous. While awaiting sentencing after his conviction, he set fire to his jail mattress, screamed and yelled like a madman, and was eventually tried and convicted on a separate charge of arson. For his wild and erratic behavior, he was deemed a habitual criminal and given a life sentence.

Despite all this craziness, one man had never given up on the Jaycee Lee Dugard abduction—Detective Sergeant Jim Watson. He had been on the case six long years and he was now fifty-two years old. He had poured out his heart and soul trying to recover the little girl, but it was time to turn the case over to a younger man. Being the thoughtful individual he was, Watson often wondered, "Did I do everything I could have? Did I screw up? Was I the best person to have handled the case?"

But then he took solace in the fact "There's other investigators out there with similar cases of their own, and they haven't found their kids either."

In a changing of the guard without pomp or circumstance, Detective Jim Watson placed the Jaycee Lee Dugard case into the capable hands of Detective Sergeant Randy Peshon, the man who had spent forty-eight hours straight searching for the lost girl back in 1991. Like Watson, he had never given up hope in finding the missing girl. In addition to his officer duties, he had joined the El Dorado Search and Rescue team. Rescuing lost people in the wilderness became the underlying theme of his life, and he must have felt a great deal of satisfaction when at least in this endeavor he saved the lives of more than one lost skier and snowboarder.

The rumors were flying a mile a minute in early December 1997 around Lake Tahoe about the possibility of James Daveggio and especially Michelle Michaud being involved in the Jaycee Lee Dugard kidnapping. There were indeed enough similarities in the Michaud and Daveggio case concerning Juanita Rodriguez and Vanessa Samson with the Jaycee Lee Dugard incident and other kidnapping cases that Detective Randy Peshon was ordered to attend the interagency meeting of law enforcement officers sponsored by the Sacramento office of the FBI. Suddenly, a dozen different police agencies

were interested in James Daveggio and Michelle
Michaud in regard to kidnapped and missing girls
in their jurisdictions. The same jurisdictions that Detective Jim Watson had noted years before "haven't
found their missing kids either."

FBI Agent Tom Griffin of Sacramento set the
tone. "We're looking at every case there is that they
[Daveggio and Michaud] might be involved in. It's
part of the investigation. We'd be remiss if we
didn't." FBI Spokesperson Carole Micozzi went on
to say, "Part of the investigation is to determine
what forensic evidence we have in these [unsolved]
cases. Do we have evidence? Do we have sightings?
Do we have reason to believe they were in the
area?"

Sergeant Bob Mitchell of the Sacramento Police
commented, "They appear to be involved in a lot
of stuff. Everyone's going to be looking at old
cases."

The gathering of officers took place in Sacramento all afternoon on December 17. The Sacramento Sheriff's Office listened to the array of
evidence shared at the roundtable of detectives and
FBI agents and soon decided that there was nothing
to link Daveggio and Michaud to unsolved crimes
in their jurisdiction. But as for the others, the similarities were just too compelling to dismiss. The
Pleasanton Police in particular were very interested
in Daveggio as a suspect for the murder of Tina
Faelz less than a half mile from his home at the
time. He had been a student at Foothill High where
she attended classes and probably knew of the culvert shortcut where she had been murdered.

Detective Lieutenant Dave Hoig and Detective
Monte De Coste of Alameda were looking at Daveg-
gio for the first time as a suspect in the murder of
Kellie Poppleton in Sunol, where he had once

tended bar. Michael Ihde was already a suspect in that slaying as well. Detective Randy Peshon was there to look at both Daveggio and Michaud as possible abductors of Jaycee Lee Dugard in Lake Tahoe. That they had been in and out of the Tahoe area a lot and knew its roads and backstreets was now becoming more and more evident. People all over town came forward and stated that they particularly remembered Daveggio and his purple Harley motorcycle. He was known at several motels, restaurants and a biker bar; an attendant at the Shell station knew him too.

A Hayward, California, police detective was there because of an abduction in 1988 that closely mirrored the Jaycee Lee Dugard case. On November 19, 1988, another blond-haired girl, Michaela Garecht, who bore more than just a passing resemblance to Jaycee Lee, was abducted at the Rainbow Market on Mission Boulevard in Hayward in the presence of her friend, Trina Rodriguez. Trina saw a man between the ages of twenty and twenty-eight with dirty-blond hair talking to Michaela. "Dirty-blond hair" is exactly the way that rape victim Janet Stokes described her assailant, James Daveggio, at the Tracy trial in 1985. Daveggio at the time fell right into these parameters, being of about the same weight and build. Trina heard the man say to Michaela, "You looking for your scooter? It's over by my car."

The car in question was a two-toned 1970s American sedan, similar to the Jaycee Lee Dugard abduction vehicle. When Michaela Gerecht walked over to retrieve her scooter, she was grabbed around the waist and thrown screaming into the vehicle just before it roared off in front of Trina Rodriguez's startled eyes. Even though there was a massive manhunt within the hour, just like at Lake Tahoe with Dugard, the vehicle, kidnapper and little girl were never found. Unfortunately, the kidnapper had left only a partial palm print on Gerecht's scooter and in 1988 there were no police files on palm prints as there were of fingerprints.

Michaela's mother, Sharon, expressed a plea to the kidnapper that echoed the words of all parents of abducted children. "We don't know who you are or where you are. All we really want from you right now is for you to return our daughter. Drop her off on a street corner. Give her instructions to wait five minutes and go to the phone and call home. I'm not sure that I can forgive you for what you have already done, but if you could please just let her go, then maybe I could forget."

The litany of names of Bay Area girls who simply disappeared under similar circumstances now sounded like a mournful dirge around the environs of Pleasanton: Amber Swartz-Garcia (1988, Pinole), Nikki Campbell (1991, Fairfield) and especially Ilene Misheloff (1989, Dublin) walking home near the school where James Daveggio and Michael Ihde had once buddied around.

Dublin Police were so intrigued about Daveggio as a suspect that they assigned three detectives to look into the matter. Heading the group was Lieutenant Chuck Farrugia. Attending the Sacramento conclave, he commented about Daveggio being a prime suspect in the Misheloff case, "It looks good." Then he added as a note of caution, "But it means absolutely nothing at this point."

What looked so good was the fact that Ilene Misheloff had been a Wells Middle School student at the time of her disappearance—the same campus where Daveggio had a daughter going to school. The same school that was adjacent to Valley High Continuation, Daveggio's former school. The same school where Daveggio had stopped for a visit on the day before he kidnapped Vanessa Samson.

Back on January 30, 1989, thirteen-year-old Ilene Misheloff was walking home from Wells Middle School to her skating practice. It was 3:00 P.M. and she was to meet her ice-skating coach at the woman's home on Alegre Drive. Misheloff was already a wonderful ice-skater with plenty of awards and ribbons to prove it. Dreams of someday making it to the Olympics were not far-fetched. She had that kind of technical skill and soulful grace.

Misheloff's usual route took her from the school, down Amador Boulevard and toward Mape Park. Someone saw her pass the Foster Freeze around 3:10 P.M. Then she moved off, toward a ditch that runs along the edge of Mape Park, out of the witness's line of sight. This was a common shortcut for teenagers on their way home from school. The whole situation was eerily reminiscent of Tina Faelz and her shortcut across the drainage ditch from Foothill High in Pleasanton.

She was wearing a charcoal-gray pullover sweater to ward off the cold, a horizontally striped pink-and-gray skirt, black low-top Keds, and carrying a dark blue backpack. Somewhere in that maze of ditches she passed beyond all human recall and simply vanished. Unlike Tina Faelz, neither she nor her body was later found.

By 6:00 P.M. Ilene Misheloff's mother was frantic and phoned the Dublin Police Department. There was little hesitation between the call and response, since authorities were still very mindful of the Michaela Garecht disappearance just over the hill in Hayward not long before. The Dublin police quickly sent out patrol cars to the area and cops walking on foot. Before long they were joined by investigators from the Alameda Sheriff's Department and Alameda Office of Emergency Services. The search concentrated on the maze of ditches running alongside Mape Park; while out in the hills behind the Misheloff house, units of the sheriff's posse saddled up and began riding through the rugged terrain on horseback. It was a scene out of the Old West as they scoured rugged Martin's Canyon. Even a helicopter from the East Bay Regional Park District Police, Randy Peshon's old unit, was called for and began circling overhead, looking for the missing girl.

Misheloff's father, just like her mom, was beside himself and couldn't sit still. He told a reporter for the *Tri-Valley Herald*, "I searched in the creek behind the house. I kept it up until the batteries in the flashlight were completely discharged. I was just frantic afterward and it's been a long frightening night."

Neighbors soon learned of the Misheloffs' plight and came by the house all evening long. The Kevin Collins Foundation sprang into action, printing and distributing 30,000 flyers around the area. One more person came by the house, someone who might never have been there except for the terrible thing that had transpired in her home the year before—Michaela Garecht's mother. She came armed with a long spool of yellow ribbon. Before long, friends and neighbors of the Misheloffs had yellow ribbons dangling around light poles all over town— a terrible premonition of the pink ribbons that would soon be floating around South Lake Tahoe in remembrance of Jaycee Lee Dugard.

The father of missing Amber Swartz-Garcia was there too, chipping in on an 800 number with the phone company so that the Misheloffs' main line would be free if Ilene called home or the abductor called in. It was assumed all along that this was an abduction. Ilene was not the type of girl to run away from home on a spur-of-the-moment whim.

They were a fraternity all their own now, these parents of lost children, inhabiting a world that only they could comprehend. A short distance away, beneath the photographs of the graceful, athletic girl posing in skating costume, the Mishloffs' rabbi, Ira Book, gazed at all of them and mused, "You're dealing with the ultimate nightmare for a parent. A child has been taken. I don't think there are any magic words that are going to make it any easier."

In the center of the swirling police search, the parents sat alone, the eye of the hurricane. Out in the streets helicopters flew overhead; tracking dogs sniffed through the underbrush; a mannequin was dressed up in clothes similar to the ones Ilene had been wearing, just in case it would jog someone's memory. The quietude of the pleasant suburban streets had been ripped apart forever, and ombudsman Tim Hunt of the *Tri-Valley Herald* wondered aloud in print: "In [this] valley we blissfully think we've insulated ourselves from the drug wars of Oakland and the gangs that plague other East Bay cities. But this week we discovered that senseless crime isn't limited to the places where disappearances are so routine that they warrant only a couple of paragraphs in the back of the local newspaper."

A sense of fear and loss and sin had come to this upscale Eden as it had to Hayward and Pleasanton and Lake Tahoe. Amber Swartz-Garcia's father shouted in his rage, "Our children can't go to school without being shot at with an AK-47, and they can't walk home from school without being kidnapped. They can't even play jump rope in front of the house. They are not safe anywhere!"

He wondered who could be doing all of these terrible things, as if a monster lived just beyond the horizon. But the monster was not from beyond the horizon—he had been one of them all along.

Everyone in the involved law enforcement communities had an opinion about James Daveggio being the perpetrator in the cases of their missing children. Everyone was being cautious as well. Dublin detective sergeant Michael Hart said, "We're waiting to see what they [the FBI] come up with and we have to put a time line on him [Daveggio] to find out where he was in 1989."

But there was no doubt in anyone's mind, he was the best suspect they had come up with in a long, long time. There was still a long way to go, but as 1997 passed into the new year, evidence against James Daveggio and Michelle Michaud was coming in at an ever-increasing rate. None of it, as far as they were concerned, boded well for their futures.

Chapter 29

Move . . . Countermove

The intricate legal chess game involving the lives of James Daveggio and Michelle Michaud now moved from the realm of policemen and FBI agents to the courtroom. Michaud was assigned legal counsel, Reno attorney Mary Boestch, on December 12, 1997, and on December 15 she entered a plea of not guilty in the Juanita Rodriguez case.

Right from the start Boestch was wary and tight-lipped with reporters, and her client matched her taciturn manner. But it was a telling first revelation in her strategy when Boestch moved to quash the government case at the outset. She argued that the arrest of Michaud was illegal in the first place because FBI Agent Chris Campion had lied when he spoke through the door at the Lakeside Inn saying he was a manager and that Daveggio was ill in the casino area.

David Hagen, U.S. district judge, the man who would be presiding over the case, was a dignified, lean man with graying hair and beard. He had an aspect about him that typified the best of the small-town Nevada-style open-mindedness and sense of fair play. Noted for his intelligence and thoughtfulness, he carefully considered Mary Boestch's request and after much consideration let the arrest order stand.

In the meantime, Daveggio had been assigned court-appointed attorney Michael Kennedy. In his thirties with an effusive manner, flashy suits and long dark hair tied back in a ponytail, Kennedy was in stark contrast to the conservatively attired and reticent Mary Boestch. Kennedy divided his time between Reno and Las Vegas; he knew with this case he had a "big one" on his hands. Not only would it have high media awareness, but it would be difficult as well. Kennedy was up to the challenge.

While Boestch and her client hid behind a wall of silence, Kennedy came out swinging right off the bat for Daveggio. The analogy of the chess game was now more true than ever. Boestch and Michaud waited in the corner for things to develop while Kennedy and Daveggio moved their pieces all over the judicial chessboard, countering the moves made by the federal prosecutors.

There were two federal prosecutors on the case now attempting to link James Daveggio and Michelle Michaud to the abduction and rape of Juanita Rodriguez—Daniel Bogden and Ronald Rachow. While Bogden radiated youth and enthusiasm, a spark plug in the crime unit against drugs and racketeering, Rachow was a more sedate warrior of the legal battlefield. He looked like a television version of a veteran prosecutor—gray short hair and a penchant for gray suits. But even though he spoke quietly, he still managed to have a commanding presence and well thought-out delivery. When he wanted, he could insert sarcastic barbs hidden behind his smooth sentences. There wasn't much that got past him, and any openings the defense gave him, he pounced on.

The two dissimilar prosecutors were in no hurry for the trial to get under way as evidence came pouring in from all points of the compass. Criminalist Renee Romero was joined by criminalist Maria Fassett at the Washoe County Crime Lab as they scanned the evidence obtained from the minivan. They had a wide array of evidence to peruse. They first searched for hair that might have come from Juanita Rodriguez, and if a root sheath was attached, DNA testing using the PCR method could definitely say it came from a certain portion of the population to which the victim belonged. Even without the root sheath, microscopic analysis could say that the hair had the same characteristics as the victim's hair.

Broken fingernails were also searched for, since they, much like a bullet, have individualized striations on them. They could be matched to a victim even months after a crime had been committed.

Also a key element were clothing fibers that could be matched with a fair degree of accuracy to the victim's clothing. Under a high-powered microscope they had very significant characteristics.

Meanwhile, another lab in Reno, a California Department of Justice lab in Berkeley and still another DOJ lab in Santa Rosa began to take in samples for analyzing. In an ironic twist of fate, Daveggio was ordered to produce some blood and it was sent to a lab in Pleasanton not far from where Vanessa Samson had lived. Even the Child Abduction and Serial Killer Unit at Quantico, Virginia, was looking at James Daveggio and Michelle Michaud. Especially Michelle Michaud. "It is one of the first cases in which a woman has allegedly taken an equal role in a series of sexual assaults," FBI officials said. Unlike Charlene Gallego, who had been termed "an enabler" and only picked out young girls for her husband to rape, torture and kill, Michaud in time became just as involved in the rapes and murders as Daveggio. So few women in the United States fell into this category that the FBI took a long, hard look at her case. They worried she was just the tip of the iceberg in a growing trend of violent female criminals. It was only half jokingly referred to by some as the "Thelma and Louise Syndrome."

There was so much information gathering, in fact, that Judge Hagen continued the case scheduled for mid-January 1998 until September 8, 1998. Neither counsels for Daveggio nor Michaud objected. In fact, they were glad for the delay, for on February 5 and March 27, 1998, both Mary Boestch and Michael Kennedy had to view literally hundreds of physical evidence items seized by law enforcement agents.

After June 26, 1998, Boestch and Kennedy had even more physical evidence to review. On that date law enforcement agents seized a computer tower and two cases of computer discs belonging to Daveggio, along with clothing items, and as the search warrant stated, "Fibers, hairs, and trace evidence." With all this mountain of evidence, criminalist Rene Romero had more ammunition than ever in the case against Daveggio and Michaud.

Meanwhile, a curious thing was happening. Even though Daveggio and Michaud weren't separated by a great distance now, both being confined in separate parts of the Washoe County Jail in Reno, it became more and more apparent to Daveggio that Michaud was slipping away. Just what that witchy woman was up to he couldn't say for sure. But as the summer of 1998 progressed and the pile of evidence grew, Daveggio and his attorney could feel a decided chill deepening on Michaud's part. What was at first just a hunch became almost a certainty as July turned into August. Michaud at some point was going to cut her losses and leave James dangling alone in the wind.

Before that could happen, Michael Kennedy struck first. On August 8, 1998, he made a motion to sever James Daveggio's trial from Michelle Michaud's. The deadly link that had been forged in the smoky recesses of Bobby Joe's nearly two years before was now totally and irrevocably broken.

Another significant event happened "off stage" on August 25, 1998—Police Chief Bill Eastman was rushed to Valley Care Medical Center directly from his office, complaining of chest pains. He had suffered a mild heart attack and would retire within the year after serving as head man in Pleasanton for eighteen years. He said, "It's time. I've enjoyed my career, but being a police chief is not my whole identity in life."

At least he had one great satisfaction upon retirement. The murder of Vanessa Samson, unlike that of Tina Faelz, would not go unpunished.

Back on the judicial scene, on September 11, 1998, Judge Hagen granted the severance that Daveggio sought, and Michaud's trial was set for November 17, only two months away. Daveggio's trial was scheduled for December 15. But nothing was going forward in an orderly manner with these two involved. It was as if the cases had taken on the aspects of Daveggio's and Michaud's own erratic personalities. The two who had been lovers were now sworn enemies and as the government's case against Michaud was just coming to trial on November 11, 1998, all of the minivan exhibits were admitted into evidence over the objections of Mary Boestch. Boestch requested once again that all of Michaud's statements to the FBI made on December 5, 6 and 8 be supressed because Agent Chris

Campion had lied to her at the motel door when he said that he was the manager and James Daveggio was sick in the casino area. But that motion was denied by Judge Hagen again. Even more damaging government evidence was admitted on November 16, 1998—the findings of criminalist Renee Romero who had indeed found two hairs matching Juanita Rodriguez's in Michaud's minivan.

Everything was lining up to place Michelle Michaud right in the crosshairs with James Daveggio. But Michaud was never one to sit back and let fate take its course. On the afternoon of Monday, November 16, 1998, just one day before her jury trial was to begin, she made a conditional plea of guilty to Count 2 of the charges: Aiding and abetting a kidnapping. By doing this, she added one big bonus for herself. She could come back at a later time with her lawyer and approach the Ninth Circuit Court of Appeals. This court could then decide whether or not to overturn Judge Hagen's decision to include her taped statements to the FBI and Desiree Carrington on December 5 through 8. If indeed the Ninth Circuit Court overturned Judge Hagen's decision, Michaud could return, change her plea to not guilty, and ask for a new trial. Without all the statements, it might be very hard to prove that she even aided and abetted in the kidnapping of Juanita Rodriguez and she might get off scot-free, at least on the Reno kidnapping case.

Her conditional plea of guilty to Count 2 caught everyone by surprise, including prosecutors Ron Rachow and Daniel Bogden. They were set for a lengthy, hard-fought trial. They well knew Michaud's lawyer, Mary Boestch, was no pushover. But Michaud, staying true to form, twisted the proceedings her way. James Daveggio could have learned a lesson in control from her.

Bogden was particularly surprised because he had to give up so little for a plea bargain. In return for her plea of guilty to a charge of kidnapping, he and Rachow dropped the charge of conspiracy. He expressed a certain buoyancy of stunned relief when he told reporters, "One down, one to go!" But his buoyancy might have been less exuberant if he knew what tricks Michaud still held up her sleeve.

Even after her plea of guilty, Michaud and Boestch had to face Judge Hagen to formally enter the plea before the court. Michaud came quietly into the courtroom, wearing wire-rimmed glasses and sporting neatly combed shoulder-length hair. She looked nothing like the defiant hooker standing before the camera at the Sacramento Police Department as they snapped her mug shot in 1991. She now matched the popular conception of a mousy librarian. She wiped away tears with Kleenex as Judge Hagen began to ask her questions.

Boestch maintained her sphinxlike silence until Judge Hagen asked of Michaud, "What did you do to assist the kidnapping of Juanita Rodriguez?"

Boestch jumped up and objected.

Judge Hagen rephrased the question. "Is it true that you were driving the green minivan when James Daveggio abducted the woman from Reno and then drove across state lines to California?"

"Yes, sir," Michaud answered quietly.

Judge Hagen cautioned her that she would be under strict sentencing qualifications. "It could be quite different from the sentence you have in mind right now. Do you understand that?"

"Yes, sir, I do," Michaud answered.

Judge Hagen then ordered Michelle back into custody at the Washoe County Jail until James Daveggio's trial. As she was escorted out of the courtroom by federal marshals, it did in fact seem as Daniel Bogden had stated, "One down, one to go."

Across town, James Daveggio's lawyer, Michael Kennedy, had a few tricks of his own up his sleeve. He had noted in the testimony that Juanita Rodriguez had given to Detective Desiree Carrington and others that she had referred to her male attacker's voice as high-pitched. Now that was odd. Everyone who knew James Daveggio could attest to his raspy low voice. It was his trademark and had earned him the name Frog.

Kennedy obtained the services of Dr. Steve MacFarlane, professor of speech pathology at the University of Nevada, Reno, to examine and test Daveggio's voice. As Dr. MacFarlane explained to the court about his planned examination, "The first type requires visualization of the actual vocal cords and there's a whole rack of equipment as it were, and an examining chair, much like a dental chair that allows us to put a scope in and see the larynx and high-speed photography and slow motion. The second one is smaller but essentially like a desktop computer that allows us to measure airflow through the vocal cords in a second of time. And the third is actually a computer that has a monitor that allows us to do an acoustical measure of the voice. That is another big piece of equipment that we do sort of a voice print. I've done that in some cases to identify people who have done telephone scams and things. All of the equipment could fill a van."

All this equipment was at UNR at the Redfield Building in the Speech Pathology and Audiology Department. Judge Hagen expressed his concerns about security, but Dr. MacFarlane assured him that other prisoners had been brought there in orange jumpsuits and shackles by federal marshals with no problem. Bowing to that knowledge, Judge Hagen allowed Daveggio to be tested.

Linking Daveggio up to the equipment and testing him, Dr. MacFarlane learned that Daveggio had an aberration on the left side of his larynx as well as additional tissue near the front of the larynx. It was a congenital condition and had affected his voice since birth, giving it a rough husky quality. That someone would ever accuse him of having a "high-pitched" voice seemed highly unlikely.

This was Michael Kennedy's first chink in the government's argument. But as he studied all their evidence, he found even more. He discovered that the rape victim Juanita Rodriguez never mentioned her attacker as having tattoos, whereas Daveggio had several prominent ones all over his body and he had been undressed during the attack. She also had told the Washoe County Sheriff's sketch technician that her attacker had brown hair and brown eyes. Daveggio had blond hair and blue eyes.

These were small victories for Michael Kennedy, but they were better than nothing. After all, if not even the victim could positively identify James Daveggio as her rapist, then who for sure could say he was guilty beyond a reasonable doubt? Kennedy wouldn't argue that Rodriguez hadn't been raped— he would simply say Daveggio hadn't been the one.

But before he could congratulate himself very much, he should have been paying closer attention to Michelle Michaud. In early January 1999 she approached a detective with the Washoe County Sheriff's Office and told the officer that if she was released she could infiltrate the Mustang Ranch bordello as an undercover agent. The government at the time was trying to prove that Joe Conforte, who was wanted for tax evasion and on the lam in South America, was in fact still controlling the brothel through manager Shirley Colletti, who was a former Storey County commissioner.

Michaud also reiterated the statement she had made to Rick Bourne that she was in the room when a bail bondsman in Sacramento was shot in the head and killed by a member of the Hell's Angels. If allowed her freedom, she could also infiltrate *that* organization.

The authorities took her seriously for a while and mulled over her request. When they eventually passed on her proposal, she still had one major trick up her sleeve. On the night before James Daveggio was to start his trial on February 23, 1999, she decided to be a witness for the prosecution against him. More than anyone else, it would be Michaud who put the nails in his coffin.

Chapter 30

Decision in Reno

James Daveggio's lawyer, Michael Kennedy, went through the roof when he found out what Michelle Michaud was up to. He argued before Judge Hagen, "The government's own investigation in this prosecution has produced evidence that its star witness, Michelle Michaud, is a pathological liar." Way back on December 5, 1997, Michaud's sister, Misty Michaud, had described Michaud to the FBI as "overdramatic, attention-seeking and a pathological liar who can be very convincing." Misty's boyfriend, Rick Bourne, who also knew Michelle well, told FBI Agent Tom Osbourne that "Michelle has multiple personalities." The law enforcement report itself described her as "a prostitute, drug addict and pathological liar." Kennedy requested that Michaud undergo a psychiatric evaluation before being allowed to testify against Daveggio. He argued that she was incapable of telling the truth.

Assistant U.S. Attorney Ron Rachow argued, "The government strongly opposes the defendant's [Daveggio's] request that Michaud be required to submit to a psychiatric or psychological examination prior to being allowed to testify at the defendant's trial. In support of his allegation that Michaud is a pathological liar, he relies on statements made by two untrained lay persons. Based on the flimsiest of threads, in an attempt to avoid Michaud's testimony at the trial, the defendant tries to discourage her appearance before a jury by asking this court to compel her to submit for an examination or otherwise be prohibited from testifying.

"A trial court cannot order a nonparty witness in a trial to be examined by a psychiatrist. The most the court can do is condition such a witness's testimony—*United States* v. *Ramirez*. The credibility of Michaud, like any other witness, is for the jury to decide."

In the end Judge Hagen found for the People, allowing Kennedy the small satisfaction of having Daveggio's trial postponed until May 12, with the admonition to the jury before trial by the judge that "Michelle Michaud is on a conditional plea of guilty . . . and you have heard testimony that Michelle Michaud, a witness, has received favored treatment from the government in connection with this case. You should examine Michelle Michaud's testimony with greater caution than that of an ordinary witness."

Michael Kennedy could count this as a small blessing. But even with this caveat, he knew that he had a tough uphill battle to fight. Michaud's testimony was sure to be compelling.

On May 12, 1999, James Daveggio finally faced his moment of truth at the Federal Court House in Reno, Nevada. The courtroom, situated on the seventh floor, fronted a foyer with large plate-glass windows facing the snowcapped Sierras. If Daveggio looked closely enough out those windows as he entered the court, he could have seen the exact spot where he had married his second wife, Donetta. If he'd looked a few blocks farther up the street, he could have seen the location where Juanita Rodriguez was swept off the corner of Washington and Sixth Streets on a cool September night in 1997.

Daveggio was now neatly groomed, wearing glasses, a plaid blue shirt, dungarees and athletic shoes. His mustache was carefully trimmed and his hair cut short. Marshals led him to the defendant's table and he eased himself into a comfortable revolving chair. Across from him in the jury box entered eight men and four women of varying backgrounds.

Assistant U.S. Attorney Ron Rachow started the proceedings in his opening statement by saying, "This is not a hard case. It is an important case. This is a serious case. But it is not a hard case."

The first witness that the prosecution called was Juanita Rodriguez. She spoke in a halting, tear-choked voice of her abduction on Washington and Sixth Streets and the terrifying ride that ensued. She began sobbing so uncontrollably that Judge Hagen took the unusual step of allowing her mother to sit by her on the stand. Through streaming tears, Rodriguez said, "I was so afraid. I wasn't thinking right. I remember what the man looks like in my mind. It's the man that's wearing glasses back there."

She pointed at James Daveggio.

When asked to recall the details of her ordeal, she replied, "This is really hard for me. All I tried to do was forget. I don't want to remember."

She recounted to the rapt jury details of the assault and the moment when "he asked the woman [Michaud] to play some music and she did. There was this particular song and he was singing along and I asked what it was about and he said it was about a man who killed in Reno just for pleasure.

"Later I asked him to take me back to Reno, but he said that he knew he did bad. He kidnapped me. He abused me. He raped me, and he didn't want me to do something stupid."

She also told of how she had concocted the story of a newborn baby to save her life and that the driver became interested at that point.

"She started asking me questions, like, 'How old is the baby?' I guess she felt sorry for me. Finally, he [Daveggio] asked her [Michaud], 'What do you think?' She thought about it for a while and exited the freeway. She told me to count to twenty and not to turn around. So I didn't even look back. Later I heard freeway noise and made my way there."

Michael Kennedy on cross asked why Juanita Rodriguez had never noticed any tattoos on her assailant, even though he had his shirt off. Daveggio obviously had very prominent tattoos on his chest and arms. Rodriguez couldn't remember them and explained this lack of memory because she was so traumatized at the time.

Kennedy didn't deny that Rodriguez had been in Michaud's van and had been raped, but he contended the assailant was not James Daveggio. Then he wanted to know why Rodriguez had told the Placer County detectives that her assailant had a "high-pitched" voice. Anyone who knew Daveggio at all realized he had a low voice that had earned him the nickname Frog.

It was on this point that Rodriguez's lack of the command of the English language caused her problems. An immigrant from El Salvador, she had originally used the term *"alto fuerte"* to describe the attacker's voice. This would most likely be translated as "high." But it could also be translated as "strong." To make the point, she dropped her own voice and tried to mimic that of her assailant's. It came out low and raspy.

Next in line for the prosecution was a string of veteran FBI agents and sheriff's department detectives, including Bill Summers and Desiree Carrington. All of them had a pile of damning evidence against Daveggio, especially the team's leader, Special Agent Lynn Ferrin. He was cool and collected on the stand and brought forth his testimony with precision and ease. But the unorthodox insertion of Ms. Elzy from the San Jose Planned Parenthood Office was even more damaging. She explained that in 1993 James Daveggio had come there for a vasectomy. A few weeks after the procedure he would have had no detectible sperm in his semen. It was the very missing puzzle piece that had baffled criminalist Renee Romero early on. She had studied the swabs taken from the rape kit used on Juanita Rodriguez and found that there was no trace of DNA in the ejaculant. Now it all made sense. Only sperm in an ejaculant carries the DNA material.

Renee Romero explained on the stand, "You need sperm in the semen to collect DNA. Of this I found no trace." Then she explained how a vasectomy would leave no trace of sperm with its DNA markers intact. On another front she had also been busy. Amidst all the bottles, blankets, clothes, lint and dust collected from the green minivan after Daveggio's and Michaud's arrest, she and the crime technicians were able to lift two dark pubic hairs that neither matched Michelle's nor James's. Romero analyzed these hairs using a DNA technique known as PCR testing. It gave her a "highly probable" match that the hairs came from Juanita Rodriguez.

Michael Kennedy attempted to dismiss Romero's work and that of the Washoe County Crime Lab as shoddy and corrupted by impurities in the testing, by using his own expert in the DNA field, Dr. Christie Davis. Dr. Davis contended that PCR testing was prone to contamination because foreign material, like that picked up in the van, will skew the results. But in the cross-examination Ron Rachow quietly and methodically denigrated Dr. Davis's qualifications. He had her admit she'd never made a report on Rene Romero's findings; she had only taken 1 1/2 pages of notes; she had never looked at the actual slides that Romero had used and she had spoken at a conference that included many DNA experts opposed to the death penalty.

Kennedy had better luck with his next technical expert, Dr. Stephen MacFarlane. He was calm, well-spoken and had impeccable credentials. His testimony even brought a moment of levity to the proceedings as he made his voice go all the way from a deep bass to a high falsetto to show the range of the human voice. From his testing of Daveggio at the University of Nevada, Reno, he had discovered that the extra tissue at the front of Daveggio's larynx caused his voice to be generally low and raspy. Juanita Rodriguez's contention that her assailant was *"alto fuerte"* became a matter of semantics rather than a point against Daveggio.

But all the law enforcement and technical witnesses paled in comparison to the prosecution's star witness against James Daveggio—Michelle Michaud. When asked to give her present address, she replied, "Nine eleven Parr Boulevard"—in other words, the Washoe County Jail.

Michaud's voice was shaky and she constantly cried throughout her testimony. Some witnesses thought the tears were genuine. Others thought she was putting on a good act.

Assistant U.S. Attorney Daniel Bogden asked her,

"Do you remember coming into this courtroom and pleading guilty to the count of kidnapping on November 16, 1998?"

Michaud: "Yes, sir."
Bogden: "Does that agreement set forth all the terms of your plea agreement for your plea of guilty to Count Two, kidnapping and aiding and abetting?"
Michaud: "Yes, sir."
Bogden: "Have there been any other arrangements, negotiations or deals given to you by the United States government?"
Michaud: "No, sir."
Bogden: "Who did you perform the kidnapping with?"
Michaud: "Mr. James Anthony Daveggio."

That out of the way, Daniel Bogden took her back through the days leading up to the kidnapping, the gambling, the search for more and more money. When it came to the actual event of the abduction, Michaud said, "We were driving around. We didn't have any money, kind of bored. He [James] was kind of angry. Put off and we didn't have nowhere to go. We were in the van when we drove around. . . . That's when he saw the girl. She was kind of small. I believe she had long dark hair. It was dark out. We had went up a block. James had gotten out of the van and got in the back through a sliding door, and I got into the driver's seat. He told me to turn around and come back and circle up. I'm not good at roads or directions as far as—if he doesn't tell me where to go or where to turn, I don't know where to go. So we come down past a bridge like, and he told me to turn around slowly and come up, and he told me to go slowly, but not too slow.

"And she was walking this way. She got a little past the van. He started to open the sliding door, but I didn't stop. I tried to keep going. But he jumped out of the van, anyway, and he fell down and hurt his knee, so he was cussing and kind of mad. This all happened really fast. I'm not exactly sure how he pulled her in, but they struggled there for a second, and all she kept saying was, 'What have I done? What have I done?'

"And he got her in the van and shut the door. . . . [She was] directly behind me in the other captain's chair. He told her shut the fuck up or he was going to kill her, and she just got kind of quiet. He told her to take her shirt off. Everything is very excitable at the moment. He's yelling at me to go forward. I'm taking wrong turns. I don't have a sense of direction. He had me turn around, go down one street, and I took the wrong street. He wanted me to turn at another street, and he's yelling at me.

"And then he has me turn around and go down another street, and then we're going straight down the street, and I frequently take the wrong freeway turnoff because I get confused with east and west, north and south. I'm crying and I'm shaking and I'm trying to drive. I'm not crying out loud. The tears are just falling silently down my face.

"I had turned around one time. It was dark. He asked me what I was looking at and told me to turn the fuck around and watch the road. The only other times he really yelled at me is when he thought I was going too fast. He didn't want to draw attention to us.

"He instructed me to put in his Johnny Cash tape, and he has two favorite songs on that tape.

'A Boy Named Sue' and that one about—I think it's 'Folsom Prison Blues,' where it says, 'I shot a man in Reno, just to watch him die.'

"When we came up to the—is it the agricultural?—the little building you have to pass before you go over the line. There was a little bit of light, and I had turned around, and James was sitting in the seat . . . the captain's seat behind the passenger seat. She's on the floor and her head is on his lap and he has the pillow over her head. She was so quiet. I thought she was dead. I thought he smothered her right there. There was a gentleman at the little building there. I had the window down and he asked me where I was coming from, and I said Reno."

Bogden: "You didn't tell him you had someone in the back who had been kidnapped, did you?"

Michaud: "No."

Bogden: "You kept driving?"

Michaud: "Yes, yes, all the way down the freeway."

Bogden: "Do you know what he was doing to that girl?"

Michaud: "I didn't see, but I could surmise; she . . ."

Bogden: "You could hear it, couldn't you?"

Michaud: "She would whimper, she would cry, and she would talk. She said she had a young baby that her mother was watching, and she was talking about how she was going to school and she wanted to get back to her baby and to please not kill her."

Bogden: "Did she seem smart?"

Michaud: "I thought she was very smart talking about her child."

Bogden: "Why?"

Michaud: "Because she was begging for her life, and he started to talk back to her."

Bogden: "Who made the decision to let her go?"

Michaud: "I'm not sure it was my decision. He said find a place to stop at."

Bogden: "Did Mr. Daveggio ask you what we should do with her?"

Michaud: "I think it was put to me in the sense that he [had] a plan, 'Are we going to stick with the plan or what are we going to do?' I didn't answer him because I didn't know what he was talking about. It was a little bit later she asked if we were going to drive her back to Reno and James told her, 'That's up to Micki.'"

Bogden: "Did you ever try to help her?"

Michaud: "I helped her stay alive when we let her go."

Bogden: "Why did you stop the van?"

Michaud: "Because he was done; he was done with her."

Bogden: "Was the victim ever released?"

Michaud: "Yes."

Bogden: "Where did that happen?"

Michaud: "When I pulled off the exit—it was Gap, that's the only word I remember. When we pulled off the exit, we went up and around an overpass bridge. There was nothing but hills on the sides. He opened the side sliding door. He instructed her to get out. I went around and I came up behind her and I told her, 'Stay here. Don't move. Don't turn around and look at the van. Don't go walking around at night again because you never know what can happen to you.'"

After Michaud's graphic testimony, Daveggio's lawyer, Michael Kennedy, had an uphill job trying to refute it. After all, she had been Daveggio's partner in crime and supposedly witnessed everything. But he gave it his best shot. He already had told the jury in his opening statements that Michaud was a convincing pathological liar. Now he went about trying to prove it.

He showed that on certain documents Michaud had lied to the government agents right from the beginning.

Kennedy: "They [the FBI] asked you about a girl in Reno and you said, 'There is no girl in Reno.' Correct?"

Michaud: "Yes, I did say that."

Kennedy: "You told them, 'I've told you everything I know.' Correct?"

Michaud: "Yes."

Kennedy: "Was that a lie?"

Michaud: "Yes."

Kennedy: "In fact, Mr. Bogden at the November 1998 suppression hearing held in your case asked you, 'Isn't it true that you've said on twenty-two occasions that you've done nothing wrong?' "

Michaud: "If it is written, yes. I'm sorry I don't remember. Oh, God."

(She then tried to qualify how she saw herself in all of this.)

Michaud: "I'm sorry, I'm not seeing myself being involved because I didn't plan it with him. I didn't know he was going to do it until he did it, and I didn't pull her into the van. I tried to stop it that way, but I couldn't, when I tried to keep going."

Kennedy: "Could you have stopped the van?"

Michaud: "I could have."

Kennedy: "And you didn't, correct?"

Michaud: "At the expense of my family being hurt, no, I didn't."

Trying another angle, Kennedy began to show the dangerous company Michaud kept besides Daveggio. He said, "During that time period [the 1980s and 1990s] you met a lot of folks who you would call shady characters, right?"

Daniel Bogden was out of his chair in an instant, objecting as to relevance.

What followed was the longest and most contentious sidebar discussion out of the jury's hearing, in the whole trial.

Kennedy pounded away at his point as he, Judge Hagen, and Assistant U.S. Attorney Bogden huddled together. Kennedy argued, "She comes to the case with not only bias but motive, so I'm going to question her about her associations today with various members, her knowledge of individuals who are in the Hell's Angels, Misfits Motorcycle Club, and other things over the years. She met in January 1999 with authorities saying that if she was released she could infiltrate those groups and tie the Mustang Ranch, in this area, to certain crime activities, showing that she has knowledge of a lot of individuals who fit the basic descriptions of the individual in this case, and so that she has motive to those associations."

Judge Hagen asked, "How does that give her motive to lie?"

Kennedy responded, "If an individual from the Hell's Angels, or a different person who did not have tattoos, committed this crime, then she would be in danger for fingering him. The authorities put Daveggio together [with her], so Daveggio is obviously in custody right now, that gives her motive. My defense in this case is that she is lying about the person who did this. . . . She has connections, going back between California and Nevada, with individuals who are very capable of committing this crime."

Bogden chimed in, "Your Honor, this line of testimony . . . we've given Mr. Kennedy lots of leeway, but this is totally irrelevant to the facts at hand."

Both Kennedy and Bogden were now talking at the same time, and in exasperation Judge Hagen said, "Wait, wait, wait! Stop! I know it's not relevant to the alleged crime, but the purpose of cross-examination is also to test the credibility of the witness, and I'd like to hear from you [Mr. Bogden] on the issue of credibility."

Bogden answered, "Well, I mean, every single person in the United States. He can ask her questions on who doesn't have tattoos if that's his theory or that's the way he's going. These are hearsay statements that he's making."

Judge Hagen finally said, "OK, here's what I'm going to do. This is getting too time-consuming. Mr. Kennedy will ask the questions he wishes to ask; you [Bogden] will make the objections you wish to make; I will rule on the objection. We're not going to keep coming back here discussing this issue at sidebar."

Back before the jury, Kennedy continued down this path, showing Michaud's association with known criminals, such as the Hell's Angels and Joe Conforte, and Bogden objected at every instance until Judge Hagen announced it was time to get on with a new line of questioning.

Kennedy had one last card to play. He brought in Misty Michaud, Michelle's sister. Whereas Michelle had been on the stand for two days, Misty was there for five minutes. Kennedy's question was succinct and to the point. Would she characterize Michelle as truthful or a liar?

Misty responded, "I love my sister dearly, but I'd say she's untruthful."

After seven days of testimony the parade of witnesses was over. Now it was up to the jury of eight men and four women to decide if James Daveggio was guilty or innocent of the abduction and rape of Juanita Rodriguez. On Wednesday, May 19, 1999, they reached their verdict after less than two hours of deliberation. As Daveggio sat quietly at the defense table, flanked by his attorney, the only sign that he was agitated was the constant drumming of his right-hand fingers on the tabletop.

Judge Hagen read the note and asked the jury foreperson, "How do you find the defendant, James Anthony Daveggio?"

On all counts the verdict was the same: "Guilty."

The federal trial was finally over after more than a year of delays. In Reno, James Daveggio and Michelle Michaud had been fighting for their freedom—in the Alameda County trial they would be fighting for their lives.

Chapter 31

The "Rock" Returns

In the interval between James Daveggio's federal trial and Michelle Michaud's Reno sentencing, the Mustang Ranch closed for business. The feds had been contending for years that ex-owner Joe Conforte was still running operations secretly from South America and receiving payoffs. The government had originally closed the bordello in 1990 after Conforte declared bankruptcy and auctioned the ranch off to recover some of the back taxes to the IRS.

Victor Perry, the one and only bidder, bought the property for $1.49 million on behalf of Mustang Properties, Inc. Perry had a brother named Peter, who was Conforte's lawyer. A.G.E., a conglomeration, whose members were all associates of Conforte, took over the establishment. The government soon alleged that they were secretly transferring millions of dollars to Conforte in South America. There was no doubt that he wanted to come back and take over operations. He'd even placed a full-page ad in one of Nevada's newspapers stating that fact.

The FBI looked closely into the illegal actions of

Mustang madam, and former Storey County commissioner, Shirley Colletti, as well as brothel bookkeeper Joann Olcese. When the heat came down on them, they decided to talk, alleging that Conforte was still skimming profits from the bordello. In a trial that took place in the spring of 1999, a jury found both Colletti and Olcese guilty of racketeering.

The end came for the Mustang Ranch on Monday, August 9, as a mob of reporters, television cameramen and curious onlookers surrounded the pink stucco ranch house, while a file of working girls moved back and forth taking possessions to their cars. At 5:00 P.M., former Storey County sheriff, and now president of the Mustang operations, Bob Del-Carlo handed over the keys to the padlocked gate to Agent Ronald Meseberg of Customs Service.

It's hard to say how much Michelle Michaud was involved in Mustang Ranch's demise. Whether she gave key evidence about Joe Conforte and the others, or whether it was just one more set of lies in an attempt to gain her freedom, only the FBI knows for sure. Whatever she had to say apparently wasn't enough to convince them to use her as an undercover operative.

It not only wasn't enough for the FBI—it wasn't enough to sway either the Alameda County prosecutors or Judge David Hagen either. On August 12, 1999, Michaud once again found herself in Judge Hagen's federal courtroom in Reno for sentencing. In a tearful, dramatic statement during her ninety-minute sentencing phase, she said, "I'm so sorry for not being able to stop things he [Daveggio] has done."

Attorney Mary Boestch tried to portray Michelle Michaud as another of Daveggio's victims.

"He physically assaulted her," Boestch said. "He

terrorized her. She does not fit the profile of a
woman who is a cold-blooded criminal."

Boestch asked for leniency in Michaud's sentencing because she had cooperated with authorities after her arrest. Judge Hagen saw things differently
and replied, "I believe that what Ms. Michaud saw
was the murder [of Vanessa Samson] in California
[on the Douglas County Jail television] has been
discovered and thinks, 'I'm going to do something
right now to distance myself from that 85 [murder
charge].' My first thought [about the Juanita Rodriguez case] was what a horrible, horrible crime
this was. The victim was trussed up like an animal
in the back of a minivan."

Judge Hagen dismissed the battered-woman syndrome that Boestch was trying to use and contended that Michaud had ample opportunity to
escape the clutches of James Daveggio. As Michaud
sat weeping, he sentenced her to twelve years and
eight months for the kidnapping of Juanita Rodriguez.

The government, meanwhile, was trying to make
the court be even harder on James Daveggio. Assistant U.S. Attorney Daniel Bogden said, "Daveggio
chose his Reno victim due to her gender, age, physical size and due to the fact she was a small-in-stature
female victim walking alone at night. This pattern
of choosing defenseless, vulnerable female victims
occurred both prior to the Reno kidnapping and
following the Reno kidnapping. Without a doubt,
defendant Daveggio is one of the most heinous, violent, cruel, dangerous and remorseless defendants
that this court or most other courts in the state of
Nevada has sentenced. This criminal [Daveggio]
acts, in this case, unusually heinous, cruel, brutal
and degrading to[ward] the victim. If allowed to
return to the streets, he poses an immediate and

imminent threat to innocent females who may cross his path. Incapacitation and imprisonment is the only way society can be protected from this repeat and obviously non-rehabilitative criminal rapist."

Both Bogden and Rachow sought a two-level increase in Daveggio's sentencing, which would mean a great deal more prison time. Daveggio's lawyer, Michael Kennedy, shot back that the government had not sought the same two-level increase against Michelle Michaud, had filed this motion late, and that Daveggio did not know beforehand that Juanita Rodriguez was a "vulnerable" victim.

Judge Hagen ruled in Kennedy's favor, and at least in this he won a small victory for his client. But it was one small victory in a war that was steadily going against Daveggio. Only eleven days after Michaud had been sentenced in front of Judge Hagen, it was Daveggio's turn. Unlike Michaud, who cried constantly, he remained stoic and sat almost motionless during the hour-long sentencing phase. Prosecutor Daniel Bogden once again summarized Juanita Rodriguez's horrifying ordeal, stating that she now suffered from post-traumatic stress disorders. "She has a chronic fear of death," he said, "with the belief she will not wake up in the morning and will die young. What kind of life is that?"

When asked to make a comment, Daveggio, dressed in a jail uniform, only said, "On the advice of [my attorney] Mr. Kennedy, I don't have anything to say, Your Honor."

In the end Judge Hagen was twice as hard on James Daveggio as he had been on Michelle Michaud. He sentenced him to twenty-four years in prison, saying, "He [Daveggio] controlled the depraved nature of the forcible sexual acts. The victim was trussed up like an animal."

The Nevada phase of the Daveggio/Michaud saga was now over. But the California phase was just getting into high gear, thanks to the efforts of Rock Harmon.

Back in November 1998, Rock Harmon and Alameda district attorney Tom Orloff had convened a grand jury to look into the crimes James Daveggio and Michelle Michaud had perpetrated in their county. They had plenty of technical evidence to back up their charges. Way back on December 19, 1997, Brian Burritt of the California Department of Justice Lab, in Berkeley, received several items from the Washoe County Sheriff's Office that had been found in Michaud's van. One large envelope and one smaller envelope contained three blood tubes and a stain from the liquid blood. He also obtained a napkin from her van with a dark stain on it, two curling irons and a green gag ball. With these came a blood sample from James Daveggio, drawn by criminalist Maria Fassett, and a blood sample from Michelle Michaud, drawn by criminalist Renee Romero.

Brian Burritt explained what he did next. "The first thing generally is to examine the packaging. I'll look at the packaging, see what notations are made on them, if there's any case numbers, item numbers, descriptions of evidence, that sort of thing. Then make notes and document what I'm observing there.

"The next step is to open up that item or the envelope or container and just visually examine the item and try to assess what I'm going to collect and what I'm going to analyze. I looked at Q12701, the curling iron, and looked for any possible biological stains, since that's what I'm focusing on is DNA testing, the biological evidence. So in an effort to also preserve any other evidence that might be there, such as latent prints, I didn't want to overly handle the item such that I smear a latent print that was there or some other type of evidence.

"I observed in the tip portion of that item some brown stains that looked like they might be biological material that I could test. There's a concave area in that tip and that's where I observed the stains and collected them. I collected a portion of the stains with a damp Q-tip cotton swab."

In his search he noted a brown pellet of material that appeared to be biological in nature. He didn't know what it was at first, so he did a presumptive test for dried blood. The test came up positive, so he did a test for coagulated blood. But when he tried to extract it, the material didn't act the way a solid blood sample should act. At this point he surmised it might be fecal material. His test in this area proved that his assumption was correct.

On the smaller of the curling irons, which had a deeper tip, he also found a more pronounced amount of brown material. He pried it loose with a scalpel blade. Preserving and putting these samples aside for a while, he concentrated on taking minute samples from the napkin that appeared to have bloodstains on it, and a sample from the green ball gag that had apparent teeth marks on it. From his test on the green ball gag, he found that the ball surface contained epithelial cells, which generally come from a person's mouth.

On all the samples that he had gathered, Burritt ran DNA tests, noting, as Renee Romero had already done, the kind of DNA test performed depended on the amount of DNA material gathered. The PCR test was more general in nature, but needed very little DNA material. The RFLP test was much more precise, but needed a greater amount of DNA material. Burritt had enough potential

DNA material on the paper napkin to run both a PCR and RFLP test. The results he found were that the DNA located there was consistent with the DNA found in Vanessa Samson's blood. Only one in 8.9 billion people in the PCR test, and only one in 22 billion people in the RFLP test, were likely to have the same DNA as found on the napkin. From the blood samples he had received from Maria Fassett and Renee Romero, he discovered that James Daveggio's and Michelle Michaud's DNA did not match the DNA picked up from the paper napkin. Only Vanessa Samson's DNA matched.

The same results came in from the curling irons and ball gag. The DNA was consistent with Vanessa Samson's and not Daveggio's or Michaud's. When Burritt ran a test for semen stains in Samson's panties and from a vaginal swab, he found that there was no semen present. But even this was damaging evidence against Daveggio. As Renee Romero had discovered in the Reno case, Daveggio had undergone a vasectomy and had no semen in his ejaculant.

The curling irons were becoming a double whammy against Daveggio and Michaud at this point. Not only did they contain DNA material from Vanessa Samson, proving that she had been in their van, but these same items contained fingerprints, and Bonnie Paolini, who was an expert latent print analyst at the California Department of Justice Lab, was about to find out to whom the fingerprints belonged.

On the AM/PM cup she had received from the Washoe County Sheriff's Crime Lab, she used a superglue fuming method and then a rhodamine laser method, picking up prints she dusted with fingerprint powder. She photographed her results and used a lifting tape to place the prints on a lift card. On the cup she had found not only a print of Daveggio's right thumb, but his left thumbprint twice. She also found prints from Michaud's right thumb, right middle finger and right ring finger. But most damaging of all, she found Vanessa Samson's right thumbprint on the same cup.

Bonnie Paolini also received the two curling irons that DNA expert Burritt had looked at. She said, "My initial processing method was to superglue it [the larger of the curling irons]. I examined the item to see if there were any visible latent impressions. There were not. At this point I removed the duct tape that was wrapped around the center area of the curling iron. I then processed the pieces of the duct tape, and I reprocessed the curling iron itself, to possibly develop any prints underneath the duct tape area. I processed these items with superglue fuming again and used the laser on them. I found Michelle Michaud's right thumb on the middle of the duct tape. There were three pieces wrapped around on the middle of the curling iron. On the middle piece of duct tape, I was able to develop her right thumb on the sticky side of the tape."

Ms. Paolini also found Michaud's fingerprints on the curling iron itself, underneath the duct tape area, as well as Michaud's palm print on the metal.

On the smaller curling iron she found Michaud's right middle fingerprint on the nonsticky side of the duct tape, and left index fingerprint on the curling iron's metal shaft.

There were Daveggio fingerprints on the *Dead of Night* book about serial killers, especially on the photographs. His fingerprints were also on the *Submissive Young Girls* audiotape.

With all this evidence, and much more—including testimony from Patty Wilson (Jane Doe #1);

Daveggio's daughter (Jane Doe #2); Robert Maisonet, the clerk at the Livermore adult book store; David Valentine and David Elola, the roofers near the place Vanessa Samson was kidnapped; Mukesh Patel, the manager of the Sundowner Inn; Everett Brakensiek, the Alpine County deputy who found Vanessa Samson's body; and law enforcement experts in forensic science, Toni Leal, Curtis Rollins, Brian Burritt and Bonnie Paolini—Rock Harmon had enough evidence against James Daveggio and Michelle Michaud to make a book a foot thick.

He sought several counts against them. In legal terms he stated, "The County of Alameda hereby accuses James Anthony Daveggio and Michelle Lyn Michaud of a felony to wit, Oral Copulation Acting in Concert with Force, a violation of subdivision (d) of section 288 (a) of the Penal Code of California, in that or on about the third day of November, 1997, in the County of Alameda, State of California; said defendants did willfully and unlawfully participate in an act of oral copulation with Jane Doe #1, against the will of said victim and by force and fear of immediate and unlawful bodily injury to said victim, while voluntarily acting in concert with themselves, personally and by aiding and abetting."

The second count dealt with the same victim and concerned Acting in Concert with Force.

The third count concerned a similar charge of oral copulation on a victim under the age of eighteen years old (Daveggio's daughter, Jane Doe #2) on November 27, 1997. Both of these acts took place in the Dublin area near Pleasanton.

The fourth count was directly tied to Vanessa Samson.

"The fourth count of this indictment further accuses James Anthony Daveggio and Michelle Lyn Michaud of a felony, to wit, MURDER, a violation

of Section 187 (a) of the Penal Code of California,
in that on or about the second day of December,
1997, in the County of Alameda, State of California,
said defendants did then and there murder Vanessa
Samson, a human being. SPECIAL CIRCUM-
STANCES AS TO BOTH DEFENDANTS."

Rock Harmon went on to sum up to the grand
jury all the findings in layman's terms. He said,
"Now, I want to define the crimes that we've
charged for you. In Counts One and Two we've
charged the crime that's different than Count
Three. Counts One and Two—the victim was Jane
Doe Number One—and defendants are charged in
or accused in Counts One and Two of having committed the crime of unlawful oral copulation, a violation of section 288A (D) of the penal code. Oral
copulation is the act of copulating the mouth of
one person with the sexual organ or anus of another person. Any contact, however slight, between
the mouth of one person and the sexual organ or
anus of another person constitutes oral copulation.
Penetration of the mouth, sexual organ or anus is
not required. Proof of ejaculation is not required.

"The phrase 'acting in concert' means two or
more acting together in a group sexual attack, and
includes not only those who personally engage in
the act constituting the crime but those who aid
and abet a person in that.

"So that's Counts One and Two.

"Count Three, it's a different crime. Some of the
basics are the same. The title of this instruction is
'Unlawful oral copulation with person under 18
years.' The third count is the one alleged against
the victim Jane Doe Number Two.

"Defendants are accused of having committed
the crime of murder, a violation of Penal Code Section 187. . . . Kidnapping is defined as the unlawful

movement by physical force or a person without
that person's consent. . . . The definition of unlawful penetration by a foreign object, which is a crime
which can form the basis for the first-degree felony
murder. Every person who for the purpose of sexual
arousal, gratification or abuse causes the penetration, however slight, of the genital or anal opening
of another person by any foreign object, substance,
instrument or device, against the will of that person,
is guilty of the crime of unlawful penetration by a
foreign object. It means a purpose to injure, hurt,
cause pain or discomfort. It doesn't mean that the
perpetrator must be motivated by sexual gratification or arousal or have lewd intent.

"Let me explain why we charged the first two
counts. There were two separate events like that.
One where she [Patty Wilson] was forced to orally
copulate Daveggio, and the other where Michaud
orally copulated her. There's no question that each
of them by driving and all the other actions,
Michaud holding her arms back, that this was a cooperative effort to do it. The crime against Jane
Doe Number Two [Daveggio's daughter], you probably wonder why did we charge a different crime
against her. Mostly, [because] there's no question
emotional duress is as powerful as physical duress.
The fact that Michaud said to Jane Doe Number
Two, 'Your father's going to have sex with you,' it
shows that there was a discussion of this, there's a
facilitation. Maybe she left the room to make it easier for him to get away with this. Then she performs
oral copulation on him for fifteen minutes while
he's orally copulating his daughter. It seems clear
there's mutual gratification in there.

"Okay, we've charged the crime of murder. We
have alleged it's first-degree murder. The crime of
first-degree murder occurs, even if somebody's ac-

cidentally killed, in the commission of specified crimes. You commit a burglary; you're driving away; you collide with a school bus; you kill three people. That's first-degree murder. So here's a question. Was Vanessa Samson killed during the commission of one of those crimes? Well, in my example the burglary was over, you're trying to get away, and so how would that apply to this? Well, you're kidnapped until you're free. I mean that's the simplest way to think of it. That kidnapping doesn't end when the roofers see the van pull away. It's not over then. That's the beginning of it. In the sense of liability, that kidnap was not over until Vanessa was dead. As a result of being kidnapped, she was murdered.

"So the special circumstances. We have shown to you, the hunting, and that's the most telling, chilling, and not just the vague term that's left floating out there that may have come from the *Dead of Night*. You know that statement was made on the twenty-seventh and twenty-eighth [of November 1997]. And what do we know? On the thirtieth, these things were purchased. [The curling irons]. On the first, the gag was purchased. I mean the things were actually used as the instruments of torture or death. They were bought in anticipation of this.

"There's a tendency in this society, when you view these male/female couples like this, you think the male's got to be the killer. Right? And that the woman's just helping out. Well, we know that both of them shared that hunting comment on Thanksgiving Night by Mr. Daveggio, and on Friday morning by Michelle Michaud. But we also know that it had to be Michelle Michaud that prepared these instruments. You can see there's just a Phillips screw. These clips come right off. And in some macabre accommodation to not cause her too much discomfort that duct tape was put over where the holes were. And there's no other conclusion you can reach that she's the one that did that, three layers of duct tape, sometimes her prints are on the underside of the tape, sometimes they're in the middle. So it seems obvious that this, as hard as this is to accept, that people do these kinds of things. They really, really do these kinds of things.

"So have we proven that there was a rape by a foreign instrument? The fecal matter, especially the one with the deeper tip. That seems obvious. The marks on her [Vanessa Samson's] buttocks suggest two things. Number one that these [curling irons] were both used. Number two, it's hard to picture that one person was wielding one of these or two of these, as opposed to both of them.

"So the evidence by virtue of the hunting comment, the evidence, by virtue of the shopping trips to purchase the items, which unquestionably were used in this, [and] the two prior incidents where they went on this bizarre self-centered spree, not to do this to strangers, but to do it to blood relatives and friends of theirs.

"It all really just means, if you don't know who the killer was, who strangled Vanessa Samson, then, in order to find either or both of the special circumstances to be true, I've had to show there was an intent to kill by each and both of these people. The other incidents, the hunting trip, all the preparation, seem to leave not much question on those things. So I want to close with that idea."

If Rock Harmon ever worried about how the grand jury would view any of these counts, he needn't have. In short order the grand jurors came back with findings that the suspects should be indicted on all counts, including special circumstances, which left the door open for the prosecution to seek the death penalty.

Just as in the Reno federal trial, the Alameda prosecution would take a "tag team" approach. Rock Harmon had been, and would keep working, the technical end, especially as concerned DNA tests, while Alameda County assistant district attorney Jim Anderson would take the lead in other realms of the prosecution.

Jim Anderson was known in the area as a strong death penalty advocate with a hard-nosed approach. He had no sympathy for either James Daveggio or Michelle Michaud because of what they had done to their victims. That he meant business could readily be ascertained by his previous "big" trials. On November 24, 1997, armored car guard Thomas Wheelock had set up an elaborate trap and shot his armored car partner Rodrigo Cortez to death and stole $300,000. He escaped with the money and was on the run for four days until captured hundreds of miles away in Utah. Hauled back to Alameda County, he faced Jim Anderson, who from the start wasn't fooling around with this cold-blooded killer. He had Wheelock indicted by an Alameda grand jury on a murder charge with special circumstances even before a preliminary hearing.

Wheelock's public defender, Michael Ogul, cried foul and said, "The district attorney had decided he doesn't want to honor the rights Mr. Wheelock would have in a preliminary examination . . . such as getting discovery, getting to watch the witnesses testify, get to cross-examine the witnesses."

But Anderson denied any gamesmanship and announced that the jury had more than enough facts to speed the case to superior court. When the arraignment of Wheelock was finally held, Rodrigo Cortez's mother, clad in black, rose from her seat and burst into sobs, railing at the assailant, "Why'd you kill my son?"

She had to be escorted from the courtroom, but not before DA Jim Anderson assured her that he would have Thomas Wheelock executed for the crime.

But even though Jim Anderson was an absolute death penalty advocate, he knew when to cut his losses and let a suspect plead to life in prison without the possibility of parole. Such a case happened in July 1998. Jerrol Glen Woods, a fifty-year-old carpet cleaner, had killed a popular Oakland pediatrician, but it wasn't a clear-cut case of murder for cash, which carried special circumstances with the crime. As Anderson said, "He claims he killed her, saw the purse lying there, and robbed her as an afterthought, which doesn't make it a felony robbery. I think the guy should die, but we have to play the cards we're dealt."

As autumn 1999 rolled around, both James Daveggio and Michelle Michaud hoped that prosecutors Jim Anderson and Rock Harmon had been dealt a hand of low cards. But things did not look promising as far as they were concerned. As Rock Harmon reiterated, "They are both going to be really surprised when they understand the nature of the evidence we have against both of them."

While waiting to be extradited to California, both James Daveggio and Michelle Michaud whiled away time as best they could in their respective jail cells. Daveggio in particular had few visitors or contacts with the outside world, though his mother still believed in his innocence, especially in relation to the Vanessa Samson murder. "I never killed anyone," he told her, and she believed him. She knew that James had done many bad things in his life, but she didn't believe he was capable of murder. In her mind he had been about as good a son as could be under trying circumstances, and the thought that he murdered a young lady was too much to contemplate. Surely the authorities and his erstwhile partner, Michelle Michaud, must have been trying to pin the Vanessa Samson murder on him.

Michaud, meanwhile, watched time slowly go by in her own isolation cell at the Washoe County Jail. Her father was so ashamed of what she had done that he wouldn't come and visit or even write. The one member of the family who did was sister Misty. She still loved her big sister and was loyal to her. Even more surprisingly loyal was one of Michelle's former sugar daddies. Despite having been terribly used, tricked into letting her run up his credit card at the Circus Circus Hotel, and displaced for a while in her affections by James Daveggio, he faithfully went to visit her at the jail. He was in his late seventies now, and not spry as he used to be; nonetheless, he made the 150-mile journey part of his weekly routine. When Michaud complained that her prison-issued eyeglasses weren't strong enough, he went out and bought her a pair of glasses that matched her prescription.

She barely resembled the elegantly dressed hooker who had sipped champagne at The Rustic, or held listeners spellbound with sexual tales at Bobby Joe's. Her luxuriant hair was starting to fade in color and she looked very plain without make-up and dressed in a drab prison uniform. But in one regard prison life was good to Michelle. She could no longer take crank. Her weight began to improve, even with jail food, and she no longer looked emaciated, especially in the face.

The one person neither Daveggio nor Michaud saw during this period of waiting was each other. Daveggio still seethed at what he viewed as a betrayal on her part, especially when she agreed to testify against him in the Juanita Rodriguez case. Marie Ward, Michaud's former neighbor, heard from her that she was now receiving threatening letters in jail. Michaud confided to Ward that she thought Daveggio was having someone on the outside send them to her just to torment her. Whether it was true or just part of Michaud's paranoia, Ward couldn't say. All she knew was that they disturbed Michaud greatly.

Michaud at least got a break from Daveggio's nearby presence in the early part of October 1999 when he was transferred to the federal prison in Lompoc, California, on the central coast. But it was a short reprieve in her worries. On October 12 she was on the move herself, giving up the familiar confines of the Washoe County Jail, which had been her home for nearly the past two years. She was bound for the prison facility that Michael Ihde had called his childhood home—Santa Rita Prison in Dublin.

The morning of October 15, 1999, found Michelle Michaud being escorted by marshals into the Alameda County Superior Courthouse in Oakland. A large white monolith of a building, it looked almost like a mausoleum perched on the edge of Lake Merritt, where prosecutor Rock Harmon often took his morning jogs. Wearing a yellow jumpsuit and hair neatly combed back, Michaud appeared for her hearing in a somber mood. As prosecutor Jim Anderson stood up and began to read the charges, Michaud sighed heavily and constantly looked up at the ceiling.

But she was brought down to earth in a hurry

when Anderson announced that he was seeking the death penalty against her. Her knees buckled and she told a bailiff, "Give me a minute" before being escorted from the courtroom. She did not enter a plea at this point and waited to be assigned a lawyer. She was to be only the second woman from Alameda County scheduled for death row.

Prosecutor Jim Anderson was well aware of Michaud's testimony in the Reno federal trial against James Daveggio and how she cast him as a sexual predator and herself as an abused and unwilling accomplice. He said, "Whatever happened up there will have no bearing on our case over here whatsoever. The only abuse going on was what she and he were doing to the victim."

He added that he and Rock Harmon didn't need a confession in the Vanessa Samson case. "There's prevalent physical evidence, including DNA, to prove the couple's guilt."

Michaud's formal arraignment was postponed until she could be assigned a lawyer, but from here it was only jumping from the frying pan into the fire. She was scheduled to be right back in the Alameda courthouse on October 28, and this time James Daveggio would be there as well. No matter how hard she tried, she couldn't get rid of him.

Chapter 32

End of the Line

Two days after her first appearance in the Alameda County Court, Michelle Michaud spoke to Scott Marshall, a reporter for the *Contra Costa Times*. It was the first interview she had granted since being arrested at the Lakeside Inn nearly two years before. Escorted into the visitation room by two Santa Rita prison deputies, she slowly sat down on a hard plastic chair across from the reporter. She clutched a telephone and wearily stared at him on the other side of a thick Plexiglas window. The voices of nearby prisoners and visitors bounced around raucously and erratically on the concrete and cinder-block walls of the stark room, but Michaud spoke softly through a stream of tears to the reporter.

"I don't know how many people will believe it," she said, "about the real Michelle. The real culprit is James Daveggio. Are you going to meet him?" she asked anxiously. "You'll learn a lot if you meet him."

Then she spoke of her own conditions at the Santa Rita Prison, where she was kept isolated from the nearly 4,000 other prisoners.

"The clothes they gave me are awful. They're smelly hand-me-downs. It's awful in here."

She seemed depressed and tired, speaking in a soft monotone to the reporter. She only began to perk up when she announced, "I spend a lot of time reading the Bible. I've been reading Romans. I like it."

Then she mentioned that Romans referred frequently to love.

But it wasn't long before her mind drifted back to more depressing subjects.

"I want a lawyer. I don't trust anyone. There's a lot of deceiving going on," she said angrily.

Then she blurted out, "I'm not a monster!"

But if she didn't perceive herself as a monster, many others did. She was about to be reunited with one, though she didn't know it.

On the morning of October 28, 1999, at the Alameda County Superior Courthouse, James Daveggio was brought into Department 11 for his arraignment on the Vanessa Samson kidnapping and murder charges. His beard was almost white now and the multiple tattoos on his arms were clearly visible, protruding from the sleeves of his pink jail uniform. He wore a pair of dark-framed glasses and a bland, almost bored expression, which was captured by a gallery filled with television and print photographers and newspaper reporters.

They weren't the only interested parties there—the Samson family sat in the courtroom as well. When Daveggio was escorted into the court by a sheriff's deputy, Vanessa's brother, Vincent, stood up and glared at the prisoner.

The commotion of the photographers and television crews hit a fever pitch as one more person entered the side door into Department 11—Michelle Michaud. She blinked in absolute dismay and fear when she suddenly realized who was standing next to her, separated by only one burly court bailiff, her former lover James Daveggio. All too graphically, his presence reminded her that this was the man she had followed down a road of kidnapping and rape, to eventually be accused of murder. The same man she had turned on and helped to convict in Reno. A fact he was not likely to forget.

Michaud quickly lowered her head and only once or twice glanced at Daveggio. He remained totally impassive and didn't look at her at all. But other eyes were staring at them in the crowded court-room, especially those of the Samson family. Va-nessa's mother turned toward *Contra Costa Times* reporter David Holbrook and said, "There are the people who killed my daughter. But I don't feel any-thing. I'm not angry."

Vincent Samson was less subdued. He muttered after looking at the pair, "They're pathetic!"

At last James Daveggio and Michelle Michaud were reunited, but not in the manner they might have hoped for. Vincent Samson was right; they did look pathetic. Daveggio appeared old and care-worn, with his scraggily beard. His bright blue eyes, which so many women had found attractive, were now bloodshot and puffy.

On seeing his photo in the newspaper, ex-wife Donetta Rhodes commented, "He looked awful! Did you see those puffy eyes? That's what struck me the most. Those puffy, bloodshot eyes."

If anything, Michelle Michaud looked even more pathetic. With her unkempt hair and faded yellow prison jumper, she was the picture of dejection. She constantly bit her lower lip, as if on the verge of tears. No one who had known the exuberant, foul-mouthed prostitute at Mustang Ranch or Bobby Joe's would have recognized the mousy-looking, teary-eyed, middle-aged woman who now stood in Judge Dean Beaupre's courtroom.

James Daveggio listened impassively as ADA Jim Anderson stated that he would indeed seek the death penalty against this pair. Daveggio seemed to be miles away from the menacing words and clicks of journalists' cameras. But not so Michelle Michaud. Her body visibly shuddered as the impact of every word struck home, as if the words themselves were like tiny lethal injections being jabbed into her shackled and firmly restrained arm.

After more than twenty years, James Daveggio was entering Santa Rita, the prison facility where his old schoolmate Michael Ihde had lived as a child. If by some means he could have climbed into a guard tower, he would have easily seen their old school and Wells Middle School nearby, where his own daughters and Kellie Poppleton had attended classes. Not far away was a series of ditches where Ilene Misheloff disappeared one wintry day in 1989. If his gaze had traveled even farther to another ditch, he could have picked out the spot where Tina Faelz bled to death—not far from his old home on Clovewood Drive. Near that ditch where freeways 580 and 680 intersected was the very hotel where he and Michelle had made their plans to "go hunting."

There in the distance was the exact spot where he and Michelle Michaud had driven her van on the morning of December 2, 1997, and emerged from the mist on the corner of Singletree and Kern Court.

Even though all these facts came to light after their arrests, a fog of suspicion and innuendo still surrounded them and Michael Ihde. Law enforcement agencies still pondered if Michael Ihde had been responsible for the rape and murder of Kellie Poppleton. Other police departments wondered how much Michelle Michaud was connected with the Jaycee Lee Dugard kidnapping.

But of these three, it was James Daveggio who was the main target of law enforcement's speculation and continuing interest. His possible involvement in unsolved cases read like a *Who's Who* of missing Bay Area girls: Amber Swartz-Garcia, Michaela Garecht, Tina Faelz and Ilene Misheloff. Even by the time of Daveggio's arraignment at the Alameda County Courthouse, the FBI and other law enforcement agencies were still looking at his possible connections with these and other crimes.

In the winter of a new millenium, there was more than just these unanswered questions and speculations. James Daveggio, Michelle Michaud and Michael Ihde were now behind bars for very tangible and proven crimes. Michael Ihde had raped and nearly killed Gloria Hagelwood of Jackson, California. He had raped and murdered Lisa Ann Monzo as well as Ellen Parker of Vancouver, Washington. Michelle Michaud had helped James Daveggio kidnap Juanita Rodriguez and transport her across state lines as he raped her. He had also raped Janet Stokes in Tracy. There were arrest warrants out on him in four different counties concerning all the raped and molested teenage girls.

Now as the winter fogs once again returned to Pleasanton in the year 2000, the grand jury charges against James Daveggio and Michelle Michaud were in binders that covered hundreds of pages with graphic and damning evidence about the two rapes of young Pleasanton women in November 1997, and the kidnap, rape and murder of Vanessa Samson. About the only ones denying those charges were James Daveggio, Michelle Michaud, their lawyers and James Daveggio's mother.

True to the end, Daveggio's mother, Darlene, still believed in him and told a *San Francisco Chronicle* reporter, "I told him I love him. I was crying a lot. He told me, 'Mom, I swear to you, I did not kill anyone.' "

But even a sliver of doubt crept into her voice as she said, "If there's even the remote possibility that my son could have done this to someone's child, I am so sorry. If I could take it back and give them my life instead, I would."

As to Michaud's and Daveggio's denials, veteran Alameda Sheriff's Department lieutenant Dave Hoig had an interesting comment. He had seen his share of serial killers over the years and said, "It is fairly common that a serial rapist or killer will not admit to a crime that law enforcement agencies are pretty sure they've committed but can't yet prove. The suspect will deny it even when they are already sitting on death row for other murders. It's pretty obvious that a person can't be put to death more than once, but still the killer won't admit to unproven crimes. But there's one thing they have to remember—there are no statute of limitations on murder. Things change over time; new officers come on board and look at old crimes. Technology and forensic science become better. And the case with Michael Ihde is a perfect example. Years after he murdered Lisa Ann Monzo, someone talked and it led eventually to his conviction. Criminals like him and James Daveggio and Michelle Michaud can't feel too safe just because they've gotten away with something so far. The one thing they have to remember is that time is on the side of law enforcement, and they never stop looking at old cases, especially when it involves a missing child or a murder."

The fact of the matter was that by the year 2000, James Daveggio and Michelle Michaud still faced more years of trials and courtroom procedures. But no matter the outcome—guilty, acquittal or plea bargain—they weren't going anywhere for a long, long time. The gray walls of the Santa Rita Prison that James Daveggio had looked at from afar when he lived in Pleasanton, in the shadow of Mount Diablo, the Devil's Mountain, were now their home.

Chapter 33

A Time of Farewells

In the new century for the parents of Amber Swartz-Garcia, Michaela Garecht, Ilene Misheloff and Jaycee Lee Dugard, there were no final farewells, only open wounds that never quite healed. Jaycee Lee Dugard's mother, Terry Probyn, could no longer stand the strain of missing her daughter in the familiar setting of South Lake Tahoe. She moved to another area far away. She left behind a practical memorial to her daughter—a video called *A Child's Life,* with local self-defense expert and friend Ken Bowers. On the tape, available to the public, he put together a comprehensive instructional video for the prevention of child abduction. It taught simple but effective techniques for children to evade or fight back against abductors. The video is dedicated to Jaycee Lee Dugard.

In the introduction Terry Probyn faces the camera, looking sad but determined to tell her story so that others might escape Jaycee Lee's fate. She says, "My message to you today is to empower your child. I think, reflecting back, and I know it's Monday morning quarterbacking, that if I would have given her [Jaycee Lee] the knowledge to help herself, she would be with me today. Jaycee was caught off guard. She wasn't expecting someone to come up behind her and cut off her path. She froze. I'd have given her knowledge to run the other way or possibly help herself find an avenue out after she had been taken. If I'd have done this, she'd be home."

Then in words echoing Michela Garecht's mom, she says, "All I can think about is not being able to hold her, hug her and kiss her. I'll never give up looking for her. Ever."

Sergeant Randy Peshon, too, has never given up looking for Jaycee Lee Dugard. As he told a *San Francisco Chronicle* reporter in the waning days of 1999, "You name it, we've tried it. Just here in my office are twelve working binders and there's 150 to 160 volumes of paperwork stored at the FBI in Sacramento. It eats at you and it never goes away. Even now deputies talk among themselves about it at work, speculating, trading theories, looking for things we might have missed. For her family, the community, those of us who worked on the case, there is no closure. People used to feel safe sending their kids to the bus stop and now they take them there. The community lost its innocence."

For four other families and friends, the tributes and farewells had already come and gone, still resonating like distant echoes by the time James Daveggio and Michelle Michaud faced their day in court in Alameda County. For the family of Tina Faelz there still was no hard evidence as to who had killed their daughter and the case was like an open wound that would not heal. For the parents of Kellie Poppleton, the one key clue linking her death to the killer was still missing. But at least the friends and family of Lisa Ann Monzo could get some closure knowing that her murderer, Michael Ihde, was paying the ultimate price for her death with his own life. And the parents and friends of Vanessa Samson knew that someday the killers of Vanessa would also pay a terrible price.

Vanessa Samson's funeral had been a large one; more than 800 people from Pleasanton came to say good-bye to her. A memorial was conducted by her priest, Father Daniel Davidson, at St. Augustine Catholic Church. He said to the gathered throng, "Evil will not ultimately overcome." He chose to speak of the goodness in her life rather than the terror of her death.

Then with an escort of police motorcycles and an honor guard, including Police Chief Bill Eastman of Pleasanton, Vanessa's body had been transported to her final resting place.

"This is how 'Nessa would have liked it," her brother, Vincent, said. "She was always smiling and laughing. She had a lot to give to people. We are especially thankful for the motorist who found her. If he didn't happen to be there that day, we wouldn't be able to do any of this today."

So the young woman who had always been smiling and laughing was buried not far down the hill from pioneer Charles Garthwaite, the old '49er who had chosen Pleasanton over any other place he could have picked in California. He had known it as a place of goodness and light, and so had she. The dark shadows that were cast by others remained there for a while, and then they faded with the morning sun.

In a subtle way the smiling and effervescent Vanessa Samson was now a sister to the sad and lonely Kellie Poppleton who had inhabited the other, darker side of Pleasanton. Though they died years apart and were interred miles apart, there was a common thread of friends and family who remembered the girls with love and promises never to forget. In the years that followed, they kept their promises.

A stranger visiting Kellie Poppleton's and Vanessa Samson's final resting places will notice that fresh flowers keep appearing at their graves. No matter the day of the week or time of the year, the bright petals add an array of color to an otherwise somber scene. It's an unspoken testimony that friends and family have indeed not forgotten these girls and still surround them with memories and love.

From the Files of
True Detective
Magazine